The War against al-Qaeda

The War against al-Qaeda

Religion, Policy, and Counter-narratives

Nahed Artoul Zehr

Georgetown University Press | *Washington, DC*

The publisher is not responsible for third-party websites or their content. URL links were active at time of publication.

Library of Congress Cataloging-in-Publication Data

Names: Zehr, Nahed Artoul, author.
Title: The War against al-Qaeda : Religion, Policy, and Counter-narratives / Nahed Artoul Zehr.
Description: Washington, DC : Georgetown University Press, 2017 | Includes bibliographical references and index.
Identifiers: LCCN 2016031233 (print) | LCCN 2016040145 (ebook) | ISBN 9781626164277 (hc. : alk. paper) | ISBN 9781626164284 (pb. : alk. paper) | ISBN 9781626164291 (eb)
Subjects: LCSH: Qaida (Organization) | Terrorism—Religious aspects—Islam. | Islamic fundamentalism. | Afghan War, 2001–
Classification: LCC HV6432.5.Q2 Z44 2017 (print) | LCC HV6432.5.Q2 (ebook) | DDC 363.325—dc23
LC record available at https://lccn.loc.gov/2016031233

♾ This book is printed on acid-free paper meeting the requirements of the American National Standard for Permanence in Paper for Printed Library Materials.

18 17   9 8 7 6 5 4 3 2 First printing

Printed in the United States of America

Cover design by James Keller.

For my parents, Samir and Afifa Artoul

Contents

Acknowledgments   ix
Note on Terms and Translations   xiii

   Introduction: A Different Kind of War   1

1 Foundations: A Just War Analysis of the
   War against al-Qaeda   17

2 Traditions: The Moral Constraints of War in Islam   53

3 Narratives: Al-Qaeda's Dual Nature   79

4 Tactics: Al-Suri and al-Qaeda's Model of War   105

5 Counter-narratives: Moderate Muslim Voices
   and a Debate within the Tradition   143

   Conclusion: Operationalizing Counter-narratives
   in the War against al-Qaeda   173

Selected Bibliography   197
Index   205
About the Author   217

Acknowledgments

In the late fall of 2011, I sat in on a seminar in the Joint Military Operations (JMO) Department at the US Naval War College. I was a freshly minted PhD who had landed her dream fellowship to spend an entire year at a graduate training school for military officers, where I learned about war and the military in ways that are unavailable to most academics. I had been invited to attend this particular seminar because of the topic, "Is al-Qaeda a global insurgency?"

About thirty minutes into the discussion, one of the students, a navy captain, asked me to reply to the prompt. I responded, and as the conversation continued, I realized the import of what the officer had asked of me. For this officer, the way this group was conceptualized had a direct impact on how the US military would respond to the threat. At the time, major decision makers had deemed al-Qaeda a global *insurgency*, and the military was engaged in the task of learning how to fight *counter*insurgency war (discussed in more detail in chapter 1). This was a significant shift from the conventional state-on-state conflicts that the US military was used to fighting and, moreover, a shift from the type of war that it was very good at winning. I understood very clearly, then, that the way in which we conceptualize any group or threat has consequences—or, to put it more plainly, that different ways of thinking about the nature of a phenomenon will generate different types of responses. For these reasons, I decided to focus my research more specifically toward understanding the *practical* consequences of conceptualizing "al-Qaeda"—a term that, by the time I was sitting in this seminar, had become ubiquitous in any conversation on war, national security, or international politics.

For this I wish to thank the Department of Defense's Minerva Initiative, which funded my position as Minerva Research Chair at the war college from the fall of 2011 to the summer of 2012. Moreover, my time there would not have been so pleasant without the friendship and guidance of Dr. Martin Cook, who was the Adm. James B. Stockdale Professor of Professional

Military Ethics at the time. Thank you also to my office mates, Kevin Brew and Sarah Sewall, who provided a warm, welcoming, and stimulating environment and engaging conversation (among other things!). A sincere thank you also goes to the folks on the "fourth deck" in JMO who, despite my being a stranger among them, were welcoming and engaging hosts, were generous with their time and energy, and were always willing to answer my questions.

Of course, the research on this book began well before my fellowship and was possible only because of the work and support of my intellectual community. I had the good fortune of working with Howard Rhodes while we were both at the University of Iowa. He became an adviser, a mentor, and a true-blue friend. He introduced me to the field of just war and provided invaluable feedback on my writing. His counsel and friendship continue to serve as guiding marks for my professional life. I wish to express gratitude to those who read the work in its early form. Feedback from Aline Kalbian, Sumner B. Twiss, and Adam Gaiser steered the work in directions that were much more fruitful than those I had originally intended. Aline Kalbian's and Sumner Twiss's comments helped me better understand how to use the tools of my subfield to highlight the contribution of this work, and Adam Gaiser's probing questions on US foreign policy and "counter-narratives" pushed me to do more research in this direction. Their comments helped me to shape this project into its current form.

A special thank you is owed to my intellectual forebearers in the just war community. I wish to thank James Turner Johnson, whose foundational work on the just war tradition has formed my understanding of the field and its importance. His intellectual influence permeates this book's pages. All students of just war owe him a great debt. Thank you to G. Scott Davis for his support and for taking my work seriously. Although I never had the good fortune of being his student (at least not directly), his work has been critical to the way I understand the just war tradition. Moreover, his comments on my scholarship have always demonstrated a keen ability to understand both its strengths and its shortcomings, and to do so in ways in which I could understand how to capitalize on the former and (try to) fix the latter. To John Kelsay, I wish to express my very deepest gratitude. My own work would not have been possible without his groundbreaking books on comparative ethics, the just war tradition, and Islam. Through our conversations on the field of comparative religious ethics, I was able to imagine the framework for my own projects and to garner an understanding of myself as a scholar. More so than this, though, his support of me and my work has been the force moving me forward when the moments of self-doubt impeded my way. Having him as an adviser and mentor has been my very sincere honor and privilege.

I wish to express my gratitude to Western Kentucky University and the Society for Values in Higher Education for funding the Symposium on Peace, Islam, and Counter-narratives that I organized in the fall of 2014. This symposium allowed me to pursue a number of questions that had emerged from my work on the manuscript and to invite a community of scholars and practitioners who were interested in the same issues. Thank you to all the participants for their diligence and enthusiasm for the project and for the important work that they have done and continue to do. I would also like to thank my colleagues (at Western Kentucky and elsewhere) and my students, all of whom have provided a pleasant and stimulating environment as I pursue the questions that I take up in this book. Thanks in particular to my graduate students, whose thought-provoking comments in seminars helped me clarify my thinking and whose sense of humor always gave me perspective.

A special thank you is owed to the team at Georgetown University Press. Thank you to Richard Brown, my editor, who believed in this book from the beginning, and to Vicki Chamlee, whose careful and percipient work was a critical contribution to the final manuscript. Thank you also to Glenn Saltzman and to the marketing and editorial and production teams for their careful and attentive work on this project.

Writing a book takes a level of stamina and dedication that is exhausting. My biggest debts are to those who helped see me through this process. Thank you to multiple colleagues who provided support along the way and, in particular, to Betsy Barre, Kate Temoney, Rosemary Kellison, Shannon Dunn, Julie Fortune, Emily Cox, Brooke Knorr, and Molly Reed. Thank you to Jordan Napier and Brenna Dailey, as I would not have finished this book without you. A sincere thank you to my friends and especially to Tamara Monet Marks, Melissa Carpenter, and Sarah Saffold. I am forever grateful for your sincere and deep friendship and for your encouragement and support through the years that I have been working on this book. A tremendous thank you, from the very bottom of a daughter and sister's heart, to my family on both the Artoul and Zehr sides. In particular, my parents—Samir Artoul and Afifa Artoul—have been an unending source of love and encouragement. Their insistence on excellence has encouraged me to reach beyond what I might have otherwise thought to be possible. Thanks go especially to my dad (a native Arabic speaker) for looking over my translations and ensuring their accuracy.

To my daughters, Nurah and Nadeen, you have flooded my world with hope and light, and you have changed me fundamentally in the process. The two of you are my whole heart. I love you relentlessly and enduringly, and I strive, every day, in all that I do and in every decision that I make to demonstrate that love to you. I hope one day you will read this work and that you will be proud of it. And to my husband, Joel, while the girls are my heart, you are my soul. Words can neither express nor do justice to my love, respect, and appreciation for you. Your love sustains me. Thanks for believing in me when no one else did and in the moments when I could not believe in myself. YAMSM. Forever.

Note on Terms and Translations

The term "al-Qaeda" is used to refer to a set of ideas or to a specific religious narrative that is explicated in this book. The term "al-Qaeda phenomenon" refers to the proliferation of groups that have been inspired by this narrative. In writing about both the set of ideas and the proliferation of groups, at times these terms are used synonymously. When referring to al-Qaeda as a specific organization—one headed by Osama bin Laden or Ayman al-Zawahiri—I do so in such a way that this use is clear.

Common English spellings are used for a variety of Arabic words—such as "al-Qaeda," "Quran," "shariah," and so on—and proper nouns are capitalized. Transliterated terms in direct quotations are left as the author had them, although I removed the diacritical marks for uniformity.

With my own translations, I sought to make the English as smooth as possible while staying relatively close to the Arabic. In particular, Abu Musab al-Suri's writing is heavy and unwieldy at times; the Arabic is dense, and he is verbose. I have done my best to translate his writing so that it is easy for the reader to understand without my taking unnecessary liberty with his ideas.

Introduction
A Different Kind of War

As I write this introduction, the international community is consumed by the rampant and wanton destruction that the Islamic State (ISIS) has unleashed on Iraq and Syria. Images of beheadings, executions, and the indiscriminate slaughter of religious minorities and the testimonies of forced sexual slavery have filled our computer and television screens. Such images, coupled with a series of ISIS-linked terror attacks in Paris and Brussels in 2015 and 2016, have ignited a robust public debate regarding the best way to respond. This book hopes to contribute to the debate, yet this book is not about ISIS—at least not directly. However, it seems fitting to begin with a discussion of this group, primarily because, as I have been writing and editing, my thoughts have been occupied with the idea that ISIS is another product of what I refer to as the "al-Qaeda narrative." Let me take a moment to explain.

On June 29, 2014, ISIS declared the establishment of a caliphate. Explaining the significance of the occasion, the new caliph, Abu Bakr al-Baghdadi, issued the following statement:

> O Muslims everywhere, glad tidings to you and expect good. Raise your head high, for today—by Allah's grace—you have a state and Khilafah [caliphate], *which will return your dignity, might, rights, and leadership.*
>
> It is a state where the Arab and non-Arab, the white man and black man, the easterner and westerner are all brothers.
>
> It is a Khilafah that gathered the Caucasian, Indian, Chinese, Shami, Iraqi, Yemeni, Egyptian, Maghribi (North African), American, French, German, and Australian. Allah brought their hearts together, and thus, they became brothers by His grace, loving each other for the sake of Allah, standing in a single trench, defending and guarding each other, and sacrificing themselves for one another.

Their blood mixed and became one, under a single flag and goal, in one pavilion, enjoying this blessing, the blessing of faithful brotherhood [emphasis mine].[1]

This was followed by a statement from ISIS's official spokesperson, Abu Muhammad al-Adnani.

The time has come for those generations that were drowning in oceans of disgrace, being nursed on the milk of humiliation, and being ruled by the vilest of all people, after their long slumber in the darkness of neglect—the time has come for them to rise.

The time has come for the Ummah of Muhammad (*sallallahu 'alayhi wa sallam*) to wake up from its sleep, remove the garments of dishonor, and shake off the dust of humiliation and disgrace, for the era of lamenting and moaning has gone, and the dawn of honor has emerged anew.

The sun of jihad has risen. The glad tidings of good are shining. Triumph looms on the horizon. The signs of victory have appeared.[2]

Through these dramatic declarations, ISIS sought to communicate an important point: The establishment of the caliphate, a historical Islamic institution, was a momentous and watershed moment for contemporary Muslims, as the symbol and source of Muslim strength and unity had been restored. ISIS maintained that no longer would Muslims be dominated and humiliated at the hands of outsiders. No longer would they be subject to the political, cultural, and economic interference of others. No longer would Muslims be the agents for someone else's interests. Rather, "the time has come," the group announced, for Muslims to liberate themselves from a period of stagnation and weakness and to rise anew.

ISIS's declaration was sneered at by the US administration and dramatically contested by a number of influential Muslim personalities, including figures who have been important in the jihadi community. Despite this, ISIS has continued to insist on the legitimacy of its caliphate and has managed to bring a significant amount of territory under its control. As ISIS continues to grow in strength and numbers, the international community is taking notice, attempting to understand the reasons for its military success and appeal. To this end, analysts have elaborated on the novel and unique nature of ISIS and have taken great pains to elaborate the differences between ISIS and its mother organization, al-Qaeda.[3]

ISIS is, indeed, unique in important respects. It is, after all, one of the only jihadist terrorist groups that has managed to capture significant amounts of territory and to execute some measure of administrative control (including raising an army, collecting taxes, and so on). And certainly its military strength and success are significant reasons that it continues to attract what appears to be a relatively steady stream of recruits, supporters, and sympathizers. Yet, more specifically, the appeal of ISIS is directly tied to its having done what every other major jihadi group has sought to do but has failed to accomplish—that is, to establish an Islamic state.[4]

Of course, the term "state" is a misnomer. ISIS can make no claims to legitimacy in terms of the international community of nation-states or in light of the moral traditions and the respective understanding of legitimate authority.[5] However, that it has decided to identify itself through the language of a "state" is significant. It helps us understand its nature and appeal. Further, it helps us identify ISIS as the product of a narrative, revitalized in the eighteenth and nineteenth centuries, that was radicalized, or removed from any appreciable moral constraints, and given tactical and strategic life by a series of ideologues whose work has culminated in the birth of al-Qaeda and the al-Qaeda phenomenon.

This narrative is the primary subject of *The War against al-Qaeda*, a project that conceptualizes al-Qaeda as a meaning-giving and action-guiding narrative that has given groups like al-Qaeda and ISIS meaning and direction. I focus on the specific religious narrative that directs a *multitude* of groups—what I refer to as the "al-Qaeda phenomenon"—that are motivated by the idea that the use of *indiscriminate* force put toward the goal of achieving a "proper" Islamic state is a critical and indispensable part of Muslim revitalization in the contemporary world. Understood in this way, ISIS and its declaration of a caliphate represent a climax in the story—the narrative—of a marginal interpretation of Islamic history and ideas that existed before al-Qaeda and ISIS and that entered the world stage through the life and work of bin Laden and his organization.[6]

The description of the al-Qaeda phenomenon as a meaning-giving, action-guiding narrative begins with a set of ideas developed by a group of jihadi thinkers who have influenced al-Qaeda's worldview. While these figures preceded the movement that bin Laden and others fostered, and thus could not be a part of this group, it nevertheless serves our purpose to think of them as al-Qaeda ideologues who helped shape how those associated with this group see the world. Understanding al-Qaeda thinking, then, requires investigating the reasons these figures provide for their actions. According to their ideologues, these reasons are religious or theological in nature in that they are linked to a framework that is connected to ideas about God and God's will. When al-Qaeda's ideologues attempt to understand contemporary events that affect or concern them, they apply this framework to understand how God's dictates can provide clarity and meaning to these events. In other words, they use this religious framework to answer the question, what is going on? Moreover, in attempting to understand how they ought to respond to contemporary events, they again reference this religious framework and determine how to proceed or to answer the question, what should we do?

In telling this story, this book argues for a shift in focus regarding how the al-Qaeda phenomenon is conceptualized and, hence, approached by the international community. It is an observable fact that human beings organize information into conceptual models to help them categorize and understand the world around them. This is a fundamental human activity, born out of a desire to give information clarity and meaning. Moreover, as the phenomena of daily life can be understood and organized in multiple ways, the activity of conceptual organization has real and practical consequences. Deciding how information will be organized, or choosing the form or the model that such information will take, directly determines the *type* of response that is constructed and applied.

This point is indispensable in the war against the al-Qaeda phenomenon. The specific way that al-Qaeda is characterized has strategic implications, for it directly affects the framework, or the *counter*-model, that the US military and policy communities will choose to apply. Important for our purposes, then, determining how to respond to al-Qaeda requires that al-Qaeda must be conceptualized in a way that accurately reflects its nature—that is, its fundamental qualities, features, attributes, dispositions, and inclinations. To understand how we ought to respond to the al-Qaeda phenomenon, we must first ask the questions, what is al-Qaeda, and what does it seek to be?

I argue that approaching al-Qaeda in this way will demonstrate what I call its dual nature, reflecting that it is both *rooted* in but significantly *departs* from the Islamic tradition's understanding of proper statecraft and the just use of force. Its dual nature is a critical factor when thinking about how to construct a response to the al-Qaeda phenomenon and its long-term defeat, for its real weakness, its center of gravity, is its departure from the very tradition that it uses to both direct and legitimate its strategy and tactics. To this end, this book uses the wisdom of two moral-ethical traditions, the Western and Islamic traditions on the just use of force, to provide a constructive critique of the war against al-Qaeda. Both traditions, as repositories of moral wisdom and guidance, provide a critical lens for forming a response to the al-Qaeda phenomenon that takes its meaning-giving and action-guiding narrative into consideration.

This is not, then, a book about al-Qaeda that focuses primarily on recruitment, numbers, radicalization, historical formation, and so on. The book certainly incorporates some of that material, but it does so to focus on the religious ideas that formed and drive the al-Qaeda phenomenon and seeks to explicate the implications of understanding it through this lens. Understanding this in detail, though, requires that we recall the history of al-Qaeda's declarations of war against the United States and the US military's response.

The War against al-Qaeda

Osama bin Laden issued his first declaration of war against the United States on August 23, 1996, in a tract called "A Declaration of Jihad against the Americans Occupying the Land of the Two Holy Sanctuaries." Those familiar with his earlier statements will note the recurring reference to the "occupation" of Saudi Arabia and Palestine, a central and continuing theme in his diatribes against the West.[7] According to bin Laden, emancipating the two holy sanctuaries (in Mecca and Medina) is the stepping-stone to the liberation of Muslim lands from Western domination and oppression. All Muslims, he argued, must participate in the armed struggle to unshackle the holy sanctuaries from Western occupation and to unify the greater Muslim world.[8]

The full force of this agenda, however, was not apparent until bin Laden produced the "Jihad against the Jews and Crusaders," issued on February 23, 1998. In this short epistle (approximately fifteen paragraphs), bin Laden provides a list of American "crimes and sins," including the ongoing American occupation of the Arabian Peninsula, the damage inflicted on the Iraqi people as a result of the First Gulf War and continuing economic sanctions, the Americans' support of Israel, and a set of pernicious economic and foreign policies that seek to weaken, fragment, and ultimately destroy the Arab-Muslim states. Such actions, he argues, constitute an aggressive war on Muslims' lands, a war that ultimately seeks to destroy Islam and its people. For bin Laden, an American war of aggression against Muslims is an empirical fact. Furthermore, the injunctions and duties of Islam regarding the situation at hand are exceedingly clear. He argues, "The ruling to kill Americans—civilian and military—is an individual duty on every Muslim capable of this, in any country in which he is able to do it, so that the al-Aqsa Mosque and the Holy Mosque will be liberated from their grip, and that their armies will depart (تخرج) from all Muslim land, defeated and incapable of doing harm."[9]

Bin Laden's militant organization, al-Qaeda, wasted no time making good on its declaration of war. As noted by Washington insiders like Daniel Benjamin, Steven Simon, and Richard A. Clarke, the story of al-Qaeda's attacks on US interests begins well before the dramatic climax of the attacks on September 11, 2001.[10] Within the span of thirteen years, al-Qaeda had initiated a series of impressive attacks against the United States, including the bombings of the US embassies in Kenya and Tanzania (both in 1988), the World Trade Center in New York City (1993), the Khobar Towers housing US military personnel (1996), and the USS *Cole* in Yemen (2000).

Since then, al-Qaeda has been associated with attacks on the commuter train systems in Madrid and London (2004 and 2005), and its ideas are thought to be the driving force behind a growing line of lone-wolf jihadists such as Faisal Shahzad, Nidal Malik Hasan, Dzhokhar Tsarnaev, and Tamerlan Tsarnaev (discussed in more detail in chapter 4). As analysts have noted, al-Qaeda after 9/11 has transformed from a centralized and hierarchical organization with camps based in Afghanistan to a network of networks that spans the globe.

The United States responded to these actions with its own declaration of war. Since then, the war against al-Qaeda, or the "Long War" as it has come to be called, has become a central tenet in the US canon of national security. In the attempt to "disrupt, dismantle, and defeat" bin Laden's al-Qaeda, its affiliates, and now ISIS, the United States has entered two large-scale and ferociously complex military engagements in Iraq and Afghanistan and has undertaken the use of extraordinary tools of counterterrorism, primarily the use of drones. From the inception of hostilities, major military and policy decision makers determined that this kind of war was different, necessitating a decisive shift from a focus on conventional combat to the realm of irregular warfare. As a consequence, the relevant decision makers made a concerted effort to categorize al-Qaeda. Academics, analysts, and other interested parties put forward conceptual models of al-Qaeda that were focused on its structure, organization, and tactics.[11]

Two military counter-models were put forward in the attempt to understand and combat the al-Qaeda network—counterinsurgency and counterterrorism. The counterinsurgency model construes al-Qaeda as a worldwide militant Islamist insurgency that has penetrated Iraq and Afghanistan. Relying on the classic principles of military counterinsurgency doctrine, policy and military decision makers determined that both "fronts" (Iraq and Afghanistan) must be secured to ensure an overall defeat of al-Qaeda. The counterterrorism model, meanwhile, understands al-Qaeda as a network of terrorists violating both domestic and international law. Under this second line of thinking, defeating al-Qaeda requires the traditional tools of counter-terrorism—arrests and detentions—and, in instances where such tools are not available, the use of drone weapons in the hopes that arresting or killing high-level leaders would eventually lead al-Qaeda to implode.

Neither approach has produced sustainable levels of progress or success in Iraq and Afghanistan. Moreover, the power vacuums in both states—and in the region more broadly speaking—have clearly been a contributing factor to the rise and spread of ISIS, indicating that the religious ideas that drive the al-Qaeda phenomenon have not been disrupted, dismantled, or destroyed. Interestingly, the dominant conceptual models of al-Qaeda tend to note that its religious underpinnings play some kind of role, though these ideas are sidelined in favor of a focus on organization and tactics.[12] This book seeks to fill that gap and, in doing so, offers an additional approach to combating the al-Qaeda phenomenon, but it first requires refocusing our understanding of what al-Qaeda is and what it seeks to be.

Rather than investigating the al-Qaeda phenomenon through its orga-nization or its tactics, I argue that the international community ought to approach al-Qaeda as a set of ideas that have undergirded the formation, development, and proliferation of these groups. This is not to argue that structure and tactics are not important to understanding al-Qaeda, but we ought to think about al-Qaeda's strategy and tactics through the religious narrative that gives it meaning and consequence.

The Argument

I make this argument about al-Qaeda in five separate but interconnected chapters. Chapter 1, "Foundations," sets the stage for shifting focus by draw-ing on the tools and methods of the Western just war tradition. I use them to make the case for reevaluating the current strategic frameworks that have organized, and continue to organize, the use of military force in the Long War. Chapter 1 provides a just war critique of counterinsurgency and counterterrorism as they have been applied in the war against al-Qaeda. While a constructive critique of counterinsurgency and counterterrorism may be had from multiple lenses, I chose the just war lens for two reasons.

First, as Mark Totten notes, the just war tradition provides the "grammar" for Americans' debates on warfare, as the tradition's values and commitments structure the way that Americans think and debate major policy dimen-sions on the use of force.[13] Although there is no extensive agreement in the relevant debates concerning US foreign policy on these issues, Americans are generally persuaded by the ideas that force ought to be guided by morality and ethics, and that, furthermore, the terms of such guidance have been provided largely by the body of moral wisdom referred to as the just war tradition. Specifically, this tradition reflects a relatively broad American consensus on the relationship between war, justice, morality, and statecraft, arguing that the use of force—in the pursuit of justice—is sometimes necessary but should *always* be limited.

Second, the tradition provides what Alex Bellamy refers to as "moral anchorages." These moral and ethical commitments ought to "guide political decision makers and the way that democratic societies debate and evaluate what is done in their name."[14] As US president Barack Obama notes in his 2009 acceptance speech for the Nobel Peace Prize, even as the United States confronts "a vicious adversary that abides by no rules," the United States must "remain a standard bearer in the conduct of war. This is what makes us different from those whom we fight."[15] The ideas of the just war tradition, then, ought to set certain moral and ethical boundaries for US military action.[16]

Positioning itself against pacifism and realism, the just war tradition argues that war is a moral activity, and as such, it is always limited by and subject to ethical restraints as determined by a set of categories that developed over time. These categories highlight the values contained in the just war tradition and provide parameters that guide decision-making. They are organized into two distinct yet interrelated branches. The first set—legitimate authority, just cause, right intention, reasonable hope of success, proportionality of ends, last resort, and aim of peace—is categorized under the label of *jus ad bellum*. These criteria address the question of determining when the use of force is just. The second set—proportionality of means and discrimination—is categorized as *jus in bello* and concerns determining how to appropriately use force once it has been decided that military means are the proper course of action.[17]

These categories guide the ethical deliberation on the use of force by pointing to values and commitments that, through processes of reason and deliberation, define the political and social goods of just and proper statecraft. They bracket the use of force by erecting limits beyond which we may not tread without jeopardizing our obligation to these principles. It is this framework, then, that guides the analysis and critique of the counterinsurgency and counterterrorism efforts as they have been applied in the war against al-Qaeda.

Chapter 1 demonstrates the *limits* of military counter-models in the war against the al-Qaeda phenomenon. I want to emphasize the point that this discussion does not mean the use of force is an inappropriate or unnecessary tool in the war against al-Qaeda; rather, I argue that any approach to the al-Qaeda phenomenon must note the limits of the proposed counter-models and, relatedly, of US military power. In doing so, it seems prudent to shift our attention from conceptualizations of al-Qaeda that focus only on strategy and tactics to what is, I contend, the driving force behind the al-Qaeda phenomenon—that is, the specific religious narrative that gives it meaning and direction.

This narrative is described in chapter 2, "Traditions," and chapter 3, "Narratives." They work together to demonstrate two points. First, they detail the way in which al-Qaeda's ideologues reference early Islamic history to make sense of contemporary events. Chapter 2 provides a judiciously selected narrative of events in early Islamic history, beginning with the life of Muhammad and the earliest Muslim communities and then moving forward to a "transition" phase in the eighteenth century. It uses these events to highlight the moral constraints of war in the Islamic just war tradition, focusing particularly on notions of legitimate authority and discrimination.[18]

Once the historical components of this narrative are established and the moral constraints are brought to the reader's attention, chapter 3 builds on this foundation by turning to the work of three al-Qaeda ideologues: Muhammad abd-al-Salam Faraj, Abdullah Yusuf Azzam, and bin Laden. Each of these figures made significant contributions to the development and evolution of the al-Qaeda narrative. Demonstrating the development of this narrative through the work of al-Qaeda's ideologues illumes what I refer to as its "dual nature." On the one hand, this narrative is rooted in Islamic history, ideas, and symbols; on the other hand, it departs from the tradition in critical ways. Importantly, when we look at the work of these thinkers, we note that they used religious commitments to both understand and give meaning to current social ills and to provide guidance for how these problems can and should be alleviated. For al-Qaeda's ideologues, understanding why Muslims suffer—why they remain in a position of weakness vis-à-vis the West—requires that the interpretive lens of the Islamic tradition be brought to bear on a slew of issues that, according to these thinkers, affect Muslims today. It refers to the set of Islamic ideas and history that allow Muslims to see the true cause of their suffering and weakness.

Of course, it is important to clarify that al-Qaeda's ideologues do not typically provide elaborate treatises on a variety of religious questions and problems; rather, their writing is narrowly focused on the issue of jihad and its permissibility and necessity in the lives of contemporary Muslims. This has led, at times, to suspicion regarding al-Qaeda's use of religious ideas and terms, causing analysts to argue that al-Qaeda uses religion as a guise—or as a way to galvanize support for what are, in reality, social, political, and economic concerns. In response, I note that untangling religious ideas from political, social, and economic issues and concerns is nearly impossible, and the attempt to do so often does not offer additional clarity or insight but rather false dichotomies ("Is this religion or is this politics?"). Indeed, it is the combination of political, economic, and social ills *coupled* with the theological narrative that has led to the birth of al-Qaeda and the al-Qaeda phenomenon. Moreover, the lack of nuance and theological sophistication of the type we would expect from those with formal training in Islamic jurisprudence does not render the arguments or positions put forward by these thinkers as any less religious. Quite the contrary, what we see are thinkers who attempt to determine how the dictates of their faith—what they understand as the commandments of God to the pious—can help them understand and respond to a series of immediate concerns.

While al-Qaeda references this history, though, it categorically ignores a number of critical moral restraints developed from historical Islamic discourse on the use of force. Chapter 4, "Tactics," demonstrates how this departure on the part of the al-Qaeda narrative has led to the development of a strategic and tactical model that is lacking in any appreciable limits. To this end, none have made a more prolific contribution to the development of al-Qaeda tactics and strategy than has Mustafa Abd al-Qadir Setmariam Nasar, better known as Abu Musab al-Suri.

Al-Suri's work and contributions to the al-Qaeda phenomenon's strategic and tactical model are the subject of chapter 4. He spent most of his adult life supporting, working, and traveling to further a variety of jihadi groups, including those in Syria, Algeria, and Afghanistan, and allegedly spent time as bin Laden's media adviser. Al-Suri was, at heart, a theoretician writing strategic and tactical tracts that sought to align tactics and strategy with the reality of current conditions. In his 1,600-page manifesto, *The Global Islamic Resistance Call* (دعوة المقاومة الإسلامية العالمية), al-Suri provides an extensive assessment of jihadi groups (including al-Qaeda) to understand how past mistakes and successes could be applied to the current state of political, religious, social, and economic conditions that confront Muslims in a post-9/11 world, which he calls "The New World Order" (النظام العالمي الجديد). In these current conditions, he writes, Muslims are subjugated and oppressed at the hands of outsiders as well as of their own governments.

In his *Call*, al-Suri argues that the jihad must transform itself and respond to the post-9/11 environment in which al-Qaeda training camps have been destroyed and regimes across the world have initiated serious crackdowns on secret jihadi groups. The old ways of operating are no longer feasible in the New World Order. These old methods, he writes, are too vulnerable to government infiltration and crackdown. For these reasons, he argues for a new strategic or tactical model of jihad that is less vulnerable to such forces and that allows Muslims anywhere and everywhere to join the fight. At the heart of his model is the idea that all Muslims have the individual authority to wage this "war" against the internal and external forces of oppression. Therefore, the import of his thinking is the connection that al-Suri makes between the al-Qaeda narrative described in chapter 3 and his strategic and tactical model for jihad. In this way, al-Suri's work as a military theorist and strategist demonstrates the critical connection between al-Qaeda's theological narrative and its actions in the world.[19]

At this point, we arrive at the implications of conceptualizing al-Qaeda as a meaning-giving and action-guiding narrative. In taking al-Qaeda's religious underpinnings seriously, it becomes necessary to argue that in addition to the use of military force, the war against the al-Qaeda phenomenon requires responding to its theological narrative. A number of influential Muslim figures have taken on this task and tackled issues of "radicalism," "militancy," and "extremism" in Islam by offering interpretations of the textual sources that directly counter the religious arguments made by al-Qaeda's ideologues. Their ideas are the subject of chapter 5, "Counter-narratives." As the reader will note, these figures are of many different persuasions and have different interpretations of how the textual sources ought to be understood. The point of presenting figures as diverse as Bassam Tibi, who understands himself as a secular Muslim, and Yusuf al-Qaradawi, a traditionally trained Islamic cleric, is to show that contestations of the al-Qaeda phenomenon come from figures across the theological spectrum.

Naturally, the concluding question to pose is, to what extent ought US policy toward al-Qaeda incorporate counter-narratives into its response to the al-Qaeda phenomenon? Sectors of the foreign policy community have recognized the importance of responding to al-Qaeda's narrative. The conclusion describes what I refer to as the "counter-narrative initiative"—that is, the attempt of academics, foreign policy influencers, and US State Department personnel to respond to the ideas that undergird the al-Qaeda phenomenon. Moreover, it provides a constructive critique of this initiative by investigating the ethical issues involved in the counter-narrative initiative. It is encouraging that a section of the policy community is recognizing the importance of religion in understanding al-Qaeda. That policymakers are paying attention to al-Qaeda in this way is encouraging; however, their policy recommendations, at times, are leading us in a disconcerting direction or, at the very least, one that ought to be investigated in more detail. The counter-narrative initiative is fraught with a variety of issues that must be raised and addressed. The conclusion, then, provides a constructive critique of the counter-narrative initiative in US foreign policy and offers suggestions for how to move forward.

This Long War is indeed a different kind of war. What I offer in *The War against al-Qaeda* is an additional lens from which to view the al-Qaeda phenomenon—one that I believe is a critical addition to the current strategic and tactical models. It does so with the understanding that other approaches—ones that focus on political, social, and economic factors as well as strategy and tactics—have much to contribute. This book, though, focuses specifically on the religious narrative that drives the al-Qaeda phenomenon. Concentrating on this point provides a multifaceted perspective on the al-Qaeda phenomenon in the hopes of, ultimately, offering additional approaches to respond to groups like al-Qaeda and ISIS. It is my hope that this book will be read alongside other projects that offer their own unique contribution to the tremendous task of understanding what al-Qaeda is, what it seeks to be, and how to apply that knowledge to the Long War.

To begin, we must establish the consequences of conceptualizing al-Qaeda primarily through its organization and tactics. We must ask, what are the practical implications of understanding al-Qaeda primarily through the lens of organizational theories that describe it as a network of networks?[20] How does one fight a global threat that is both decentralized and shifting?

Notes

1. "Khilafah Declared," *Dabiq* 1 (June 2014): 7, http://media.clarionproject.org /files/09-2014/isis-isil-islamic-state-magazine-Issue-1-the-return-of-khilafah.pdf.

2. Ibid., 9.

3. For example, al-Qaeda under Osama bin Laden and Ayman al-Zawarhiri is a diffuse network of groups with relatively limited central control, while ISIS is an organization that controls territory and has a hierarchical model of rule. There are other important differences beyond these factors. For instance, Jessica Stern and J. M. Berger argue that ISIS is a hybrid between a terrorist group and an insurgency that has made extraordinary use of social media. See Stern and Berger, *ISIS: The State of Terror*. William McCants demonstrates how ISIS's apocalyptic beliefs have influenced its strategy, helping to pave the way for its split from al-Qaeda. See McCants,

ISIS Apocalypse. For a pithy summary of McCants's analysis of the difference between al-Qaeda and ISIS, see especially pp. 145–55.

4. For a particularly interesting account of one of these stories, see Ebrahim Moosa, "My Madrassa Classmate."

5. Nahed Artoul Zehr, "Moral Sovereignty and Legitimate Authority in a Global War" (working title as research is in progress). This paper critiques the alleged legitimacy of ISIS from the Western and Islamic just war tradition.

6. To make these claims, I use the analytical tools of a subfield of religious studies called religious ethics. As a work of religious ethics, this study begins from questions that investigate how individuals and communities are motivated and how action is legitimated, by way of religious commitments. Understood this way, religious ethics involves the critical investigation and description of a community's religious and moral life as it seeks to use these important values, ideas, and symbols in responding to a series of contemporary moral and ethical issues and problems.

7. Bin Laden, "Open Letter to Shaykh Bin Baz"; and bin Laden, "Second Letter."

8. For those interested in the history of al-Qaeda's formation, see Wright, *Looming Tower*; and Miller, *Audacious Ascetic*. Wright's book has become one of the standard accounts of the history of al-Qaeda's formation. Miller's book is an excellent source that problematizes the standard account while also demonstrating the evolution in bin Laden's thinking as al-Qaeda moved toward the attacks of September 11, 2001.

9. My translation. Bin Laden et al. (The World Islamic Front), "Jihad against the Jews and Crusaders."

10. Benjamin and Simon, *Age of Sacred Terror*; and Clarke, *Against All Enemies*.

11. For example, four of the most influential models approach al-Qaeda in this way. Robert Pape argues that al-Qaeda is most appropriately conceptualized through a broader theory of suicide terrorism. Marc Sageman conceptualizes al-Qaeda through its recruitment and radicalization processes and contends that al-Qaeda ought to be approached as a social movement through which ordinary people become radicalized and militant. He maintains that al-Qaeda is best understood through its recruitment, a four-part process in which an individual comes into contact with a militant group through some kind of personal tie or kinship network. Jonathan Schanzer and Jason Burke—both of whom focus on organizational models—argue that al-Qaeda is best understood as a conglomeration of its cells and affiliates that work together in various ways. Moreover, the dominant models describe the importance of religion in some way. All of them agree that religion, or "ideology," has something to do with understanding al-Qaeda; yet they tend to ascribe religion a marginal role. See Pape, *Dying to Win*; Sageman, *Leaderless Jihad*; Burke, *Al-Qaeda*; and Schanzer, *Al-Qaeda's Armies*.

12. For example, Pape argues that al-Qaeda uses suicide terrorism as a strategic

tactic in much the same way that other national liberation campaigns used it against democracies (which are especially vulnerable to terrorism). He aims to debunk the idea that using suicide terrorism as a tactic is peculiar to "Islamic fundamentalism." Rather, religion, he points out, plays a qualified role in what is a more primary factor that explains suicide terrorism—that is, foreign occupation. He writes that "religious difference"—more than Islam or any other particular religion—"hardens the boundaries between national communities and so makes it easier for terrorist leaders to portray the conflict in zero-sum terms, demonize the opponent, and gain legitimacy for martyrdom from the local community" (80). For Sageman, the contact with, or access to, those who are of a militant mind-set is what ultimately determines whether an individual will choose to join the jihad, as "social bonds play a more important role in the emergence of the global Salafi jihad than ideology" (51).

13. Totten, *First Strike*, 80–83.

14. Bellamy, *Fighting Terror*, 2.

15. Text of President Obama's acceptance speech is found at https://www.white house.gov/the-press-office/remarks-president-acceptance-nobel-peace-prize.

16. James Turner Johnson provides critical insight on both of these points. He describes the just war idea as a historical and moral "tradition" constructed through the relationship between "historical reflection and moral valuing." He argues that moral values are "derived" from a community's historical experience. Thus, when an individual or a community is engaged in historical reflection, it is engaged in a normative act. He insists that historical reflection, through memory, serves to guide moral reasoning and action in the present. Through the act of remembering, a community gazes on the "unconscious imprint of the past upon the present" and intentionally and significantly determines what aspects of this imprint are significant for the present circumstances at hand. Furthermore, it is through this process of historical reflection that moral wisdom and insight are gained and moral communities are forged. By linking moral wisdom from the past to the present, a moral tradition is built and maintained. See Johnson, *Just War Tradition*, 14; and Johnson, "On Keeping Faith," 97–115.

17. For an excellent chart summarizing the just war criteria, see Johnson, *Morality and Contemporary Warfare*, 28–29.

18. The careful reader will note that I use Western just war categories to describe the moral constraints of war in the Islamic tradition. I do so for two reasons. First, the Western just war tradition has been the focus of sustained and concentrated academic attention, leading to historical and applied work that identifies sources and developments. A similar investigation into the Islamic sources has recently been revived. Asma Afsaruddin's *Striving in the Path of God* is an excellent example of this type of work. Second, the comparative work that has been done on these two traditions, particularly that of John Kelsay and James Turner Johnson, demonstrates their

affinity (and important differences) in talking about war. Thus, we can proceed with our investigation under the assumption that while certainly more needs to be done, we can be comfortable using these comparative terms to move forward important work in these areas.

19. William McCants argues that al-Suri has also played an important role in ISIS's thinking. See McCants, *ISIS Apocalypse*.

20. See, for example, Burke, *Al-Qaeda*, 12–13.

Foundations

A Just War Analysis of the War against al-Qaeda

This chapter explicates, analyzes, and critiques the counterinsurgency and counterterrorism frameworks as they have been applied in the war against al-Qaeda to demonstrate the strategic and tactical difficulties of counter-insurgency and counterterrorism in that war. This chapter argues that the attempt to understand al-Qaeda through its tactics and organization—as a "network of networks"—has led to military counter-models that are hampered in their ability to degrade, dismantle, and defeat the al-Qaeda phenomenon.

The point is made through the language and moral commitments of the Western just war criteria. As noted in the introduction to this book, they provide a set of "moral anchorages" that guide US democratic discourse and decision-making.[1] Just as important, the criteria also have realist and ground-level concerns as they help clarify the issues and realities that decision makers confront in determining if, when, and how to use force in response to a specific set of circumstances. In this way, the Western just war criteria help form pointed questions regarding the nature of the threat or the adversary, the means available, the intentions of the use of force, and the probabilities of long-term success.

Historically, just war analyses of war against irregular forces (insurgents or non-state actors) have focused on the criteria of legitimate authority and *jus in bello* discrimination and proportionality. It makes sense, then, that we would begin our assessment of counterinsurgency and counterterrorism in the war against al-Qaeda from the same starting point. In particular, the legitimate authority criterion helps probe into the nature of al-Qaeda and the question of whether it is useful to think of al-Qaeda as a global insurgency.

Yet we cannot stop there as the al-Qaeda phenomenon presents us with a complex case that ought to engender additional considerations. While issues of authority and *jus in bello* commitments remain significant, providing an ethical analysis of counterinsurgency and counterterrorism requires that a larger spectrum of just war reasoning be brought to bear. In particular, the criteria of overall proportionality of ends and reasonable hope of success are useful to us. Both direct our attention to the point that a just use of force must make a sincere and conscientious effort to attend to the *feasibility* and *efficacy* of war planning and conduct. This is not to argue that war planning must ensure victory or make prophetic determinations on how events will develop. Any framework or counter-model for the use of force, however, must reflect the ends and aims to which it has been tasked, must demonstrate planning that is reasonable and prudent, and, furthermore, must be capable of determining whether the proposed use of force remains capable of achieving its desired ends.

The analysis here demonstrates that the standard frameworks are not particularly successful in characterizing al-Qaeda or determining a proper application for the use of force. In the attempt to fight what has been construed as a global insurgency, the United States remains engaged in two large-scale counterinsurgency campaigns and heavily embroiled in the political, social, and economic issues of Afghanistan and Iraq—both of which have been critically hindered by questions regarding the ability of either country's government to sustain the level of legitimacy required to secure its territory against the threat posed by militant groups. In its attempt to respond to al-Qaeda through the lens of counterterrorism, the United States has resorted to what are, arguably, extraordinary uses of force that require the aid and cooperation of multiple states. In light of the transnational nature of the al-Qaeda phenomenon, sustaining these policies, particularly on a broad scale, appears highly problematic.

It is important to note that this chapter neither categorically rejects the dominant models or military counter-models nor argues that understanding organization, tactics, and recruitment are inconsequential to understanding al-Qaeda—for, certainly, this is not the case. That said, this chapter aims to establish the point that we ought to acknowledge the limits of the military counter-models in the war against the al-Qaeda phenomenon.

Models and Counter-models in the War against al-Qaeda

Insurgency and Counterinsurgency War

Counterinsurgency was the primary military framework for the first decade of the war on terrorism, specifically as that war unfolded in Afghanistan and Iraq. Before describing it in detail, our discussion will benefit from a foundational understanding of the concepts and theories of insurgency and counterinsurgency. In particular, it is important that we establish the relationship between politics and insurgency that is the characterizing feature of insurgency and counterinsurgency war.

While specialists trace guerrilla tactics to the ancient world, insurgency is a modern phenomenon.[2] Only in the modern period do we see the systematization of guerrilla tactics into the method of war that we refer to as "insurgency." Figures such as T. E. Lawrence (Lawrence of Arabia), Mao Tse-tung, and Che Guevara—all of whom led successful insurgency wars—argued that guerrilla tactics could be formalized in such a way that a substantial and growing group of guerrilla fighters could face and eventually defeat a large-scale conventional army with superior numbers and material capabilities.[3] In opposition to the traditional military theories of Carl von Clausewitz and Antoine-Henri Jomini—both of whom understood guerrilla war as ancillary to conventional warfare—Lawrence, Mao, and Guevara sought to demonstrate that the irregular nature of guerrillas (their ability to navigate difficult terrain, to hide and ambush, and to live among the people) could be used for strategic and decisive military advantage.

Importantly, however, in their discussions of tactics, Mao, Lawrence, and Guevara emphasized a more foundational point: Insurgency is defined and directed by a specific set of political goals. In this light, understanding counterinsurgency in the war against al-Qaeda requires emphasizing that insurgency war is characterized by a specific political objective—the overthrow of the standing political regime so that the guerrilla forces may replace it with one of their own. This form of war is distinct in the way that insurgencies, at the very heart of the matter, *contest the political legitimacy and authority of a standing regime.* More specifically, insurgency war is defined through the use of guerrilla tactics by a local movement or a group that contests and *ultimately aims to dismantle its own constituted, standing government in the hopes of reestablishing another on different political and social terms.* It is, by definition, a *local* war fought by and against *indigenous* actors.

Because of this, support from the local population is critical. Counterinsurgency doctrine operates under the assumption that both insurgency and counterinsurgency campaigns are engaged in a war for the people, at the fault line of which lies the struggle to possess political authority. As Mao so astutely observed, guerrilla fighters move among the people as fish do in water, drawing on the masses for their lifeblood and sustaining themselves on the people's energy, material resources, and cooperation. Removing the fish from the water kills the guerrillas, extinguishing their sustenance and drive.

In a war that is initiated, organized, and fought on this level, the guerrilla fighters are both materially dependent on the citizens and politically committed to winning them over to the cause. The citizens' support is critical to the political and revolutionary transformation that the guerrilla fighters seek to produce.[4]

The designation of insurgency war as a *political* battle for the hearts and minds of the local population is the driving force behind counterinsurgency frameworks and theories.[5] As an example, let us draw on the work of counterinsurgency expert Sir Robert Thompson, who served as the permanent secretary of defense in Malaya, as the head of the British Advisory Mission to Vietnam, and eventually as the special adviser of pacification to US president Richard Nixon. Thompson highlights the political emphasis of irregular war explicitly in his five "Basic Principles of Counterinsurgency," which are still drawn on extensively by those who are interested in counterinsurgency theory and doctrine.[6] As Thompson states, "An insurgent movement is a war for the people. It stands to reason that government measures must be directed to restoring government authority and law and order throughout the country, so that control over the population can be regained and its support won."[7]

As insurgents capitalize on the *failure of governments*, according to Thompson's principles, counterinsurgency must (1) have a clear political aim, (2) function in accordance with the law, and (3) have an overall plan. This way, he argues, government (4) can give priority to defeating political subversion (rather than guerrillas) and do so through (5) securing its own base areas. Thus, three out of five of Thompson's principles aim at establishing, maintaining, or strengthening the political authority and legitimacy of the standing government.[8] *Counter*insurgency, then, is a tactical response to the *political* aims of insurgency war.

With this point established, let us turn to counterinsurgency as it was applied in Iraq and Afghanistan.

Counterinsurgency in Afghanistan and Iraq: Battlegrounds in the War against al-Qaeda

Relatively quickly, developments on the ground in both campaigns led military decision makers to categorize Iraq and Afghanistan as counterinsurgency wars. In Afghanistan the 2001 US-led invasion did not seem to do much to quell the strength of the Taliban, who were able to regroup by 2002. Aided by recruitment from Pakistan's tribal areas, they continued to launch attacks against US and Coalition forces. US efforts, however, were not limited to fighting the Taliban; US forces also faced a complicated array of actors such as Hezb-i-Islami, the Haqqani network, and an assortment of foreign fighters.

In Iraq, as soon as US forces toppled the Saddam Hussein regime in 2003, the country erupted into a seemingly unending spiral of violence and crime that eventually turned against US and Coalition forces. This violence quickly became sectarian, with clashes between Sunnis and Shiites growing bloodier and more rampant. The rise of Shiite cleric Muqtada al-Sadr, who seemed to be increasingly radicalizing sections of the Shiite classes, the al-Awda group of Hussein loyalists, and the burgeoning presence of jihadi foreign fighters (from places such as Syria, Yemen, Lebanon, Chechnya), severely compli-cated US post-invasion efforts in Iraq. The Americans' hopes for a decisive victory and a quick transition to a post–Saddam Hussein government were strangled by the weight and complexity of the various insurgent groups that emerged.

Facing this reality, American decision makers argued that based on the facts on the ground, both the Afghan and Iraqi conflicts were best described as insurgency wars and required the application of counterinsurgency mil-itary doctrine—a type of warfare that would necessitate the US military's taking on a host of changes in strategy and tactics in its attempt to win both campaigns. Thus, the counterinsurgency framework became the primary military counter-model for the first decade of the war against al-Qaeda. Important for our purposes, both campaigns were framed as counter-insurgency wars given their direct relationship to the war against al-Qaeda. Therefore, addressing the complicated and messy political realities of Iraq and Afghanistan became the cornerstone of US strategy in defeating the al-Qaeda phenomenon.

This connection between the campaigns in Iraq and Afghanistan and the war against al-Qaeda is explicated in the work of counterinsurgency advo-cates and experts, such as Gen. Stanley A. McChrystal, David Kilcullen, and John A. Nagl, who have been among its most prominent supporters. It is important to note that Kilcullen's most recent assessments of the counter-insurgency models are more tempered than his earlier work.[9] However, his framing of the issue has played a profoundly influential role in directing the counterinsurgency discussion as his construal of al-Qaeda as a "transnational militant Islamist insurgency" took root within the military and policy world.[10]

Kilcullen argues that al-Qaeda is a transnational militant Islamist insur-gency. In contrast to a "traditional terrorism problem," Kilcullen's model defines the al-Qaeda network as a transnational organization attempting to overthrow various local governments through the use of insurgency tactics (including terrorism).[11] Al-Qaeda fighters, he contends, are insurgents taking part in a global jihadist movement, one headed by Osama bin Laden's al-Qaeda and linked through a series of social factors and interactions. While the various groups under the al-Qaeda network are separated by geographical borders, they remain linked through shared language, ideology, schooling, and other cultural factors. These social ties are coupled with material publications and other media outlets that serve to distribute and disseminate the al-Qaeda message in the attempt to move the aims of this global insurgency forward. According to Kilcullen, al-Qaeda and the various groups under its umbrella provide either material or "inspirational" assistance, cooperation, and guidance through a sponsorship system.[12]

Employing a four-part process of provocation, intimidation, protraction, and exhaustion, al-Qaeda utilizes guerrilla tactics on a transnational scale to bleed the United States and its allies through an exhaustive war of attrition. Described by Kilcullen as the "accidental guerrilla" phenomenon, al-Qaeda "moves into remote areas, creates alliances with local traditional communities, exports violence that prompts Western intervention, and then exploits the backlash against that intervention in order to generate support for its takfiri agenda."[13]

This leads Kilcullen to argue that the war against al-Qaeda requires the application of counterinsurgency doctrine, though in a way where it is reconstructed to speak to the distinguishing features of a modern and global insurgency. His recommendations draw on classic counterinsurgency theory (as discussed earlier) but in a way that applies to the broader geographical scope and ambitions of al-Qaeda. For example, in 2005 Kilcullen wrote that effective modern counterinsurgency must take note that through their transnational networks of influence, support, and funding, the insurgents' area of interest and influence are not only regional but global. In light of this, modern counterinsurgency is no longer aimed solely at defeating the insurgents but also at "imposing order" on a "complex ecosystem" composed of a network of cooperative and, at times, competitive groups.[14]

Kilcullen's ideas are echoed by other experts. For example, John Nagl, a lieutenant colonel in the US Army, affirms the "infiltration" underpinning of the Kilcullen thesis. Nagl contends that both campaigns are part of a comprehensive war against al-Qaeda, specifically in the connection he draws between insurgency abroad and terrorism threats against the Western world.[15] Seeking territories lacking legitimate and functioning governments—failed states—al-Qaeda and its affiliates infiltrate and use these spaces as combat bases, building their numbers and organizing attacks against Western targets. For this reason securing Iraq and Afghanistan is of such high strategic importance for the United States and its allies. As Nagl and Paul Yingling write, "Because free societies rely on the relatively free movement of people and goods across and within national boundaries, it is cost prohibitive to defend every vulnerable point [from terrorism]." Therefore, "the best way to prevent terrorism at home is to deny terrorists the sanctuary they seek in rogue and failed states around the globe."[16]

The most significant example, however, is General McChrystal's August 2009 assessment of Afghanistan. In the "Commander's Summary," he writes that the United States faces a "resilient and growing insurgency" coupled with a "crisis of confidence among Afghans—in both their government and the international community—that undermines our credibility and emboldens the insurgents." This assessment, he argues, requires "redefining the fight." It requires conducting "*classic counterinsurgency* operations in an environment that is uniquely complex" (emphasis mine). Therefore, he argues, the intentional objective must be the population. The war must be understood as a "war of ideas" where "perceptions derive from actions" and the goals center on a population-centric approach that seeks to regain the trust and legitimacy of Afghans in their government.[17]

McChrystal, Kilcullen, and Nagl all maintain that denying al-Qaeda territory is at the heart of the counterinsurgency tactic in the war against al-Qaeda. Proponents of the counterinsurgency framework insist that al-Qaeda must be denied safe havens and grounds for training and recruitment in both Iraq and Afghanistan. Furthermore, securing these countries may be done effectively only by constructing legitimate governments in both regions.

For example, in elaborating eight "best practices," Kilcullen articulates a counterinsurgency strategy focused on building an effective and legitimate government, integrating civil and military efforts, strengthening local authority, focusing on the population, developing government and security efforts of the host nation, and establishing a "region-wide approach that disrupts insurgent safe havens, controls borders and frontier regions, and undermines terrorist infrastructure in neighboring countries."[18] Referring specifically to Afghanistan, Nagl describes the key objectives as preventing Afghanistan from serving (1) as a terrorist sanctuary and (2) as the "catalyst" for regional instability. Such a policy calls for a military campaign with the goals of security and governance as its keystones. This is, according to Nagl, the only type of military strategy that will provide an exit for US forces from Afghanistan. He continues, "It's at the grass-roots level that you're trying to win. You can kill enemy soldiers—that's not the only issue. You also need to dry up their support. You can't just use the military. It's got to be a constant din of propaganda; it's got to be economic support; it's got to be elections. As long as you only go after the bad guy with the weapon, you're missing the most important part."[19]

Importantly then, in designating al-Qaeda as a global insurgency—and the war against al-Qaeda as a global counterinsurgency war—US military efforts shifted from conventional combat operations to efforts focused on supporting the emerging governments in both nations. For counterinsurgency proponents, fighting the war against al-Qaeda required doing what was necessary to support and strengthen the emerging governments of Iraq and Afghanistan and to gain support from the local population.

This point is particularly well described in the US Army and US Marine Corps' *Counterinsurgency Field Manual.* Published in 2006, this manual was developed by General Petraeus, Lieutenant Colonel Nagl, and a host of other experts as a response to the developing campaigns in Iraq and Afghanistan. It defines insurgency as "an organized movement aimed at the overthrow of a constituted government through the use of subversion and armed conflict. . . . Stated another way, an insurgency is an organized, protracted, politico-military struggle designed to weaken the control of an established government, occupying power, or other political authority while increasing insurgent control."[20]

As the manual notes, insurgencies are focused on constructing a new system of power, whether by replacing the standing government with another or by attempting to gain political control of a certain territory within a nation-state. Insurgencies, the manual argues, are struggles that are interstate and contain "at least some elements of civil war."[21] *Counterinsurgency,* according to the manual, is the "military, paramilitary, political, economic, psychological, and civic actions taken by a government to defeat insurgency."[22] In light of this, "political power is the central issue in insurgencies and counterinsurgencies; each side aims to get the *people to accept its governance* or authority as legitimate [emphasis mine]."[23]

Thus, the decision to classify Iraq and Afghanistan as counterinsurgency wars had a significant impact on the strategic and tactical decisions in both campaigns. American decision makers argued that the war efforts—including the full brunt of the US military's capabilities—must turn toward strengthening the legitimacy of the nascent governments emerging in Iraq and Afghanistan. This shift led to a focus on nation-building efforts—such as providing advisers and ambassadors, assisting with elections, and training indigenous police and military forces—in the hope that both Iraq and Afghanistan could transition to stable and well-functioning states that would no longer serve as fertile breeding or training grounds for al-Qaeda. The "center of gravity" is the civilian population, whose hearts and minds must be won or at least turned toward supporting their current regimes and away from the extremist elements nurtured and inspired by al-Qaeda.

A Just War Critique of Counterinsurgency in the War against al-Qaeda

Legitimate Authority and al-Qaeda as Insurgency?

It seems prudent to begin with a set of basic questions. Is labeling al-Qaeda a "global insurgency" a useful and helpful designation? Does this label help us grasp what al-Qaeda is and what it seeks to be? These are particularly important questions to ask in terms of the insurgency/counterinsurgency labels insofar as using these terms triggers a very specific set of military responses that, as outlined previously, focus heavily on nation-building efforts that are exceptionally complex, time intensive, and expensive.

A foundational feature of insurgency war is a claim to authority. Insurgency forces are claiming a particular type of authority—that is, the authority to use force on behalf of a political community whose interests they claim to represent. Thinking about whether the label of "global insurgency" is a useful one for al-Qaeda then requires that we investigate the question of whether al-Qaeda could (even theoretically) claim the right to use force on behalf of a political community. By investigating this claim, the legitimate authority criterion helps clarify what al-Qaeda is primarily by demonstrating what it is *not*.

Understanding this point in depth, however, requires that we first note the purpose and aims of the legitimate authority criterion.[24] Primarily, this criterion places limits on the use of force by arguing that only a select group of individuals may use armed force on behalf of the community it represents. This restriction is foundational to Western just war thinking in that it establishes the point that only those responsible for, or entrusted with, the welfare and protection of the political community hold the appropriate vantage point (and, hence, the authority) from which to make determinations on the appropriate use of force. Others—individual citizens, for example—are too steeped in their personal interests to claim the type of high-level perspective that is necessary for determining whether a particular use of force is required. To put this concisely, only those who are entrusted with the community's welfare may determine when and under what circumstances the use of force is necessary to protect or maintain the political community to which and for which they are responsible.[25]

It is important to note that for most of its history, the Western just war tradition was averse to granting this authority to individuals who were not formally responsible for the political community—namely those considered rebels, irregulars, or revolutionaries. When reading the work of milestone thinkers within the tradition—from Saint Augustine to Hugo Grotius—it is relatively clear that the insurrection against the standing political authority must be treated very carefully. Oftentimes the stability provided by the standing government would trump the disorder and chaos that would accompany a revolution or contestation of that authority by irregulars and even in cases in which revolutionary forces were contesting governments that were unjust.[26] The idea was that order—sometimes even an order of an unjust kind—is better than the chaos and inevitable injustice that follow the disruption of a standing regime.

This aversion has eased, somewhat, in light of a series of political developments where the authority of irregulars has been more concretely recognized. This development is significant in Western just war thinking as it adds a category of actors who are not part of the established government but are considered to have some effective authority to use force on behalf of a political community. For example, Michael Walzer, one of the most important just war thinkers of the contemporary period, argues that soldiers acquire war rights because of their status as "political instruments" or as members of a community that has a reciprocal relationship with the citizenry. Therefore, the war rights of soldiers may be extended to the guerrilla fighter under specific conditions—for example, when the guerrilla fighter exists in the same type of reciprocal relationship, living as a member of the citizenry and fighting as a military representative.

For Walzer, if the guerrilla fighters, or the insurgency army, are not accorded support and recognition by the masses, they do not acquire the rights of war. However, under the determination that such support and recognition are apparent and are freely given by the citizens, the guerrillas ought to be guaranteed certain rights and treatment such as benevolent quarantine in the case of capture. If the political support for the irregulars is such that the "guerrillas cannot be isolated from the people," then a counterinsurgency war can no longer be fought on moral grounds. He writes, "It cannot be fought because it is no longer an anti-guerrilla but an anti-social war, a war against an entire people, in which no distinctions would be possible in the actual fighting."[27]

The point to draw from this discussion, then, is that authority *can* shift from those who hold political power to those waging an insurrection against tyranny or other forms of injustice. While the classic just war tradition was more reluctant to grant this shift, modern developments have tilted the pendulum toward the idea that certain types of revolutionaries, if they demonstrate particular characteristics, may be afforded the status of legitimate authority.[28]

What does this mean for evaluations of counterinsurgency as they have been applied to the al-Qaeda phenomenon? When we consider al-Qaeda's strategy, tactics, and organization, it becomes clear that, at least in terms of the just war tradition, al-Qaeda may not claim to represent a legitimate group of irregulars or irregular forces. As a loose conglomeration of groups and lone-wolf actors who are inspired by al-Qaeda's thinking, who come from a wide range of locations, and approach armed jihad from a variety of perspectives, al-Qaeda can hold no claim to authority. It holds no legitimate authority to represent a nation or even a political group. Its claim of representing Muslims or the community of 1.6 billion Muslims spread across the globe is meaningless. Even if we were to grant, the way that al-Qaeda does, that it has some support from the global Muslim community, it is impossible to make the case that any political community has chosen or delegated al-Qaeda as its representative. Nor is it possible to argue that al-Qaeda may then represent any community's grievances.

The point of this, however, is not to argue that al-Qaeda's lack of legitimacy emasculates the international community's ability or legal or moral right to use force against al-Qaeda. Legitimate authority on the part of the adversary is not necessarily a requirement for the just use of force; rather, what we see here is that al-Qaeda is not best conceptualized through the category of insurgency. An insurgency is an irregular force that claims to represent the grievances and interests of a specific political community and against a specific standing government; thus, irregular forces have a status within just war thinking (and international law). Al-Qaeda's label of a *global* insurgency, therefore, is a misnomer, because it is not tied to a specific political community with aims to overturn its standing government. Conceptualizing al-Qaeda in this way has led to a counter-model that seeks to apply counterinsurgency theory on a transnational (and sometimes on a global) scale and has triggered a counter-model that is bound to incur a series of insurmountable strategic, tactical, and ethical difficulties.

In short, when we think of al-Qaeda as an insurgency, our moral and ethical analysis yields unsatisfactory answers. It does not produce much in the way of determining *what* al-Qaeda is. Nor does it necessarily provide much guidance on the question of *how* it ought to be addressed. While the assessments by Kilcullen and Nagl attempt to create clear relationships between the insurgencies in Iraq and Afghanistan and the war against al-Qaeda, the "denial of sanctuary" arguments invite further investigation. Even if it is possible to claim that the US military campaigns opened the way for securing stable and well-functioning states in both Iraq and Afghanistan, and ultimately denying al-Qaeda both states as sanctuaries, questions remain regarding the appropriateness of a counterinsurgency approach to al-Qaeda, for the efficacy of the counterinsurgency framework is ultimately measured not only by its ability to secure Iraq and Afghanistan but also by its ability to contain the global al-Qaeda phenomenon. Thus, the incorporation of additional just war criteria into the analysis highlights other issues that ought to be considered in evaluating this framework.

Overall Proportionality of Ends and Reasonable Hope of Success in Afghanistan and Iraq

To begin, the demands of successful counterinsurgency raise serious questions of overall proportionality. The proportionality of ends criterion leads to reflection on the harms and benefits of using force. It requires that the overall good anticipated by resorting to force be greater than the expected harm. Working under the understanding that straightforward calculations of harms and benefits are usually out of reach, this factor in just war reasoning calls for serious, conscientious, and deliberate reflection on the anticipated (and possible) ends to be achieved. Such an analysis necessitates taking into account the multiple factors and considerations involved in a counterinsurgency war against al-Qaeda.

The first is a protracted military commitment to the areas in question. As demonstrated by the campaigns in Iraq and Afghanistan, counterinsurgency is messy and slow and requires long-term pledges of support to maintain the progress that is achieved. As noted by the *Counterinsurgency Field Manual*, a population-centric approach necessitates the development of local community partnerships that will assist in locating and understanding the insurgency as well as local civilian problems and grievances. In this way, a significant amount of counterinsurgency involves troops going out among the people, attempting to gather intelligence, and all while restricting the use of firepower.[29] Building these relationships is a time-consuming task that is subject to the difficulties (and frequent disintegration) that are inherent to any political form of negotiation.

In the same way, proper counterinsurgency demands counterinsurgents to expend significant resources. They must develop an understanding of indigenous social, political, and economic structures and issues. As the manual argues, "Soldiers and Marines are expected to be nation builders, in addition to warriors."[30] The counterinsurgents must have a grasp of both local interests and local grievances. They must learn how a society works and what it is seeking. In addition, they must further recognize how power is distributed, shared, or negotiated, and that involves knowledge not only of contemporary conditions but also of the historical events that continue to impose their hold on the population. As Kilcullen notes, the local counterinsurgents are tasked with "becoming the world expert on your district."[31] Furthermore, given the protracted nature of counterinsurgency campaigns, successful operations necessitate that the trust and initiative gained through these personal relationships be transferred through various generations of troop deployments. Such requirements are a serious strain even on an institution as large and as sophisticated as that of the US military.

Moreover, the trans-territorial nature of al-Qaeda raises questions about the efficacy of this approach. US forces have become embroiled in the local and indigenous conflicts of both Afghanistan and Iraq. As noted, troops respond to local issues and problems and exert tremendous material resources and energy all while taking on increased levels of risk because of the restrained firepower policy of counterinsurgency. The cumulative effect, however, is that the United States remains involved in two complex, expensive, and material-laden wars to "secure" Iraq and Afghanistan. As a result of the counterinsurgency approach, the United States has spent serious levels of energy and resources to *indirectly* fight al-Qaeda. While al-Qaeda fighters are unquestionably involved in both campaigns, counterinsurgency appears to be directly focused on the local politics of Iraq and Afghanistan as opposed to the al-Qaeda network.[32]

Furthermore, the question of whether a counterinsurgency approach may yield long-term success in both Iraq and Afghanistan is acute. As noted, the criterion of a reasonable hope of success highlights that a just war is one in which the relevant authorities conscientiously deliberate and determine whether there is a realistic chance of attaining victory. While prophetic assurances of success are not required, this criterion does call for prudent decision-making based on sound assessments of the facts at hand. Such assessments will note that successful counterinsurgency entails that a standing government is capable of maintaining, or at least acquiring, levels of support from its citizens—ultimately leading it to hold an authority and legitimacy that is above local and diffuse power structures. This calls for a government to be committed to making the political changes that the counterinsurgency seeks and to be capable of maintaining levels of progress.[33] Up until this point, the ability of the government of either Iraq or Afghanistan to do this work is questionable at best.

Despite troop surges in 2007 (Iraq) and 2010 (Afghanistan), stability in both campaigns has proved elusive. Shortly after President Obama's speech at Fort Bragg, North Carolina, in 2011, where he announced that American troops would exit Iraq, Prime Minister Nouri al-Maliki issued an arrest warrant for Iraq's Sunni vice president. This move initiated a period of violence that by 2014 had reached levels almost as severe as those seen at the height of the war. ISIS's entrance into Iraq and Syria has only further complicated Iraq's intense and violent postwar developments.[34] As for Afghanistan, President Hamid Karzai's decade-long reign as president was fraught with corruption and duplicity. Moreover, the massive fraud that characterized the 2014 election of Ashraf Ghani, coupled with the resurgence of the Taliban and ethnic and tribal warfare, led to grim predictions regarding Afghanistan's long-term stability. Even as the United States attempts to end both campaigns, there are approximately ten thousand American troops in Afghanistan and approximately three thousand American troops in Iraq, serving as trainers, advisers, security keepers, and so on. The political instability of both Iraq and Afghanistan, therefore, render both states unagreeable to successful counterinsurgency.

Iraq and Afghanistan, as well as other regional governments, have yet to display the degree of legitimacy required for effective long-term governance. Both remain fraught with ineffective and divided central governments. Furthermore, their authority is limited, rarely extending throughout the country, as indigenous power structures take over in their absence.

At the time of writing, President Obama announced that the United States will maintain ninety-eight hundred troops in Afghanistan through 2016 and will likely maintain a level of approximately fifty-five hundred troops there until an unspecified date. This number is coupled with approximately five thousand American personnel in Iraq to aid the fight against ISIS. Both Iraqis and Afghanis continue to deal with the effects of fragmented governments, sectarian and tribal wars, and a lack of necessary services, such as food, gas, and water. Moreover, the penetration of ISIS into Iraq and Syria has severely complicated US efforts to end these wars. A complete exit of American troops remains a source of anxiety for both Iraqi and Afghani citizens as they wonder what will prevent tribal war between the various factions in both states. Such worries are intensified by developments in Egypt, Bosnia, and Yemen, where anxiety over groups affiliated or linked with al-Qaeda have colored the conversations about US military involvement (or lack thereof).

Yet thinking of counterinsurgency against al-Qaeda only in terms of Afghanistan and Iraq is not enough. Again, here we must note the global nature of the al-Qaeda phenomenon. As we have seen, this foundational point of Kilcullen's thesis and of the military's counterinsurgency approach to al-Qaeda conceptualizes al-Qaeda specifically as a *global insurgency*. Therefore, we are forced to examine how the tools of counterinsurgency may be applied on a global scale and to the various groups that are affiliated or inspired by the al-Qaeda phenomenon. And if we think in terms of the difficulties and costs of the conflicts in Afghanistan and Iraq and now in Syria and other places where ISIS may spread, it quickly becomes apparent that a global counterinsurgency war—given the limits of US military and diplomatic power—is impossible.

Counterterrorism: Foundational Terms, Theories, and Concepts

Counterterrorism in the War against al-Qaeda

The proponents of counterterrorism often begin from a critique of counterinsurgency. While they do not contest the global nature of al-Qaeda, or the global insurgency label, they directly challenge the core of the counterinsurgency framework, or the notion that large-scale nation-building efforts are a critical part of eliminating this threat.

The work of Steven Simon, a respected Middle East foreign policy analyst, well illustrates the foundational points of the counterterrorism approach. Writing in 2009, Simon and coauthor Jonathan Stevenson argued that counterinsurgency efforts have been unsuccessful in Afghanistan and, moreover, have contributed to a "spillover" effect of militants going to Pakistan in response to greater US military pressure on Afghanistan.[35] Through the Taliban's support in both Pakistan and Afghanistan, al-Qaeda has managed to rebuild its camps and to reconstruct a safe haven in the tribal areas of Pakistan. The real threat, Simon writes, is the establishment of "mini-Afghanistans" in Pakistan.[36] Of further note is the difficulty that any increase in the US military presence would place on Pakistan. Such pressure would ultimately impede Islamabad's ability to cooperate with the United States by intensifying popular perceptions of the US military's presence and involvement as an occupation and of Pakistan's cooperation as "complicity."[37]

In light of this, US policy cannot focus on guaranteeing the political legitimacy and integrity of Afghanistan while simultaneously containing al-Qaeda and the Taliban in Pakistan. Simon argues these objectives are not realistic. Rather than pursuing the costly and inefficient methods of counterinsurgency, the United States should aim only to "ensure that al-Qaeda is denied both Afghanistan and Pakistan as operating bases for transnational attacks on the United States and its allies and partners."[38]

This, Simon argues, ought to be done by increasing Washington's "effective policy of eliminating al-Qaeda's leadership with drone strikes." He quotes an anonymous senior US counterterrorism official as saying, "In the past, you could take out the number 3 al-Qaeda leader, and number 4 just moved up to take his place. . . . Well, if you take out number 3, number 4, and then 5, 6, 7, 8, 9, and 10, it suddenly becomes a lot more difficult to revive the leadership cadre."[39] The aim is to make it difficult for al-Qaeda to regenerate its leadership, eventually crushing its ability to mount attacks.

The George W. Bush and Obama administrations were on board with this logic. While the Bush administration initiated the use of drone strikes against al-Qaeda as an ancillary component of the campaigns in Iraq and Afghanistan, the Obama administration—as it sought to draw down from the war in Iraq to focus resources and attention in Afghanistan—ramped up the drone program significantly. Since the drone program was initiated in 2004, there have been (at the time of writing) 403 total drone strikes in Pakistan; most began in 2008 with the number of strikes peaking in 2010 (117 strikes). While neither administration has provided casualty numbers, independent groups have noted that these strikes have killed 1,850 to 3,079 "militants" along with 255 to 315 civilians. These numbers are coupled with 173 total American drone strikes in Yemen, which have killed a reported 942 to 1,194 militants and 87 to 93 civilians.[40]

It is important to note that traditional counterterrorism methods are still utilized. For example, the most recent cases of foiled plots—Amine El Khalifi (US Capitol bomb plot, 2012) and Quazi Mohammad Rezwanel Ahsan Nafis (Federal Reserve Building, 2012)—were discovered through traditional counterterrorism techniques. Moreover, figures such as Ahmed Ghailani (embassy bombings in Kenya and Tanzania, 1998), Umar Farouk Abdulmutallab (attempted airliner bombing, Christmas Day 2009), Faisal Shahzad (attempted Times Square bombing, 2010), and, most recently, Dzhokhar Tsarnaev (Boston Marathon bombing, 2013) were all tried and prosecuted through the US criminal court system.

However, proponents of drones, and the Obama administration in particular, have argued repeatedly that this technology is a necessary part of the war against al-Qaeda because dangerous terrorists who pose a threat to US national security cannot always be captured, detained, interrogated, and then subjected to the criminal court process. In other words, increased reliance on drone technology results from the fact that "full due process cannot always be afforded terrorists owing to the immediate threat some pose, and the operational impracticality of subjecting purportedly actionable intelligence to quasi-judicial review in very tight time frames."[41]

Despite these claims to necessity, the use of drones remains a highly debated topic. This controversy has only intensified over the number of civilian casualties and with the killing of eight American citizens, only one of whom, Anwar al-Awlaki (whose influence is discussed in chapter 4), was intentionally targeted. In response to public calls for accountability and transparency in the drone program, the Obama administration has repeatedly justified its use of these weapons in the war against al-Qaeda. Evaluating the ethical questions involved requires that we begin with these justifications, all of which have come in the form of public speeches from President Obama and administration officials when attempting to communicate the point that, from their perspective, drone strikes against al-Qaeda militants (or those suspected of being al-Qaeda militants) are well within the legal power of the United Sates. Importantly, these speeches are the only documents available to the general public that provide information regarding the targeting procedures and the administration's justifications for why these strikes are not only necessary but also legal.

Obama Administration Policy Statements on Drone Strikes and International Law

Speeches by President Obama and his advisers demonstrate four foundational points of the administration's reasoning for using drones in the war against al-Qaeda. First, Congress granted the president the legal authority to use force against al-Qaeda operatives. Given al-Qaeda's diffuse and decentralized nature, this authority extends beyond Afghanistan and into the various places that al-Qaeda operates. Second, the threat from al-Qaeda cannot always be dealt with through traditional methods. Therefore, in light of the president's authority and responsibility to the safety of American citizens, the president can and must use other means available to him. Third, the use of such technology is constrained by both necessity and imminence. As these statements argue, the United States uses drone strikes only if suspected terrorists cannot be captured, detained, and interrogated. And fourth, each strike decision undergoes a process of debate and scrutiny. Moreover, it is subject to a series of restrictions imposed by international law, such as noncombatant immunity, last resort, proportionality, and respect for state sovereignty.

Harold Hongju Koh, legal adviser to the Department of State from 2009 to 2013, described the Obama administration's legal justifications for targeted killings during a talk given at the annual meeting of the American Society of International Law on March 25, 2010. In his speech Koh stressed that drone strikes are a legitimate use of force in the "ongoing armed conflict" between the United States and the "associated forces" of al-Qaeda and the Taliban that, he argues, the United States initiated in response to the events of September 11. Thus, the Americans' use of force is justified and legitimate under the inherent right of self-defense granted under international law. Furthermore, as Congress authorized the use of all necessary and appropriate force through the 2001 Authorization for Use of Military Force, domestic law buttresses this authority.[42]

In the same vein, Koh also insisted on classifying al-Qaeda operatives as "belligerents" and "lawful targets under international law." The United States, he argued, is not required to provide al-Qaeda operatives with due process. Moreover, targeting al-Qaeda operatives does not violate the domestic ban on "assassinations," because the use of weapons systems for targeting high-level targets in an act of self-defense during an armed conflict is not a violation of domestic law. Koh insisted that the procedures surrounding targeting adhere to the principles of distinction and proportionality, with care taken to ensure that civilians are not attacked directly and that the collateral damage incurred is minimized to the greatest extent possible. Targeting decisions are made upon "considerations specific to each case, including those related to the imminence of the threat, the sovereignty of the other states involved, and the willingness and ability of those states to suppress the threat the target poses."[43]

US attorney general Eric Holder reinforced these points in a March 2012 speech at Northwestern University School of Law. In particular, Holder stressed that drone strikes are a defensive use of force that is well established both by Congress's authorization to the president to use all "necessary and appropriate force" against the Taliban and al-Qaeda and by the president's constitutional powers to "protect the nation from any imminent threat of violent attack." While he emphasized that US policy, and preference, is to capture, detain, and interrogate suspected terrorists, he also noted that "there are instances when our government has the clear authority—and, I would argue, the responsibility—to defend the United States through appropriate and lawful use of lethal force."[44]

Most interesting, however, is Holder's insistence that this legal authority reaches beyond Afghanistan, extending US authority to use drones even outside places where the United States is at war or has boots on the ground. The decentralized and diffuse nature of al-Qaeda, he argued, is such that military force can be used in countries other than Afghanistan. He maintained, "We are at war with a stateless enemy, prone to shifting operations from country to country. Over the last three years, al Qaeda and its associates have directed several attacks—fortunately, unsuccessful—against us from countries other than Afghanistan. Our government has both a responsibility and a right to protect this nation and its people from such threats."[45]

Of course, Holder was quick to note that this authority is not unconstrained and, in fact, is limited by international legal principles, including another nation's right to sovereignty. However, he went on to say, "The use of force in foreign territory would be consistent with these international legal principles if conducted, for example, with the consent of the nation involved—or after a determination that the nation is unable or unwilling to deal effectively with a threat to the United States." The same reasoning applies, he argued, for al-Qaeda operatives who are American citizens. A US citizen who serves as a "senior operational leader" of al-Qaeda and becomes "actively engaged in planning to kill Americans" is considered a legitimate and lawful target if "the U.S. government has determined, after a thorough and careful review, that the individual poses an imminent threat of violent attack against the United States; second, capture is not feasible; and third, the operation would be conducted in a manner consistent with applicable law of war principles."[46]

Holder's speech also offers a glance into the targeting process. As he noted, the strikes are bound by various criteria: *necessity* (the target must have a "definite military value"), *distinction* (only "lawful targets—such as combatants, civilians directly participating in hostilities, and military objectives—may be targeted intentionally"), *proportionality* ("anticipated collateral damage must not be excessive in relation to the anticipated military advantage"), and *humanity*, which "requires us to use weapons that will not inflict unnecessary suffering."[47]

President Obama spoke publicly about drones at a highly publicized and anticipated speech at National Defense University on May 23, 2013. The president was responding to bipartisan demands that the drone program's targeting and selection criteria become subject to congressional and public scrutiny. As with Koh's and Holder's speeches, Obama began by emphasizing the necessity of drone strikes against a force like al-Qaeda. Although the "core of al Qaeda in Afghanistan and Pakistan is on a path to defeat," he remarked, the United States still faces threats from "the emergence of various al Qaeda affiliates. From Yemen to Iraq, from Somalia to North Africa, the threat today is more diffuse." This, he notes, is coupled with a "real threat from radicalized individuals in the United States."[48]

Echoing Koh and Holder, President Obama asserted the same legal and ethical justifications for the use of drones against al-Qaeda militants. He argued,

America's actions are legal. We were attacked on 9/11. Within a week, Congress overwhelmingly authorized the use of force. Under domestic law, and international law, the United States is at war with al Qaeda, the Taliban, and their associated forces. We are at war with an organization that right now would kill as many Americans as they could if we did not stop them first. So this is a just war—a war waged proportionately, in last resort, and in self-defense.[49]

Moreover, as Koh and Holder did, Obama also insisted that the use of drone technology is necessary in cases where the authority and power of the host state is limited or where the host state lacks the ability or the desire to capture terrorists who threaten US national security. In addition to this, however, President Obama argued that even in situations where the United States can place boots on the ground, there are cases where it is preferable not to do so, as engaging US firepower in this way could pose a threat to the local communities or "trigger a major international crisis." In fact, he notes, drone technology allows the United States to narrowly target only "those who want to kill us, and not the people they hide among"; thus, the United States is "choosing the course of action least likely to result in the loss of innocent life."[50]

President Obama also emphasized that beyond Afghanistan, the United States targets only al-Qaeda operatives, and it is, presumably, legal under the congressional mandate handed to the president after September 11. He was also careful to emphasize that strikes are conducted only under specific conditions. Insofar as the administration always prefers to capture and interrogate terrorists, he pointed out the United States initiates strikes only when capture is not possible. Moreover, the power to use drone technology is not "unconstrained." Rather, such actions "are bound by consultations with partners, and respect for state sovereignty. America does not take strikes to punish individuals—we act against terrorists who pose a continuing and imminent threat to the American people, and where there are no other governments capable of effectively addressing the threat. And before any strike is taken, there must be a near-certainty that no civilians will be killed or injured—the highest standard we can set."[51]

In summary, the administration argues that these weapons are necessary, they are discriminate and precise, they are subject to a review process, and, in the ongoing armed conflict with al-Qaeda, they are defensive and legal.

For the Obama administration, drones are the weapons of the future, ones that will allow the United States to fundamentally change the way it conducts its military business. As President Obama noted, the nature of this technology (being discriminate and requiring virtually no US military casualties) will allow the United States to move from large-scale campaigns with boots on the ground to a "surgical" approach of warfare—that is, "a series of persistent, targeted efforts to dismantle specific networks of violent extremists that threaten America."[52]

Critics of the drone program, however, have contested precisely these points. Their critiques will help demonstrate the difficulty of relying on drone strikes as the primary weapon in the pursuit of an al-Qaeda defeat.

A Just War Critique of the Counterterrorism Framework

Legitimate Authority and Reasonable Hope of Success

The question of legitimate authority, in the case of drones, is focused primarily on the issue of whether the Obama administration has the legal and moral authority to use drones not only in Iraq and Afghanistan but also in other places (Pakistan, Yemen, Syria, etc.) where it claims al-Qaeda poses a threat to US security. The Obama administration argues that drone strikes are a legitimate use of the president's military power. Others in the international legal community, however, have challenged the administration's legal justifications.

In a United Nations (UN) General Assembly study on targeted killings, United Nations special rapporteur on extrajudicial, summary, or arbitrary executions Philip Alston notes that the laws of war concerning drone strikes, as they have been construed in response to contemporary threats, have expanded "who may be permissibly targeted and under what conditions."[53] More specifically, Alston questions the administration's description of the war against al-Qaeda as an ongoing armed conflict, for the legality of targeted killings is directly dependent on a legitimate claim of armed conflict. Mentioning the case of the United States specifically, Alston argues that under the current stipulations of international law, the Unites States will have a difficult time demonstrating its claim to an armed conflict (a legal term that requires a certain level of hostilities) with a group like al-Qaeda, a group that neither represents a particular community or nation-state nor seems to constitute a "party" in an appreciable way. As Alston writes, the United States has yet to demonstrate how—"outside the context of the armed conflicts in Afghanistan or Iraq—it is in a transnational non-international armed conflict against 'al-Qaeda, the Taliban and other associated forces' without further explanation of how those entities constitute a 'party' under the IHL [international humanitarian law] of non-international armed conflict, and whether and how any violence by any such group rises to the level necessary for an armed conflict to exist."[54]

Both treaty law and customary international law require that the group in question be engaged in "collective, armed, anti-government action."[55] While al-Qaeda and its entities have operated in various countries around the world, none of these states (with the possible exception of Pakistan) "recognize themselves as being part of an armed conflict against al-Qaeda or its 'associates' in their territory," nor have the attacks risen to the level necessary to reach the criteria of an armed conflict. Furthermore, the ties between al-Qaeda and its affiliates are loose, such that "they appear to be not even groups, but a few individuals who take 'inspiration' from al-Qaeda. The idea that, instead, they are part of continuing hostilities that spread to new territories as new alliances form or are claimed may be superficially appealing but such 'associates' cannot constitute a 'party' as required by IHL."[56]

According to Alston, if the United States were to define its current state of hostilities with al-Qaeda as an "ongoing armed conflict," then the dangers involved would be magnified. This is particularly the case, he argues, because drones drastically reduce the risk to a state's armed forces while still yielding significant targeting capabilities. They pose enticements for policymakers and military commanders who, he writes, may "be tempted to interpret the legal limitations on who can be killed, and under what circumstances, too expansively."[57] He concludes, therefore, that while the "appeal of an armed conflict paradigm to address terrorism is obvious," it is outweighed by the "potential for abuse" when states are given an unrestricted ability to use force in ways they deem necessary or useful.

This problem is further exacerbated given that insurgency and violence on the part of non-state actors occur all over the globe. Therefore, the ability of states to respond to such unrest with force must be tempered and guided by laws that are applicable to it and not through paradigms that do not fit. As Alston writes, "If States unilaterally extend the law of armed conflict to situations that are essentially matters of law enforcement that must, under international law, be dealt with under the framework of human rights, they are not only effectively declaring war against a particular group, but eviscerating key and necessary distinctions between international law frameworks that restricts States' ability to kill arbitrarily."[58]

Alston is not alone in his critique. More recently, Ben Emmerson, UN special rapporteur on counterterrorism and human rights, also has argued that US legal reasoning for the use of drones is highly questionable under the terms of international law. Like Alston, Emmerson also contests the claim that the United States is waging an armed conflict against a global al-Qaeda. As he notes, he is unaware of another state that has declared itself engaged in a global war with members of al-Qaeda wherever they happen to be. By making this assertion, the United States attempts to lawfully assert that it can take action against an al-Qaeda fighter wherever he or she might be, but he argues the claim ought not withstand the scrutiny of the international community.[59]

Emmerson was also tasked with launching a special inquiry into the "civilian impact, and human rights implications" of US drone strikes, the conclusions of which were presented to the United Nations.[60] In his press release, he emphasizes his concern that such technology required clear and unambiguous legal justification for its use as well as guidelines for target selection. This is especially true in light of the international character of such attacks, with the United States launching drone strikes into areas (like Yemen and Pakistan) where no official hostilities have been declared.[61] Moreover, at the conclusion of an initial three-day visit to Pakistan, Emmerson categorized US drone use as "forcible military interference," arguing that the United States is violating Pakistan's national sovereignty as the strikes are being conducted without the Pakistanis' consent.

Emmerson's report to the Human Rights Council, released in February 2014, cites increasing levels of civilian casualties as a result of drone strikes in Yemen and Afghanistan. Noteworthy, also, are the report's eight pages of descriptions of multiple strikes in Afghanistan, Pakistan, and Yemen that, according to his report, killed civilians only.[62] Perhaps most interesting, Emmerson emphasizes that there remains an "urgent and imperative need" to reach an agreement on a number of significant legal issues:

> Does the international law principle of self-defence entitle a State to engage in non-consensual lethal counter-terrorism operations on the territory of another State against a non-State armed group that poses a direct and immediate threat of attack even when the armed group concerned has no operational connection to its host State? If so, under what conditions does such a right of self-defence arise? Does such a right arise where the territorial State is judged to be unable or unwilling to prevent the threat from materialising? If so, what are the criteria for determining "unwillingness" or "inability" to act?[63]

From these questions, and Emmerson's repeated calls for transparency and the release of post-strike investigations, international consensus on the legality of drone strikes in the territory of sovereign states clearly is not yet widely accepted. These points are critical to consider, especially when we highlight the difficulties the United States has faced in its relationship with Pakistan over the use of drones and over Pakistani civilian casualties. While drone strikes in Pakistan appear to have been conducted with varying levels of consent from the Pakistani government in the early stages, as of 2011, Pakistan demanded that the United States both reduce the number of intelligence personnel in its territory and immediately halt drone strikes in the northwest region. The reduction in personnel was drastic enough (approximately 25–40 percent) to severely hamper US efforts. More important, however, it signaled a deteriorating cooperative relationship between Pakistan and the United States—a relationship that is critical to the continued use of targeted killing policies.[64]

Islamabad's protests of drone strikes have continued steadily, with Pakistani officials continually noting that drone strikes are conducted without their consent. Pakistan also feels it has the means, and is making concerted efforts, to deal with suspected terrorists on its own soil through its own government and resources. Officials have continually noted that drone strikes in Pakistan—in light of Pakistani anger over civilian casualties—are counterproductive. As noted by Emmerson,

> The position of the Pakistani government is quite clear. It does not consent to the use of drones by the United States on its territory and it considers this to be a violation of Pakistan's sovereignty and territorial integrity. As a matter of international law, the US drone campaign in Pakistan is therefore being conducted without the consent of the elected representatives of the people or the legitimate government of the state. It involves the use of force on the territory of another state without its consent and is therefore a violation of Pakistan's sovereignty. Pakistan has also been quite clear that it considers the drone campaign to be counter-productive and to be radicalizing a whole new generation, and thereby perpetuating the problem of terrorism in the region.[65]

In fact, his 2014 report noted that Pakistan was one of the only places where US drone strikes had decreased. He attributed this fact to Islamabad's unwillingness to continue its partnership with the United States on the issue of drone strikes on Pakistani soil (an issue that has been highly unpopular with its citizens).[66] Of course, some will point out that Pakistan's public position on this issue may not match its stance during discussions behind closed doors. Nevertheless, Emmerson's point must be considered in analyzing counterterrorism approaches to the al-Qaeda phenomenon as it brings up the unresolved legal issues that are at the heart of discussions about drone weapons.

These unresolved legal issues render the Obama administration's claims to authority questionable. It is unclear whether the United States will be able to acquire the necessary type of authority and cooperation in the international community to sustain the large-scale use of this drone technology in the way the Obama administration, and future administrations, seeks to do.

Proportionality and Discrimination

Of course, the authority of the Obama administration to initiate these strikes—or to label al-Qaeda fighters (and those suspected of being militants) as legitimate targets—is not the only issue in question. Just as important are the capabilities and results of these weapons, particularly in regard to their abilities to be discriminate and proportional. In just war thinking, these issues are central to evaluating tactics in war. It is important to determine that a particular use of force is proportionate; that is, the harm should not severely outweigh the good that is done by destroying a military target (or by killing a suspected al-Qaeda member). Second, it is also critical that a use of force be discriminate, taking due care not only to protect civilian lives but also to minimize other forms of collateral damage. The Obama administration's statements address these issues, yet all of the administration's statements on these questions leave a tremendous amount to be desired.

This is primarily due to the covert nature of drone strikes, making an accurate assessment of the ethical questions difficult. Review processes for assessing the accuracy of intelligence and calculating the projected collateral damage (in terms of civilian deaths) have been developed; however, the US military and Central Intelligence Agency (CIA) tightly guard the details of the procedural systems and do not share them with those outside the immediate decision-making circles. Other factors remain disconcerting. There is evidence that drone strikes have been ordered without going through the proper chain of command. Furthermore, the deployment of drone strikes by private military contractors has led to increased uncertainty on the overall "integrity" of the review processes for drone technology.[67]

While official policy statements note that drone targeting is conducted in accordance with principles of distinction and proportionality, as long as the decision-making process remains classified, a more accurate understanding of the risks and benefits of drone strikes—as well as the critical questions surrounding their necessity—requires an increased level of transparency in the decision-making process. Moreover, there is the question of noncombatant immunity and civilian casualties. The criterion of discrimination prohibits the direct targeting of civilians and requires a positive demonstration of effort not only to protect civilian life but also to minimize civilian casualties. Some level of civilian casualties may still occur; however, determining the level of collateral damage appropriate to drone strikes requires accurate assessments of the risk.

The administration continues to insist that civilian casualty numbers are much lower than those given by independent groups. In fact, Senator Dianne Feinstein (D-CA) argued that classified documents show that the number of civilian casualties caused by drone strikes were in the single digits each year. This number, however, has been contested by a variety of independent agencies. An International Human Rights and Conflict Resolution Clinic (Stanford) and the Global Justice Clinic (New York University School of Law) 2012 report, based on investigations in Pakistan and including more than 130 witness interviews, argues that the administration's insistence on the precision of these weapons is highly questionable.[68] In addition, the administration uses controversial "signature strikes" in which drone operators target and kill unidentified, armed, military-aged males who appear to be engaged in or associated with suspicious activity. This standard falls well below that of international humanitarian law, which requires those who are targeted to be participating directly or continuously in some kind of combat function. This point is underscored well in Ben Emmerson's report, which provides pages of descriptions of drone strikes in which only civilians (mistaken for militants) were killed.

In light of these reports, proponents of targeted assassination policies ought to explain publicly the necessity of this technology in the war against al-Qaeda. Such procedures also ought to clarify the risk that the targeted terrorists pose. Without such information the moral questions surrounding the use of this technology are impossible to assess. Furthermore, the procedures used to determine and authorize drone strikes ought to be spelled out and subject to some level of public scrutiny so that they may be discussed and debated among policy and military decision makers in an open public forum. While the need for secrecy remains an important consideration, the legitimacy of drone technology requires that significantly more effort is made to define the conditions under which these decisions are made.

President Obama, in his National Defense University speech, made gestures in this direction. He noted that policy recommendations for choosing targets would be systematized (though they remain classified) and that responsibility for the drone program (and strikes) would move from the CIA to the Pentagon. He also indicated that he would consider additional options for increased congressional oversight. Most recently, after the Obama administration disclosed that a January 2015 drone strike against an al-Qaeda compound had inadvertently killed an American and an Italian aid worker being held hostage by al-Qaeda (despite hundreds of hours of surveillance), President Obama ordered an investigation into the strikes. All are important moves in the right direction. Increasing transparency and oversight would certainly begin to answer some of the questions that surround the use of drone technology, especially in regard to necessity and discrimination.[69] However, as the administration's developments in this direction are in the early stages, it remains to be seen how President Obama's new policy initiatives (or those of the following administration) will affect the ethical questions surrounding the use of drones.

In addition, even in the ideal circumstances where the United States is able to clarify its targeting procedures and accountability mechanisms, as well as obtain the cooperation of its allies, serious questions remain as to whether counterterrorism efforts that rely on drone technology are sustainable. While these weapons are precise, they rely categorically on accurate intelligence, which is highly sought after but relatively elusive. Insofar as al-Qaeda is operating in multiple countries around the world, and the United States must rely on its partners for accurate intelligence, the ability of the United States to obtain the required intelligence as well as the rapid strike capacity is questionable.

Furthermore, these issues are especially worrisome insofar as it is unclear whether drone strikes can cripple the diffuse and decentralized nature of the al-Qaeda phenomenon. Drones do not appear to be advancing the strategic goals of counterterrorism, for they have not clearly weakened al-Qaeda's ability to raise new leadership or demoralized its recruitment base. Moreover, the drone campaigns have created new enemies and led to fierce opposition in Muslim-majority countries. As Audrey Kurth Cronin noted in 2013 in *Foreign Affairs*, when drones are the centerpiece of American counterterrorism initiatives, the United States will lose "the war of perceptions"— particularly as they allow "tactics to drive strategy."[70]

Even those, like Daniel Byman, who argue that drones will continue to be used in the future raise serious concerns about the program. They point in particular to the fact that the United States is setting a precedent for how other countries with this technology may choose to use it and, relatedly, that the ease of drone technology will pull the United States into conflicts that it should avoid and would be more likely to avoid if it were required to put boots on the ground. This question has become particularly worrisome in the international community, for clearly the United States, as the most frequent user of drone weapons, is setting the international standard for how other countries that have or will acquire these weapons will use them.[71]

Conclusion

The structure of al-Qaeda has complicated traditional frameworks for using force. An assessment of them, through the lens of the just war tradition, demonstrates that neither counterterrorism nor counterinsurgency—applied specifically to al-Qaeda—has been particularly successful in determining the proper application for the just use of force.

Construing al-Qaeda as a worldwide insurgency has drawn the United States into two complex, bloody, and taxing counterinsurgency wars. It has become involved in a political battle for the hearts and minds of the people of Afghanistan and Iraq, forcing the United States into the local and long-term policies of both countries in ways that are not always welcome and through relationships that do not appear sustainable. Both conflicts have required US military forces to take on the difficult (and perhaps impossible) task of constructing legitimate and self-sustaining governments in both regions. In the attempt to deny Afghanistan and Iraq to al-Qaeda, Coalition forces have been absorbed into the local politics of both states. Through the lens of a population-centric approach, soldiers have engaged in the tasks of nation building and diplomacy—building schools, roads, and infirmaries and supporting local elections and referendums. The counterinsurgency approach has been appropriated in the hope of fomenting local support for both Coalition efforts and political support for emerging local governments. The results of these efforts, however, have been volatile at best. Furthermore, the cumulative effects of counterinsurgency against al-Qaeda are highly uncertain.

The counterterrorism framework does not demand the same levels of material resources or the large-scale military footprint of counterinsurgency. However, the practical considerations involved in implementing the tools of counterterrorism to confronting al-Qaeda are such that, as currently practiced, it is unlikely to lead to a broadly effective and sustainable approach to al-Qaeda. As drone technology and preemptive strikes require the use of force in the territory of other sovereign nations, relying on either practice for effective counterinsurgency appears impractical. The legal justifications that the United States makes for drone strikes have been widely contested, and its reliance on drone technology has increased other governments' suspicion of the United States. These factors have deteriorated the cooperative relationship that is necessary for the US military's continued use of drones, particularly when making every effort to abide by the criteria of discrimination and proportionality. These interactions demonstrate the difficulties of applying drone strikes as a wide-scale policy in the war against al-Qaeda.

Al-Qaeda's decentralized form of war poses serious challenges to the notion that it might be successfully eradicated solely through military means. As noted repeatedly, the assessments made here are not meant to deny that military force must be used as a tool in the fight against al-Qaeda; rather, they demonstrate the limits of this approach. Noting that al-Qaeda has penetrated Syria, Pakistan, Yemen, Egypt, Great Britain, Somalia, the Philippines, Russia, and the United States (among others), any policy that seeks to "disrupt, defeat, and dismantle" the diffuse al-Qaeda network must observe the limits of US military and diplomatic power.[72]

Notes

1. The term "moral anchorages" is Alex J. Bellamy's. See Bellamy, *Fighting Terror*,
2. For an example of just war language used by President Obama, see his 2009 Nobel Peace Prize speech, https://www.whitehouse.gov/the-press-office/remarks-president-cairo-university-6-04-09.

2. See the introduction in Beckett, *Encyclopedia of Guerrilla Warfare*.

3. See Lawrence, *Seven Pillars of Wisdom*; Mao, *On Guerrilla Warfare*; and Mao, *Selected Military Writings*.

4. See Mao, *On Guerrilla Warfare*, 50.

5. The first major treatment of insurgency warfare was C. E. Callwell's *Small Wars*. It was first published in 1896 to teach British officers how to wage "small" wars against guerrilla tactics. By the early 1960s literature on guerrilla war demonstrated a keen awareness of the systematization of guerrilla tactics. No longer considering it an ancillary method, such literature began to discuss insurgency war through "principles" and "rules," arguing that their application to certain conditions could lead to victory even against superior, conventional forces. See Lt. Col. Frederick Wilkins, "Guerrilla Warfare"; Lt. Col. A. H. Sollom, "Nowhere Yet Everywhere"; and Col. Virgil Ney, "Guerrilla Warfare and Modern Strategy"—all in Osanka, ed., *Modern Guerrilla Warfare*. See also Thompson, *Defeating Communist Insurgency*.

6. Robert Thompson's model remains the dominant one for fighting a counterinsurgency war. Assessments by Gen. David Petraeus, Gen. Stanley McChrystal, David Kilcullen, and Lt. Col. John Nagl draw on these five principles.

7. Thompson, *Defeating Communist Insurgency*, 51.

8. Ibid., 50–62.

9. Writing (in *Accidental Guerrilla*, 2009) that counterinsurgency is "feasible,"

Kilcullen further notes that conducting it on a global scale is "not recommended" or "not preferred." Instead, he calls for an approach to terrorism that is focused on risk management and prioritizes international partnerships, civilian and local agencies, and "the lightest, most indirect and least intrusive form of intervention that will achieve the necessary effect" (283). See also 271, 277.

10. While multiple examples are available, two will suffice to demonstrate this point. First, Lt. Col. Michael F. Morris argues that al-Qaeda is a new form of insurgency "featuring Salafist theology which appeals to significant portions of Muslim believers and which sanctifies terror." Countering the idea that al-Qaeda is a transnational terrorist movement, Morris argues that its broad support base and revolutionary ideology ought to place it within the insurgency category. This categorizing activity, he argues, is important as it plays a critical role in how the military constructs a response. Insurgency groups, he maintains, are structurally different than terrorist organizations. Insurgencies typically enjoy much larger numbers of fighting forces that are hierarchically organized and are therefore suggestive of a more traditional army, while terrorist cells are usually much smaller and not organized into formal chains of command. More important, however, insurgencies display a political strength that terrorist groups do not possess. Terrorists groups, Morris continues, "remain isolated from the social movements from which they sprang and their political goals become . . . more and more divorced from reality." In contrast, insurgencies represent "both a political and military challenge" insofar as they "combine ideologically motivated leadership with an unsatisfied citizenry into a challenge to existing governments." In this way, successfully countering an insurgency—such as the one represented by al-Qaeda—requires a program that allows the indigenous government to win the allegiance of its citizens by offering them a more appealing structure of government than that put forward by the insurgency. Consequently, the war against al-Qaeda also must address the political challenges that al-Qaeda presents. See Morris, "Al-Qaeda as Insurgency," 2–10.

Second, Lt. Col. Ken Tovo argues that counterinsurgency lessons from the Vietnam War may assist in the effort against al-Qaeda. Tovo is specifically thinking of the Phoenix Program, a US initiative aimed at combating the infrastructure of the Viet Cong—the component of North Vietnamese guerrillas sent to South Vietnam to mobilize political support for Ho Chi Minh. "Infrastructure," according to Tovo, refers to those who "performed support roles, such as recruitment, political indoctrination, propaganda, and psychological operations, intelligence collection and logistical support." In the same way, Tovo argues, the current "militant Islamic Insurgency" is a "loosely coordinated effort of multiple groups with nearly coincident goals and objectives." The Islamist insurgency is also supported by "infrastructure" consisting of religious and secular personalities and institutions that serve to grant it legitimacy and support (religious clerics, religious schools, and nongovernmental institutions soliciting funds in support of al-Qaeda). Given the importance of infrastructure to the political aims of counterinsurgency, al-Qaeda's infrastructure must be considered and "neutralized to defeat the insurgency." See Tovo, "From the Ashes," in Murray, *Strategic Challenges*, 20–28.

11. Kilcullen, "Countering Global Insurgency," 597–617. Kilcullen described the war on terrorism as one against a globalized Islamist insurgency. In *Accidental Guerrilla*, Kilcullen advances the globalized insurgency concept as one of four models through which to understand the current security environment. However, since Kilcullen argues al-Qaeda uses the same tactics that all historical insurgencies practiced—provocation, intimidation, protraction, and exhaustion—though with greater "scope and ambition," one can deduce that the insurgency model remains highly relevant to his work. See Kilcullen, *Accidental Guerrilla*, 12–16.

12. Kilcullen, "Countering Global Insurgency."

13. Kilcullen prefers the term "takfiri" over "jihadi" or "mujahideen." See Kilcullen, *Accidental Guerrilla*, xviii–xix, 34.

14. Kilcullen, "Countering Global Insurgency."

15. A significant amount of Nagl's writing argues that the US military is not winning counterinsurgency campaigns in Afghanistan, and only very recently was it able to turn around a failing counterinsurgency war in Iraq, because of its overriding emphasis on conventional combat. This issue, Nagl argues, stems from the US military's inability (or disinterest) to systematize and indoctrinate counterinsurgency principles acquired in Vietnam and the nonconventional conflicts of the 1990s.

16. Nagl and Yingling, "New Rules," 1; Nagl, "Winning the Wars"; Nagl, "Let's Win"; and Maass, "Professor Nagl's War."

17. McChrystal, "COMISAF'S Initial Assessment," 1-1, 1-2.

18. Kilcullen, *Accidental Guerrilla*, 265. It must be noted that Kilcullen's understanding of counterinsurgency is nuanced in a very particular way. He argues that while counterinsurgency tactics are, in fact, the best method of conducting the Long War, given the difficulty of conducting counterinsurgency, particularly on the scale necessary in today's conflicts, Western powers ought to refrain from entering into these sorts of campaigns. In other words, we ought to avoid, as much as possible, the Iraqs and Afghanistans of the future. Kilcullen also markedly focuses on the importance of using military force sparingly and of international coalition efforts to work through local and civil groups and leaders (263–89).

19. Maass, "Professor Nagl's War." Here, Nagl is elaborating on what, in other works, he has called the "key tenets of counterinsurgency": securing the population, subordinating military measures to political ends, using minimum force, and working through the host nation. See, for example, Nagl, "Let's Win," 23.

20. US Army and US Marine Corps, *Counterinsurgency Field Manual*, 2.

21. Ibid., 3.

22. Ibid., 2.

23. Ibid.

24. In the following discussion on legitimate authority and the Western just war tradition, I am indebted to James Turner Johnson.

25. See Johnson, *Just War Tradition*, 50–60; and Johnson, "Aquinas and Luther."

26. See, for example, the chapters on Aquinas, Suarez, and Grotius (especially pp. 182–86, 368–70, 394–401) in Reichberg, Syse, and Begby, *Ethics of War*.

27. Walzer, *Just and Unjust War*, 187.

28. Two publications published around the turn of the twentieth century demonstrate this shift. The first is the US Army's General Order no. 100, published in 1863, that recognized Confederate forces as legitimate belligerents (as opposed to rebels or criminals). The second is the annex to The Hague Convention IV, "Laws and Customs of War on Land," published in 1907. It stipulates the "laws, rights, and duties of war" were not just the privilege of armies but also extended to militia and volunteer corps that met certain conditions: "to be commanded by a person responsible for his subordinates; to have a fixed distinctive emblem recognizable at a distance; to carry arms openly; . . . to conduct their operations in accordance with the laws and customs of war; [and] in countries where militia or volunteer corps constitute the army, or form part of it, they are included under the denomination 'army.'" See Hague Convention IV (1907), annex, sect. 1, chap. 1, article 1, http://avalon.law.yale.edu/20th_century /hague04.asp.

29. US Army and US Marine Corps, *Counterinsurgency Field Manual*, xxix. See also Kilcullen, "Twenty-Eight Articles."

30. US Army and US Marine Corps, *Counterinsurgency Field Manual*, xxix.

31. Kilcullen, "Twenty-Eight Articles," 2.

32. See, for example, *Wrong War* by Bing West, a military veteran and expert on counterinsurgency. His assessment of the war in Afghanistan provides a window into the efficacy of counterinsurgency strategy (at the time of his writing). He argues that US forces, organized and directed by the tactical strategies of counterinsurgency doctrine, have spent a significant portion of their efforts building schools, roads, infirmaries, and the like in the attempt to respond to the economic and social needs of the Afghan people and to win the support of the population. These efforts, as West notes, neither have had the effect of winning over the population to the side of Coalition forces nor aggregated political support for Hamid Karzai. Rather, he argues, while local actors accept aid and develop levels of working relationships with Coalition forces, most remain neutral (or turn hostile). The population sits on the fence, waiting to see who will prevail at the end of the war.

33. As noted in a 2007 Brookings Institution and US Army War College colloquium brief, "The state-centric approach to COIN [counterinsurgency] works when there is a viable partner government truly committed to economic, political, and se-

curity sector reform and willing and able to make difficult decisions to see it through. In the 21st century, this is increasingly rare." Ralph Wipfli and Steven Mentz, "COIN of the Realm: U.S. Counterinsurgency Strategy" (Carlisle, PA: Strategic Studies Institute, US Army War College, 2008), http://www.strategicstudiesinstitute.army.mil /pdffiles/PUB846.pdf.

34. For an excellent summary and analysis of major events in the war in Iraq, see Brennan, "Withdrawal Symptoms."

35. Simon and Stevenson, "Afghanistan," 50–52.

36. Simon, "Can the Right War," 135.

37. Ibid., 136.

38. Simon and Stevenson, "Afghanistan," 50.

39. Simon, "Can the Right War," 134.

40. Note that the United States does not release data on drone strikes. However, efforts by various organizations have been made to track numbers of casualties. These numbers are from New America's International Security Program and its investigative project on drone strikes, available at http://securitydata.newamerica.net/. See also data from the Bureau of Investigative Journalism at http://www.thebureau investigates.com/category/projects/drones/drones-graphs/. Both were last accessed August 4, 2015.

41. Simon and Stevenson, "Afghanistan," 55.

42. Koh, speech, Annual Meeting of the American Society of International Law.

43. Ibid.

44. Holder, speech at Northwestern University School of Law.

45. Ibid.

46. Ibid.

47. Ibid.

48. Obama, "Future of Our Fight."

49. Ibid.

50. Ibid.

51. Ibid.

52. Ibid.

53. Alston, "Report on the Special Rapporteur," 3.

54. Ibid., 18.

55. Ibid., 17.

56. Ibid., 18.

57. Ibid., 24.

58. Ibid., 16.

59. Ben Brumfield and Mark Morgenstein, "Drones Killing Innocent Pakistanis, U.N. Official Says," CNN, March 15, 2013, http://www.cnn.com/2013/03/15/world /asia/u-n-drone-objections.

60. Ben Emmerson, statement, "Concerning the Launch of an Inquiry into the Civilian Impact, and Human Rights Implications of the Use of Drones and Other Forms of Targeted Killing for the Purpose of Counter-Terrorism and Counter-Insurgency," United Nations Human Rights, Office of the High Commissioner, 2014, http://www.ohchr.org/Documents/Issues/Terrorism/SRCTBenEmmersonQC.24January12.pdf.

61. Ibid.

62. In Afghanistan Emmerson noted that 40 percent of civilian casualties were the result of drone strikes. In 2013 there were forty-five such fatalities, a threefold increase from 2012. He cited twenty-four to seventy-one civilian casualties in Yemen between 2009 and 2013. Interestingly, according to his report, the numbers of civilian deaths in Pakistan had decreased significantly, with no civilian deaths from drone strikes in 2013. He attributes the number to the then ongoing talks between Islamabad and Tehrik-i-Taliban Pakistan. It is reasonable to assume, however, that the decrease in civilian deaths was also the result of a decrease in strikes on Pakistan's territory, reflecting a demand Pakistan had made to Emmerson before he submitted the report. Emmerson, "Report of the Special Rapporteur."

63. Ibid.

64. Jane Perlez and Ismail Khan, "Pakistan Tells U.S. It Must Sharply Cut C.I.A. Activities," *New York Times*, April 11, 2001. The reluctance or inability of Pakistan to root out militants led American officials, despite Pakistani demands, to continue to rely on the use of drones. Later that month, a US drone attack in North Waziristan, aimed at Pakistani irregulars who crossed the border and fought NATO and US forces, killed twenty-three civilians. The attack was met with huge public protests. It also demonstrates the reluctance of Pakistani officials to support a counterterrorism policy that uses force in this way and particularly in its own borders.

65. Emmerson, "Statement of the Special Rapporteur."

66. Emmerson, "Report of the Special Rapporteur."

67. Simon and Stevenson, "Afghanistan," 55.

68. International Human Rights and Conflict Resolution Clinic (Stanford Law School) and Global Justice Clinic (New York University School of Law), "Living under Drones: Death, Injury, and Trauma to Civilians from US Drone Practices in Pakistan," September 2012, http://www.chrgj.org/wp-content/uploads/2012/10/Living-Under-Drones.pdf.

69. The legal and academic communities have made proposals to increase transparency in the use of drones. For example, Allen Buchanan and Robert O. Keohane recommend establishing a "drone accountability regime," or an international institution that would help ensure better accountability (both among states and within states for their own drone operators) to applicable international law in lethal drone strikes. See Allen Buchanan and Robert O. Keohane, "Toward a Drone Accountability Regime," *Ethics and International Affairs* 29, no. 1 (2015): 15–37. Amos N. Guiora and

Jeffrey S. Band propose creating a "drone court" that would review executive branch targeting decisions before the strikes are carried out. See Amos N. Guiora and Jeffrey S. Brand, "Establishment of a Drone Court: A Necessary Restraint on Executive Power," in *Legitimacy and Drones: Investigating the Legality, Morality, and Efficacy of UCAVs*, ed. Steven J. Barela (New York: Routledge, 2015), 323–58.

70. Audrey Kurth Cronin, "Why Drones Fail: When Tactics Drive Strategy," *Foreign Affairs*, July/August 2013, https://www.foreignaffairs.com/articles/somalia /2013-06-11/why-drones-fail.

71. Daniel Byman, "Why Drones Work: The Case for Washington's Weapon of Choice," *Foreign Affairs*, July/August, 2013, https://www.foreignaffairs.com/articles /somalia/2013-06-11/why-drones-work.

72. Assessments of US counterinsurgency efforts in both campaigns are helpful to understanding some of the difficulties discussed. See Steven Mentz, "Learning from Iraq: Counterinsurgency in American Strategy" (Carlisle, PA: Strategic Studies Institute, January 2007), http://www.strategicstudiesinstitute.army.mil/pdffiles/PUB752 .pdf. See also Seth G. Jones, "Counterinsurgency in Afghanistan" (Santa Monica: RAND for the National Defense Research Institute, 2008), http://www.rand.org /content/dam/rand/pubs/monographs/2008/RAND_MG595.pdf.

CHAPTER TWO

Traditions
The Moral Constraints of War in Islam

The previous chapter demonstrated that conceptualizing al-Qaeda and the al-Qaeda phenomenon through a focus on organization and tactics has led to counter-models whose foundational assumptions do not apply well to al-Qaeda. While al-Qaeda unquestionably has some attributes that are particular to insurgencies and terrorism, its decentralized and diffuse nature has made both counterterrorism and counterinsurgency efforts ferociously difficult to apply and execute against it.

In shifting focus, now our attention turns to the religious narrative that gives al-Qaeda meaning, focus, and direction. Its ideologues reference this narrative both to understand the root of what they see as current Muslim ills and to provide direction for moving forward in the hope of revitalizing Muslims from their position of subjugation and weakness. Importantly for al-Qaeda's ideologues, this narrative is rooted in the past—more specifically, in early Islamic history. They argue that understanding current Muslim ills—and, just as essential, understanding their solutions—requires looking to the ways that the institutions of the earliest Muslims organized political, religious, and social life.

The most crucial of these is the Islamic state. Muslims, the ideologues argue, have been commanded by God to live by and under Islamic law, or the Shariah. Doing so requires a political institution that rules exclusively through Islamic law. Any other arrangement is unacceptable as it would entail rejecting a primary religious duty imposed on believers by God. As these thinkers look around the world and try to understand current Muslim ills, they conclude that Muslim persecution and weakness stem from the lack of a true Islamic state in the contemporary period. The Islamic state is the primary source of Muslim strength and prosperity, with Islamic history demonstrating (according to their selective reading of it) that Muslims were strong and prosperous when they lived under an Islamic state or when they obeyed God's dictates in this regard. The thinkers surmise that as Muslims have neglected this primary duty, they are suffering deeply for it. Therefore, the social and political weakness that plagues Muslims and Muslim countries can be alleviated only through the restoration of a proper Islamic state.

Of course, insisting that Muslims must live according to Islamic law is not exclusive to thinkers belonging to the al-Qaeda phenomenon. Islamic law is a ubiquitous part of Muslim life and piety. The al-Qaeda phenomenon, though, is unique in that its ideologues insist that Muslims *must* use force and engage in a war fought against all obstacles standing in their way. They include current "apostate" regimes of Muslim-majority states, any Muslims who do not adhere to their narrow interpretation of Islam, the United States and Europe (military members and civilians), and any allied country (and its citizens) involved in what they perceive as the West's pernicious policies toward Muslim societies. In fact, they argue the use of force against all of these elements is a religious *duty* and *obligation* imposed on all Muslims. Importantly then, this particular elevation of force and violence, as the foremost religious obligation of the believer, characterizes the al-Qaeda phenomenon's narrative.

Al-Qaeda's thinking on this matter is, in many ways, the culmination of ideas already present in Islamic militant thinking, for al-Qaeda is not the first to call on the historical narrative to make sense of the current international order. Its specific contribution, however, is the way in which it has built on these ideas and has decentralized and operationalized them into a model of war that is virtually indiscriminate in strategy and tactics. Understanding this point requires explicating what I refer to as its "dual nature"—a nature that, on the one hand, is deeply rooted in historical Muslim thinking on war while, on the other hand, departing from this tradition in critical ways. This view requires an investigation of al-Qaeda's narrative through two lenses.

The first is the historical narrative of Islamic thinking on war, or the jihad tradition. For al-Qaeda, social, political, and historical events and developments are understood through the lens of Islamic history and the continuing guidance provided by God's providence. The al-Qaeda model is not constructed on terms, ideas, and concepts that were invented by or unique to al-Qaeda; rather, its ideas are established on historical Islamic theories of statecraft and within a textual and historical tradition that organizes the use of force. More specifically, this theological tradition—a historical tradition encompassing Muslim discourse on the proper use of force—provides the worldview by which al-Qaeda's understanding of jihad acquires clarity, logic, and, most important, purpose.

The second lens is an explication of how the al-Qaeda model of war steps outside the moral constraints of the jihad tradition. This point is most distinct in the categories of authority and noncombatant immunity, or "discrimination" more generally. The jihad tradition has typically identified the authority to wage war with a legitimate and proper authority, or the head of the religious-political community. Furthermore, the jihad was waged for particular reasons, either to expand or to protect the territorial boundaries of the state in which Islam held sway. In light of this, the use of force was restricted not only in the ends to be achieved but also in the means through which force could be used to accomplish those ends. For example, the scholars specified categories of discrimination, indicating classes of noncombatants. In this way, war was limited.

While referencing the history, concepts, and terms of the jihad tradition, the al-Qaeda model does not require that an established political authority declare war; rather, all Muslims are not only allowed but also obligated to immediately take up arms against the West. Furthermore, the jihad is to be waged against the West in any place possible, taking strikes at Western interests both in the Muslim world and in the United States and Europe with an unlimited targeting of noncombatants. In other words, al-Qaeda's dismissal of the historical categories and restrictions has imploded the categories of noncombatant immunity and legitimate authority to the point where the use of force within al-Qaeda's model of war is unrestricted.

Therefore, understanding al-Qaeda's dual nature requires that we first understand the narrative that the ideologues who have inspired it reference and to do so in a way that highlights the moral constraints on the use of force that this narrative provides. With this in mind, the materials are divided into two separate but critically connected chapters. Chapter 2 focuses on the moral constraints of war in Islam. It starts with a judiciously selective historical narrative, beginning with Muhammad and the early Muslim community and moving through a transition phase in the eighteenth century. Though by no means an exhaustive description of the moral constraints in Islam, this chapter does serve to reference and analyze specific events in Islamic history with an eye to bringing the moral constraints on war in Islam to the surface.

Chapter 3 builds on the foundation provided in chapter 2 by turning to the work of three jihadi ideologues: Muhammad abd-al-Salam Faraj, Abdullah Azzam, and Osama bin Laden. These figures were chosen not because they are the only thinkers to discuss these ideas but because their writings demonstrate important conceptual developments that help us understand the construction and evolution of this narrative in regard to the birth of Osama bin Laden's al-Qaeda and the al-Qaeda phenomenon. Building on the ideas of one another, these figures have made significant contributions to the narrative that guides these groups by radicalizing, decentralizing, and extending the militant revivalist elements present in parts of the Muslim world in the eighteenth and nineteenth centuries. Through the work of these thinkers, the meaning-giving and action-guiding narrative that directs al-Qaeda becomes clear.

The Moral Constraints on War in Islam

A variety of social, cultural, and historical factors and influences have shaped the Islamic tradition's multifaceted perspective on war.[1] As noted in this discussion, and in the following chapters, Muslim thinking on war is contested, varied, and complex. This is a clear mark of a discourse that has changed, adapted, developed, and responded to historical events and circumstances.

As a *tradition*, however, Muslims' discourse on war demonstrates common denominators that various Muslim thinkers call on as they form their positions. In this historical tradition, appropriate conduct in war was heavily influenced by the example of Muhammad and the earliest Muslims. It also incorporated the analogical reasoning and informed opinion of the juristic class that developed the sections of Islamic law dealing with war. These thinkers relied on relevant verses in the Quran, *tafsir* works (commentaries on the Quran), early Muslim historians and their accounts of Muhammad's life, and hadiths (narratives that described Muhammad's conduct and that of his closest companions and the earliest Muslim community) for their deliberations on how warfare ought to be conducted. Therefore, many Muslims turn to these periods and sources when considering ideal ways of living and draw important guidance from them regarding piety, politics, rituals, law, and so on.

Rather than presenting a catalog discussion of each source and its position on force, this section focuses on specific events and intellectual developments in the life of the Muslim community that established a set of moral constraints on war in Islam. Insofar as this section aims to provide the foundational knowledge for understanding the way that al-Qaeda's ideologues talk about the use of force, it concentrates specifically on those events and ideas that its ideologues reference—from the life of Muhammad to the end of the "classical period" of Islam (approximately 570–1258 CE)—that formed concepts about the right and wrong ways of warring or, put differently, about the proper restraint in the use of force.[2]

The point of this discussion is not to argue for an essential picture of jihad, as the following narrative has been interpreted and reinterpreted by generations of Muslims who have turned to the classic period for guidance on proper Islamic piety and conduct. Rather, I present a summary of the events that helped develop the manifold ways that Muslims have thought about war and do so with an eye to how such events demonstrate moral constraints. As noted convincingly by Asma Afsaruddin, even within the early classical period of Islam, Muslim jurists and intellectuals had drastically different ways of interpreting this early history for guidance on their own contemporary issues and problems, arguing for both "noncombative" and "combative" meanings or interpretations.[3] My aim, then, is to demonstrate the narrative that many Muslims have consulted in their discussions about justice in war. In this way, I provide the necessary foundation for understanding how al-Qaeda both references this tradition and departs from it in critical ways.

The Example of Muhammad and the Early Muslim Community

In the Islamic tradition, history plays a particularly important role in ethical and moral deliberations because the tradition understands the past as a critical source of authority. In particular, the actions and conduct of Muhammad and that of various personalities within his immediate circle of influence have played a formative role. According to the tradition, Muhammad, deemed the last emissary to humanity from God—the "seal" of the prophets—was selected to deliver God's last message to humankind.[4] As God's chosen, Muhammad had a connection to the divine that led Muslims to interpret his example and conduct as the paradigmatic model of the Muslim life. When its historians, intellectuals, and jurists deliberated and reflected on how to live according to the dictates of God, they turned to Muhammad and his early community of followers and successors as sources of moral and ethical excellence.

This was certainly the case in the category of war. As the religious, political, and military leader of the first Muslim community, Muhammad's conduct in a series of battles and expeditions was referenced repeatedly in Muslim deliberations and played a critically formative role in discourse on war throughout Islamic history. These foundational ideas were formed within a young and growing community that was simultaneously in the process of territorial expansion. Understanding the moral constraints of war in Islam, and the nature and purpose of war among the early Muslims, requires positioning them within this specific context.

Muhammad was born in 570 CE in the western Arabian town of Mecca. Orphaned at a young age, he was taken under the protection of his uncle Abu Talib, and he eventually married a successful merchant woman named Khadija, who was several years his senior. By and large, Muhammad and Khadija had a happy and harmonious marriage that produced four daughters but no sons (all died in infancy). Muhammad developed a reputation as a successful merchant and was known as an honest and trustworthy person. He was also known to have an abiding interest in existential and introspective questions and had a habit of retreating into the caves surrounding Mecca for spiritual retreats. During one of those trips in Muhammad's fortieth year (610), he began receiving a series of revelations that he eventually understood to be messages from God, and he was instructed to impart them to the rest of his community.[5] These revelations, over time, were written down, organized, and compiled into the Quran.[6]

Muhammad's claims to prophecy were not well received by the dominant clans of Mecca, including Muhammad's own tribe, the Quraysh.[7] Despite this resistance, Muhammad gained a small number of followers in the decade following his first revelations, though both Muhammad and these early converts were subject to varying levels of persecution from the Quraysh and their supporters. Intimidation and threats led Muhammad to seek a place to which he and his small community could immigrate.[8] An opportunity came in the year 620, when Muhammad was approached by a group of people from Medina (then called Yathrib), an oasis town to the west of Mecca that was belabored by intertribal disputes. These people were hopeful that Muhammad could assist in mediating their grievances and bring some peace to Medina. In exchange for his assistance, several delegations entered into a series of political pacts with Muhammad in the years 621 and 622.[9] As a result, Muhammad and his followers immigrated to Medina, with Muhammad arriving as one of the last immigrants in the year 622 CE.[10]

The move to Medina (a journey known as the *Hijrah*), was a pivotal moment for the young Muslim community. Muhammad was able to secure a political alliance with the resident tribes of Mecca that provided the Muslims with a measure of peace and stability. It allowed for growth and development of the religious polity and of Muhammad's authority as the community's religious leader and its political head.[11] Importantly for our purposes, after establishing himself in Medina, Muhammad initiated a series of raids and eventually military battles that, within ten years, established Muhammad and the Muslim community growing under his influence as the dominant political and military power in the Arabian Peninsula.[12] Moreover, in light of Muhammad's paradigmatic example, his conduct and instruction in these battles have served as normative guidelines for later Muslims in determining the just conduct in war. From them, three noteworthy factors together establish a set of foundational points for just war in Islam that Muhammad's successors and the juristic class continued to develop.

First, the early Muslims understood their military success as evidence of a divine mandate. For the early Muslims, the growth of the community, and any victories that they had against the Meccans, were understood as orchestrated by God. In other words, they demonstrated God's favor and approval. Military success was tantamount to a divine sanctioning both of Muhammad's position as the messenger of God and of the religious community emerging under his authority. The tradition developed a connection between the Muslims' political and military success and divine intervention, with Muslim triumphs in these areas understood to be the result of God's divine favor and a sign of the truthfulness of Muhammad's position as the prophet of God's final message. This connection would eventually be developed by the juristic class into a doctrine of war that assumed that Islam—and the community of Muslims headed by its leader—was destined to take over the entire world and bring justice, peace, and order to all places and all people through the rule of Islam.

Second, the right to use force on behalf of the nascent but growing community of Muslims was Muhammad's and his alone. For example, in the first two years after Muhammad's immigration to Medina, he sent eight expeditions against the Quraysh. Muhammad led four; the rest were led by men who were "entrusted a white banner."[13] The "white banner" is a noteworthy symbolic development in the early Muslims' ideas of war. On the one hand, it clearly demonstrates Muhammad's ability to pass the responsibility of leading battles to one of his commanders, while, on the other hand, it serves to solidify Muhammad's authority by demonstrating that only he could dispatch it. The power of Muslim forces—and the decision to wage war—belonged exclusively to him as the head of the religious polity. Muhammad's actions in these terms are important, as they demonstrate that only he, as head of the early community of Muslims, could claim the authority to use force.

Additionally, Muhammad's military authority was clear in major battles against the Quraysh. In the battles of Badr (624 CE), Uhud (625 CE), and the Trench (627 CE), Muhammad led all three. Another incident illustrates Muhammad's authority as commander of the Muslim forces. In 628 CE Muhammad and a number of his followers set out for Mecca to perform the annual pilgrimage rites, but a force of the Quraysh tribe stopped them. Muhammad, despite protests from the Muslims, decided to negotiate with the Quraysh and offered them a ten-year truce, or armistice from battle, in exchange for their assurance that the Muslims could enter Mecca the following year and perform the rites without any interference from the Quraysh, who were to exit the city. The Quraysh also agreed to stop prohibiting their own allied tribes from joining the Muslims.

This truce was broken in the year 630, when Muhammad interpreted a series of clashes between tribes affiliated with the Muslims and tribes affiliated with the Quraysh as a breach of the treaty. Muhammad marched on Mecca. After negotiations with a representative of the Quraysh, he entered the city with virtually no bloodshed, demonstrating the power, authority, and appeal of the community that the early Muslims had been able to achieve in a span two decades.[14] The Treaty of Hudabiyya established Muhammad's position as the sole military leader of the Muslims and the only individual tasked with making decisions on behalf of the community in regard to the use of force. This power was solidified when, in the year after Mecca was taken, multitudes of tribes around the Hijaz accepted Islam or came to recognize Muhammad's authority in some other manner.[15]

The third factor was Muhammad's instructions for the treatment of non-combatants, or innocents, in war. For example, Muhammad al-Bukhari's *Sahih* (a widely cited collection of hadiths) asks the question, is it permissible to attack enemies with the probability of killing their women and children (unintentionally)? While the traditions on this subject indicate Muhammad's general disapproval of the killing of women and children in battle, writing that Muhammad forbade it, one hadith is less conclusive.[16] When asked whether it was "permissible to attack the pagan warriors at night with the probability of exposing their women and children to danger," the Prophet replied, "They are from them (i.e. pagans)."[17] His reply appears to indicate that the responsibility for the deaths has shifted to those who refused to submit to the Muslims. While such evidence reveals a complex notion of noncombatant immunity, Muhammad's statements clearly signal sensitivity toward, and acknowledgement of, the importance of distinguishing between combatants and noncombatants in war.[18]

Of particular interest in this regard are Muhammad's instructions to his commanders and other Muslims who undertook expeditions to various tribes throughout the peninsula in hopes of securing their allegiance to Muhammad. An example is provided by Muhammad's instructions to his general Khalid ibn al-Walid, who was dispatched on a delegation in the northern Yemeni town of Najran. Muhammad ordered ibn al-Walid to invite the people of Najran to Islam for a period of three days. If they had accepted the invitation to Islam at the end of three days, the people of Najran were to acquire the full status of Muslims, and ibn al-Walid would assign someone to remain with them and instruct them in the precepts of their new religion. If they refused, then he was to embark on a military expedition against them.[19] The tribes that did not accept Islam but recognized Muhammad's authority were offered a third option of entering treaties by which the non-Muslim tribes agreed to pay a poll tax (*jizyah*) in exchange for peace.[20] This pattern remained Muhammad's standard procedure for expeditions against non-Muslim areas and was eventually systematized into formulaic legal principles regarding proper conduct in war.[21]

What is critical to note here is the development of a protected class. Muhammad's instructions indicate that only those who had been given the choice to accept the call to Islam but declined were legitimate and proper enemies. Furthermore, if they accepted the call, they simultaneously received all the rights and protections entitled to Muslims. In addition, those who consented to pay the poll tax were included as part of the protected class; this status entitled them to freedom from harm and molestation while also granting them a set of rights (such as the freedom to practice their own traditions).

From the example of Muhammad and the early Muslim community, we see that military force was considered a legitimate means of both defending and expanding the territorial boundaries within which Muhammad (and Islam) held influence; indeed, such expansion was considered to be a sign of divine merit and approval. Yet while force was aimed at certain ends, such ends were restricted in at least two ways. First, Muhammad held the exclusive authority to initiate the use of force (or to pass that authority on to his commanders), thus centralizing authority to wage war in his hands. Second, Muhammad's instructions to his commanders demonstrate the early development of a notion of noncombatant immunity; that is, certain categories of people were offered protections and privileges and, hence, freedom from attack.

The Early Caliphate

Muhammad's death in 632 CE presented a challenge to the religious polity that he had built. The young community struggled to determine how it would conduct its affairs in the absence of Muhammad's influence and guidance. In the period immediately following his death, the community was engulfed in a series of military expeditions as Muhammad's successors sought to maintain and expand the territorial boundaries of the religious polity and to consolidate their own political positions and authority. Under Muhammad's first two successors, Abdullah ibn Abi Quhaafah and Umar bin al-Khattab (better known respectively as Abu Bakr and Umar), Muslim forces initiated campaigns against the Persians in Iraq and the Romans in Syria, eventually also capturing Palestine, Egypt, and Iran.[22] As Fred Donner notes, few events have marked world history as indelibly as the early Muslim conquests. Naturally, they have held a place of prominence in Muslim history in much the same way as they had under Muhammad, for this profound military success was taken as a sign of God's favor.[23] In this light, the early conquests, alongside Muhammad's example, have also played a formative role in Muslim thinking on war.

Shortly after Muhammad died, according to the traditional narrative, the Muslims gathered at the portico (*saqifah*) of one of the Medinan clans to discuss the question of who would lead.[24] The discussion was heated, with the community putting forward different configurations of leadership.[25] As a result of this meeting, Abu Bakr, one of the first Muslim converts and a close companion of the Prophet, emerged as Muhammad's first successor, symbolizing the Islamic community's decision to continue as a unified political entity with a single leader at its head.[26]

This vision of the Islamic polity did not go unchallenged. Almost immediately following Abu Bakr's ascension, various tribes all over Arabia began to challenge the arrangements they had conducted with Muhammad, arguing that their legal ties and obligations were to Muhammad only. His death, they claimed, dissolved those agreements. In response, Abu Bakr initiated a series of military expeditions known as the Riddah Wars, or Wars of Apostasy, to bring the revolting tribes back under the fold of Islam and Abu Bakr's leadership. In this way, Abu Bakr managed to maintain and expand the vision of religious polity that had emerged at the saqifah meeting. More important, however, Abu Bakr's insistence on a unified community under the command of a single leader maintained the concept of legitimate authority that had been established under Muhammad, with Muslims being ruled and led by one individual who, at least in theory, held the reins of power and the right to make decisions of war.

Significantly, the Riddah Wars were not limited to the tribes that were resisting previous agreements with the Islamic community. Abu Bakr and Umar, his successor, undertook military engagements against tribes that had been only minimally associated with Muhammad and those that had never had any contact with the Muslim community. Thus, the Riddah campaigns initiated a form of warfare that was concerned not only with the maintenance of the religious polity as it was but also with territorial expansion—a point that continued to develop the relationship between just cause and the extension of the geographical boundaries of territory ruled by Islam. While this connection began under Muhammad, it evolved significantly and primarily because it was more clearly and specifically articulated within juristic writings in the eighth to tenth centuries. For now, suffice it to say that the early Islamic conquests continued the connection of just, or legitimate, war with the expansion of the territorial boundaries within which Islam held sway.

Notably, military command and, with it, the power to wage war remained unified. Inheriting Muhammad's position as the political leader of the Islamic polity, Abu Bakr and, successively, Umar acquired the exclusive authority to wage the jihad. All military expeditions were conducted under their command or under the command of authorized others. The framework constructed under Muhammad was continued and thus solidified by the early caliphs during the Riddah Wars and the Islamic conquests.

The treatment of the apostate tribes (those groups that attempted to break ties with the Muslims after Muhammad's death) in these wars is critically important to the development of categories of discrimination. For example, those tribes that apostatized from Islam were treated differently than those that had never been in contact with the Islamic state prior to the Riddah Wars. The former tribes were given two choices: return to Islam or fight. Those that heeded the call would be accepted as Muslims, with all the rights afforded to such a position, while those that denied the call would be fought and granted "no respite." Every commander was instructed to "launch his attack against them [the apostates] until they acknowledge Him." According to Ibn Jarir al-Tabari's account, Abu Bakr sent a letter to the "apostate tribes from the Arabs," or those that had "turned back from" Islam after having accepted it or having "acknowledged Islam and labored in it, out of negligence of God and ignorance of His command."[27] Continuing, the letter states those tribes that accepted Islam, or "God's command," would be brought into the community; however, those that had accepted Islam and were now denying it would be fought to ensure that they would "acknowledge that which has come from God." Therefore, the letter continues, "So if [someone] has responded to the call, [the Muslim] has no cause to get at him; God shall be his reckoner thereafter in whatever he seeks to conceal." However, those who deny Islam, or "the cause of God," will be treated as enemies and "killed and fought wherever he may be and wherever he may have come to."[28]

Non-apostates were treated differently and along similar lines as those that Muhammad used to conduct agreements with the tribes of Arabia. Newly conquered areas were given three choices: submit to Islam, agree to the terms of a peace treaty with the Muslims and pay a tax, or suffer the consequences of war.[29] Examples of this exist throughout al-Tabari's work. In a detailed account of the Battle of al-Qadisiyyah, the Muslim delegation approached Yazadagird, the Persian king, and invited him to Islam. According to the account, a representative of the delegation by the name of al-Numan, speaking of Muhammad, began by stating, "We all came to understand the superiority of his message over our former condition, which was replete with enmity and destitution." Afterward Muhammad "ordered us to start with the nations adjacent to us and invite them to justice." Therefore, he continued, "We are . . . inviting you to embrace our religion . . . which approves of all that is good and rejects all that is evil." If, he continued, "you refuse our invitation, you must pay the poll tax." While this is "a bad thing," al-Numan stated, it is "not as bad as the alternative": If payment of the poll tax was refused, "it will be war." If the king was to "respond and embrace" Islam, though, the Muslims would "leave with you the Book of God and teach you its contents, provided that you will govern according to the laws included in it." After the king accepted Islam, the Muslim delegation would leave the king's territory and, furthermore, allow him to govern his own affairs.[30]

Additional evidence is acquired through the agreements that Umar arranged with towns conquered along the road to Iran. According to them, the Muslims would provide a state of security in exchange for a tribute paid to the Muslims (a tax imposed annually) on anyone who had reached the age of puberty, though those participating in military service were exempt. Muslims would also be given safe passage and hospitality.[31] The guarantee of safety would cover "their persons, their possessions, and their religion and laws."[32]

What is made clear in these accounts is that combatants (those who could be engaged militarily) were defined by a common characteristic, *choice*. They had the option to accept Islam, to pay a tax, or to undertake a war against the Muslims. Even apostates were given the first and last options. According to these traditions, the proper use of force demanded that all potential adversaries must be informed of their options. Not only did this limit the use of military force, but it also provided standards by which using force might be deemed just or unjust. Furthermore, it served to thicken the category of noncombatant immunity that had developed under Muhammad.

At this point, it is helpful to pause and summarize. Under the early caliphs and through the wars of expansion, the framework for proper warring that Muhammad had established not only continued but also developed. As conceived by Muhammad, the conceptualization of legitimate authority as a unified community led by one leader was sustained, thereby becoming a foundational concept within the tradition and the tradition's understanding of how force may or may not be used in the service of the religious polity. Basing themselves on Muhammad's example, the early successors to his authority continued to insist on a unified political community that identified itself and its members primarily through Islam. Moreover, Muhammad's early ideas on differentiating between combatants and innocents were developed under the direction of Abu Bakr and Umar as they led the Muslim armies in wars that would eventually expand the territory of the Islamic state from the Nile to the Oxus Rivers.

The Jurists: A Doctrine of Jihad

Beginning around the eighth century CE, figures such as al-Awazai, Malik ibn Anas, and Abu Hanifa began to reflect on the material provided by Muhammad and his companions and to provide judgments on various questions having to do with right and wrong living as determined by the source materials of Islam.[33] As Majid Khadduri notes, Muslim reflection on the topic of war developed as part and parcel of the juristic systematization of Islamic law. Pulling on the examples of Muhammad and the early Islamic polity, the jurists utilized the various methods of legal reasoning in order to systematize the materials provided by the example of Muhammad and the early caliphs.[34] Taken as a whole, the product of such reflection is referred to as the Islamic "law of nations," or the *siyar*.[35] Consequently, while Muhammad's motivations may only be conjectured, the juristic tradition is more explicit in its intentions for war.

While various figures wrote on the siyar, arguably the most important were Abu Hanifa and Muhammad ibn al-Hasan al-Shaybani. The jurist Abu Hanifa sought to deduce norms and principles to govern the Islamic state's interactions with external (non-Muslim) communities. The details of this system encompassed matters of travel, trade, marriage, and combat (among other subjects). Al-Shaybani, Abu Hanifa's student, wrote a treatise that sought to record the body of principles and rulings that Abu Hanifa handed down to him. Al-Shaybani's own hand, however, is clear in the text. He not only consolidated the disparate legal materials on the subject but also made his own individual contributions to the siyar, noting his disagreements with his teacher and inserting content into the text where he saw fit.

One of the most striking parts of the text is the assumed state of hostilities that exists between the Islamic polity and the non-Muslim world. Understanding this properly, however, requires an explication of the Islamic theory of statecraft that undergirded and developed alongside the formulation of the siyar. This theory is premised on two basic claims—an understanding of human beings as social creatures who need to live in society with others and an understanding of human beings as governed by, and subject to, a divine order that is promulgated and made explicit by God and God's prophets.

These two claims led to an understanding of God's law as natural and perfect—natural in the sense that the law was the proper inclination of every creature, consequently linking human welfare to the fulfillment of this law, and perfect in that achieving peace and justice was possible only through a proper ordering of human beings in regard to their world under this law. Thus, the Islamic vision is one in which human beings, in a very real and practical sense, are governed by and, hence, responsible to God and the laws God has promulgated. Consequently, it was understood that those who respond to Muhammad's call were submitting themselves to God's governance and accepting the requisite duties associated with this act. Through their submission (which is a free and willful decision by the individual), Muslims were held accountable and responsible to God's law.[36]

These links between human beings, the law, peace, and justice coalesced into the conclusion that any proper organization of human life required a political structure whose role was to promulgate and uphold God's law for human society.[37] The state, according to this vision, was the only way to achieve peace, which is understood as the order and justice that would prevail under the auspices of properly carrying out God's commands. Consequently, the existence of "peace" in the dominant Sunni opinion necessitated the prevalence of Islam, just as justice necessitated God's law.[38] It was, therefore, understood that protecting the state, or expanding its geographical boundaries, would also expand Islam's reach and, consequently, the areas in which God's laws and God's justice held sway.

As one can imagine, this understanding of the believer's position vis-à-vis the state had significant implications for ideas regarding war, or jihad of the sword. War, according to the juristic tradition, was conducted under the view that its purpose was to extend the territory ruled by Islam. Given this division, the jihad—as the means to expand Islam—was a permanent and ongoing duty for the Muslim community. Based on a notion of God's providence, the idea of Muslim victory was understood as an eventual certainty. The Islamic polity was ordained; thus, it was divinely commanded and surely going to grow.

Historical realities, however, were such that the Islamic polity did not succeed in its goal of universal expansion. As a result, the juristic tradition divided the world into two spheres—the *dar al-harb* (the territory of war) and the *dar al-Islam* (the territory of Islam). The dar al-Islam was understood as any territory in which Islamic law held sway and where Muslims were allowed to practice their religion without molestation or hindrance.[39] In contrast, the dar al-harb is territory "outside the pale" of Islamic law.[40]

As noted by Khadduri, "It follows that the existence of a dar al-harb is ultimately outlawed under the Islamic jural order; that the dar al-Islam is permanently under jihad obligation until the dar al-harb is reduced to non-existence; and that any community which prefers to remain non-Islamic—in the status of a tolerated religious community accepting certain disabilities—must submit to Islamic rule and reside in the dar al-Islam or be bound as clients to the Muslim community."[41]

The duty of jihad, however, did not require perpetual military hostilities. Nor did it call for absolute violence, as the goal of jihad could be obtained through nonviolent means. Returning to al-Shaybani's text, one notes the tremendous amount of ink he devoted to reasoning through the arrangements conducted between the dar al-harb and the dar al-Islam. Significant portions of his text discuss the regulation of property of non-Muslims and Muslims.[42] It also determines the circumstances in which the inhabitants of the dar al-harb might be granted an *aman* (a treaty granting them safe passage and guarantee of freedom from molestation) upon entering the dar al-harb for reasons of commerce.[43] Al-Shaybani also notes regulations on peace treaties conducted with "scriptuaries" as well as those living in the dar al-harb and their political representatives.[44] In short, while such arrangements were considered temporary, in theory, they provide models for conducting peaceful relations between the dar al-harb and the dar al-Islam.

Important for the purposes of our discussion, the juristic tradition initiated several marked developments in ideas regarding legitimate authority and provided a more decentralized understanding of the concept. As al-Qaeda's ideologues would go on to reference these ideas in manifold ways, we explore them here.

To begin, the jurists distinguished between two types of jihad. The first was jihad as a "community obligation," or a *fard kifaya*. This type of jihad was a duty imposed on the community as a whole, making the community collectively responsible for it. If some members of the community carried it out, then the obligation was met; however, if an insufficient number of people took on this responsibility and it was not carried out adequately, then the entire community would be held responsible.[45] In this particular conception, the jihad is an instrument of the state that is declared and executed by the standing authority—namely, the caliph or acting head of the Muslim community. A second type of jihad emerged termed the *ribat*. Developed by the Maliki jurists during the twelfth century, a time when the borders of the Islamic polity were under attack, the doctrine of ribat claims that when Islamic territory comes under attack, the jihad transforms to an "individual obligation," or a *fard 'ayn*. In such a case, *all* believers are under the obligation to take up arms in defense of the Islamic polity until an adequate force had been amassed to repel the threat. So, notably, if a piece of Muslim land came under immediate attack, then the caliph did not have to formally declare war to trigger the duty of individual jihad.[46]

The importance of this authority is evidenced through military command. By the time of the Abbasid Caliphate, the Islamic polity was accommodating itself to the realities on the ground in the tenth century CE. Provincial governors, among military leaders and Shia secessionists, had claimed political authority and established individual rule in various areas under the jurisdiction of the Islamic polity and at the expense of the caliph's power and control.[47] In response, certain jurists argued for a reinterpretation of this institution. Two schools of thought emerged. The orthodox position argued for a single seat for the caliphate, while the other claimed that more than one caliph was a legal permissibility within the doctrines of Islam.[48] The emergent position was understood as a compromise and represented the thinking of Shafi jurist al-Mawardi (972–1058). To maintain the unity of the Islamic polity, he argued that the caliph ought to recognize the authority of the emerging peripheral powers, yet he insisted that these authorities acknowledge the seat of the caliphate as the ultimate source of rule.[49] This compromise, therefore, sought at least to preserve the image of unity regarding the Islamic polity and demonstrates its importance.

Developments were made too in ideas of discrimination. Turning to *Al-Tabari's Book of Jihad*, it becomes evident that the juristic deliberations on war included discernible notions of discrimination and that they did so early in the formation of Islamic law. In this relatively early source, al-Tabari collects and presents a variety of juristic opinions on various questions having to do with war. This book helps demonstrate places where notable jurists from the early part of the classic period agreed and disagreed. From this material, we note the general consensus is that war may not be initiated without the Muslims' having first invited the non-Muslims to join Islam. In other words, those who had not heard the "call" were technically in the category of noncombatants, as they had not yet become citizens of the dar al-harb. As al-Tabari writes, there is "unanimous agreement" among Muslim jurists that Muhammad "did not fight with his enemies from among the polytheists before [first] making the call [to embrace Islam] and showing proof [of this invitation], and that he used to command the leaders of his detachments to invite [to Islam] those whom the calling did not reach."[50]

Beyond this general level of consensus, however, lies a significant amount of disagreement among the jurists. Once the call has been offered to the non-Muslims, there is still the matter of determining additional levels of noncombatant immunity, particularly regarding women, children, and the elderly. The jurists disagree on how such individuals within the dar al-harb (once they had refused to submit) were to be accorded noncombatant status. In al-Tabari's section titled "The rules concerning the conduct of combatants and the categories of people who are immune from being put to death and injured," the juristic opinions are navigated to determine this claim.

For example, some jurists (Malik ibn Anas and al-Shafi'i) took the position that those in the dar al-harb ought to be fought primarily for their disbelief. Other jurists (Abu Hanifa and Sufan al-Thawri) maintained that noncombatant immunity is accorded to women, children, and the elderly in view of prophetic traditions that indicate noncombatant status is accorded based on the individual's proximity with the war. Furthermore, while most jurists agreed that those who have been granted immunity from attack (aman) ought not be targeted, Muslim armies may target enemy territory even if such territory contains individuals who have been granted immunity and if the attack will lead to their deaths or to other unintentional deaths of innocents.[51] What is clear, however, is that such issues were taken seriously, and they continued to occupy the attention of these Muslim thinkers in their deliberations on the just use of force. In sum, as the jihad tradition was systematized by these thinkers, it retained a clear sensitivity toward appropriately determining just and unjust killing in war.

As noted, the historical discourse of Muslim thinking on justice in war demonstrates important restrictions on the use of force that were developed over time. These constraints sought to delineate how Muslims could use force appropriately. The proper use of force was aimed toward upholding and maintaining the Islamic polity, which was directed toward peace and justice insofar as it was the area in which God's laws held sway. Such conditions also included a relatively centralized understanding of authority, as they attempted to control the number of people who could use force in the name of the Islamic polity. These restrictions also included limitations on who could be targeted and who ought to be considered innocent in war.

Transitions

The reader may be struck by what appears to be an archaic and untenable relationship between religion, statecraft, and force. It is difficult to bring the juristic bifurcation of dar al-harb and dar al-Islam into consonance with our contemporary system of nation-states and international commitments to notions of territorial sovereignty. Clearly, the vast majority of Muslims do not read the historical narrative that has been outlined here in ways that advocate for violence or for continued hostilities between Muslims and non-Muslims (detailed in chapter 4). Today, Muslim-majority countries are important members of and contributors to international bodies and treaties; therefore, they have become fully part of the system of nation-states.

As demonstrated by current events, however, the notion of war in support of God's cause has taken a more radical turn in specific and marginal Muslim subcommunities, the pinnacle of which was reached with the emergence of Osama bin Laden's al-Qaeda and eventually proliferating into the al-Qaeda phenomenon we see today. Bin Laden's al-Qaeda was responsible for the extreme radicalization—the dismissal of all moral and ethical constraints—of the outlined narrative both in terms of his decentralized agenda for terror and for his presentation of these ideas on a global stage. Al-Qaeda's roots, though, are traced back to eighteenth-century Islamic revivalist movements that emerged during the decline of the Ottoman Empire. Of course, debates over proper leadership and political organization of the Muslim community occurred at its very beginning; these questions and debates are not new.[52] However, as interpreted by al-Qaeda, these debates are better understood if placed within the context of the revivalist elements of the eighteenth and nineteenth centuries.

These elements developed as Muslim intellectuals reflected on the declining power and legitimacy of the sultans of the Ottoman Empire and as the power and influence of the European world rose. In this way the materials for such reflection were internal and external. Internally, the revivalist Wahhabist movement initiated by Muhammad ibn Abd al-Wahhab (1703–92) argued for a return to "true Islam"—defined by the practice and example of the first generations of Muslims (*al-Salaf*)—and repudiated a host of Islamic practices that were seen as innovations or corruptions of the true faith. For the Wahhabis, "pure" Islam and its revival required looking backward as they attempted to imitate the behaviors, conduct, and institutions of the community as found in the early period of the tradition.

Externally, the material, intellectual, economic, and political success of European forces against those of the Ottoman sultans and their interests initiated introspection among Muslim thinkers who were attempting to understand the sources of newfound European innovation and power. As a result, figures such as Rifaa al-Tahtawi (1801–73), Jamal al-Din al-Afghani (1838–97), and Muhammad Abduh (1849–1905) sought to revitalize Islam in ways that would help Muslim societies absorb the technological and scientific achievements of European civilization.[53] For these thinkers, Islam had entered a gradual period of decline at the end of the thirteenth century, culminating in their current position of weakness vis-à-vis the West. They sought to determine how the sources of Islam, the Quran, the hadiths, and Islamic philosophical thinking could not only revitalize Muslim societies but also help to repel Western encroachment and influence. For these nineteenth-century thinkers, Muslims needed to return to the roots of their historical success and achievement—their religion—and to rely on it as they had at the height of Islamic civilization.

In the twentieth century, such sentiments took a more radical turn. Rather than attempting to find ways to integrate the perceived sources of European success into Islamic societies, certain segments of Muslim thinkers began to argue that Western influences and ideas must be categorically rejected as they were the sources of Islamic decline. Muslims, they argued, rather than setting their sights on Europe, must reject European influences and reinvigorate Islamic ideas and practices for a renewed society.

The paradigmatic example is that of Sayyid Qutb (1906–66). Born in upper Egypt, Qutb trained as a literary critic at the Dar al-Ulum in Cairo, and by the time he was in his forties, had acquired the reputation of an important writer, critic, and intellectual in his home country. In 1948 Qutb traveled to the United States, spending time in New York; Washington, DC; and Colorado. According to his memoirs, he was appalled by the liberal morals of American society; in his mind, they scandalized Americans with indecent ideas regarding family life and sexual behavior. Americans, he thought, were not only sexually immoral but also materialistic and racist. The cause, he reasoned, was the Americans' emphasis on modern values: separation of church and state, individualism, mingling of the sexes, and democracy (secular law). All these, he argued, were destroying the moral fabric of American life. Qutb began to advocate for the repulsion of any type of Western influence in Egypt, insisting that modernity would plunge Egyptian society into the same depraved moral status that he had witnessed in America. He felt Egyptians must repel these forces and return wholeheartedly to the sources, influence, and structure of Islam. Their religion, he argued, provided a comprehensive system of guidelines that would detour Muslims from the path of depravity and onto the straight path of Islam.

When he returned to Egypt in 1950, the country was in the depth of a crisis that had culminated in the Free Officers revolution, a military coup led by Gamal Abdel Nasser in 1952. The military officers responsible for the revolution, at least in its early stages, held close ties to the Muslim Brotherhood, an Islamist, revivalist, grassroots organization that had sought to revitalize

Egyptian society through the implementation of Islamic social and political values from the ground up.[54] This relationship soured quickly, however, when it became clear that the Free Officers and Nasser, specifically, were not interested in instituting the type of Islamic society that the Brotherhood wanted. The Brotherhood created its own social communities, offering all sorts of social services to ordinary Egyptians through its membership. It also had a military apparatus (that was a guarded secret), which, in October 1954, attempted to assassinate Nasser while he was giving a public address in Alexandria.

After the assassination attempt, Qutb was charged with being part of the Muslim Brotherhood group that was responsible for the attempt on Nasser's life. He was arrested and thrown in jail. He spent that time writing *In the Shade of the Quran*, one of the most important commentaries on the Quran, as well as a series of pamphlets and letters on the current state of Egyptian society. The latter were eventually compiled into the book *Milestones*. The book begins with a general diagnosis of the ills in Muslim societies. It is worth quoting at length.

> Mankind today is on the brink of precipice, not because of the danger of complete annihilation which is hanging over its head—this being just a symptom and not the real disease—but because humanity is devoid of those vital values which are necessary not only for its healthy development but also for its real progress. . . .
>
> . . . The period of the Western system has come to an end primarily because it is deprived of those life-giving values which enabled it to be the leader of mankind.
>
> It is necessary for the new leadership to preserve and develop the material fruits of the creative genius of Europe, and also to provide mankind with such high ideals and values as have so far remained undiscovered by mankind, and which will also acquaint humanity with a way of life which is harmonious with human nature, which is positive and constructive, and which is practicable.
>
> Islam is the only system which possesses these values and this way of life.[55]

Regeneration, according to Qutb, requires that Muslims understand that the world is divided into two camps. The first is the camp of Islam, the source of all knowledge and truth. The second, he insisted, is the camp of *jahiliyya* (ignorance), which contains only depravity and barbarity due to its distance from the sources of good and truth. He saw the politicians and governments at the helm of Muslim nations as belonging in the jahiliyya camp. They were nominally committed to Islam, and this tepid commitment marred Muslim society, serving to distance Muslims from the source of their power and strength. Islam needed revitalization, Qutb argued, and this effort required a vanguard to lead the rest of Muslim society to a proper Muslim life, one centered on acceptance of the Quran and rejection of secular ideas and values.

Qutb, it must be remembered, was writing from an Egyptian prison. He was a frail man in bad health who suffered tremendously himself while witnessing the suffering of his fellow inmates at the hands of their own countrymen. Taking this into account, it is difficult to know the full depth of what Qutb was envisioning. In particular, it is difficult to know the means he thought must be put to use in order to achieve his desired ends.[56] Whether Qutb meant for his ideas to be interpreted in a militant way is unclear, but the profound effect that his writing had on a generation of militants—and in particular, to the development of al-Qaeda ideologues and their thinking—is clear. To this development we now turn.

Notes

I rely on source material written by early Muslim historians and jurists for information on both the early Muslim community and for ideas regarding the juristic doctrine on jihad. As the reader will note, I distinguish these two sections in my analysis, treating them as separate (yet related) moments in the development of the jihad tradition. In light of the state of the source material, this distinction is somewhat artificial. However, to demonstrate the manner in which certain concepts were developed and referenced within the tradition, the distinction must be made. Questions related to the historical accuracy of the early sources—specifically al-Tabari—are not germane to this project. The arguments put forward here are not interested in presenting, or establishing, the experiences of the early Muslims as historical facts but in demonstrating how they serve as precedents for later generations in the community. If the reader is interested in discussions relating to the validity of such sources, I direct him or her to W. Montgomery Watt's "Translator's Foreword" in volume 6 of *The History of al-Tabari.*

1. For an excellent discussion of these factors and influences, see Donner, "Sources of Islamic Conceptions," in Kelsay and Johnson, *Just War and Jihad,* 31–69.

2. Although this section is not a comprehensive overview of the early history of Islam, it may serve as a short primer for the reader who is not familiar with early Islamic history. For this reason, I have provided a variety of endnotes to help lead the reader to useful and widely cited sources should he or she wish to pursue further study of a particular point.

3. Afsaruddin, *Striving in the Path of God*.

4. Note that historical evidence indicates that in the early stages of the tradition, Islam was considered a religion for the Arabs and that Islam as a religion with a more universal message developed under Abbasid rule.

5. There is discrepancy in the sources regarding Muhammad's age at the first revelation, with some sources attesting that he was forty years old and others stating that he was forty-three. See al-Tabari, *History of al-Tabari*, 6:153–56.

6. Experts disagree on a date for the Quran's compilation. For a pithy but informative summary of these debates, see Harald Motzki, "Alternative Accounts of the Qur'an's Formation," in *The Cambridge Companion to the Qur'an*, ed. Jane Dammen McAuliffe (New York: Cambridge University Press, 2006), 59–75.

7. Among the multiple explanations as to why this is the case, the primary theories claim that Muhammad's message threatened the economic dominance of the Quraysh, their current religious belief system, or both. See Donner, *Early Islamic Conquests*, 52–55; and Hodgson, *Venture of Islam*, 1:172–73.

8. Muhammad encouraged some of his early followers to immigrate to Abyssinia. A portion of the early Muslim emigrants remained in Abyssinia until the move to Yathrib, while others came back before. Watt, *Muhammad at Mecca*, 100–36.

9. These pacts came to be known, respectively, as the First and Second Pledge of al-Aqabah. See al-Tabari, *History of al-Tabari*, 6:136–38. For an additional description of these events, see also Watt, *Muhammad at Mecca*, 141–49.

10. Al-Tabari, *History of al-Tabari*, 6:137–52. Al-Tabari mentions increased persecution against Muhammad after his followers began moving to Medina, and he details a failed plot to murder Muhammad.

11. This political alliance is demonstrated by a document called the "Constitution of Medina," an agreement between the new Muslim emigrants, represented and led by Muhammad, and the eight tribes residing in Medina that had accepted Islam. Muhammad was designated the head of their new federation and further granted recognition as the messenger of God. Although the document available to historians is not likely the original, it nevertheless demonstrates the formation of a distinct political-religious community and is often referenced as the starting point for the Islamic state. See Watt, *Muhammad at Medina*, 221–28.

12. As noted by Sohail Hashmi, Muhammad's reasons for initiating these raids is unknown, and historians may only speculate. However, contemporary Muslim biographers of Muhammad have challenged the "orientalist" explanation that Muhammad initiated these expeditions to provide financial resources for the new Muslim immigrants in Medina. Rather than meaning to begin war, Hashmi argues, this new evidence suggests that these raids were "intended to harass the Meccans, impress upon them the new power of the Muslims, and demonstrate the necessity for a peaceful accommodation with the Muslims." See Hashmi, "Interpreting the Islamic Ethics

of War and Peace," in *The Ethics of War and Peace: Religious and Secular Perspectives*, ed. Terry Nardin (Princeton: Princeton University Press, 1996), 153–54.

13. Al-Tabari, *History of al-Tabari*, 10–14. The white banner is also mentioned in the *Sahih* of al-Bukhari.

14. Hodgson, *Venture of Islam*, 1:194. For al-Tabari's description of this event, see *History of al-Tabari*, 8:160–88.

15. Al-Tabari, *History of al-Tabari*, 9:40.

16. Hadiths demonstrating Muhammad's disapproval of killing women and children are found in *Sahih al-Bukhari*, vol. 4, book 52, pp. 257 and 258.

17. Ibid., 256.

18. For more on this issue, see Kelsay, "Islam and the Distinction," in Kelsay and Johnson, *Cross, Crescent, and Sword*, 203.

19. Al-Tabari, *History of al-Tabari*, 9:82–83.

20. See ibid., 58–59. This period demonstrates a clear centralization of Muhammad's authority, as all such agreements were contracted by Muhammad himself or under the authority Muhammad granted to his commanders. (See, for example, ibid., 88.) Furthermore, these new contracts were administered through a system of agents, chosen by Muhammad, with evidence suggesting centralized systems of taxation and legal authority over these new territories coming under the authority of the Muslims. The superiority of Islam in matters of the economy and the law was such that by his death, "Muhammad had established a new state in western Arabia. . . . The prevalence of an overriding concept of law, the focusing of political authority in God, the umma, and Muhammad, the systematization of taxation and justice, the establishment of a network of administrative agents to supervise member groups—all these helped lend the new Islamic state a durability and a degree of centralized control over its subjects hitherto unknown in the area." See Donner, *Early Islamic Conquests*, 75.

21. The details of such agreements are provided in al-Tabari, *History of al-Tabari*, 9:85–87. Al-Tabari provides the text of one of Muhammad's letters outlining the specifics of such agreements. Tribes that accepted Islam were to be instructed in the various precepts of the religion, including the nature of God, proper ritualistic behavior (prayer and dress), and salvation and the afterlife. Those who maintained their own religion (Jews and Christians) were to pay the jizyah tax, which afforded them the "full protection of God and His Messenger, and all the faithful" (87).

22. Donner, *Early Islamic Conquests*, 91–220.

23. As Donner notes, Western scholars have found the Muslim community's explanation for the success of the conquests unsatisfactory, and they have attempted to find alternative explanations. For an overview of such scholarship, see ibid., introduction.

24. Al-Tabari, *History of al-Tabari*, 10:6.

25. See ibid., discussion starting on p. 1.

26. The issue of leadership has been critical throughout Islamic history, and its significance is demonstrated in these early sources. For example, two versions of how Ali (an early companion of the prophet, the fourth caliph, and arguably the most significant figure for Shi'a Islam) granted his allegiance to Muhammad are available in al-Tabari's writings, with one clearly demonstrating Muhammad's favor toward Ali over Abu Bakr. Furthermore, discrepancies on the first male convert to Islam (Ali versus Abu Bakr) are alive and well in the sources, also demonstrating the manner in which the Muslim scholars sought to grant legitimacy to the early companions.

27. Ibid., 10:57–59. The text of the Letter to the Apostates is found on pp. 55–60.

28. Ibid. Brackets in original.

29. For examples, see al-Tabari, *History of al-Tabari*, 11:4, 6, 7, 29, 31, 45, 96; al-Tabari, *History of al-Tabari*, 12:35–38, 68, 69, 167; and al-Tabari, *History of al-Tabari*, 13:9, 16, 21.

30. Al-Tabari, *History of al-Tabari*, 12:36.

31. See al-Tabari, *History of al-Tabari*, 14:9, 26, 27, 28, 29, 30, 33, 36, 37.

32. Ibid., 30.

33. For introductory sources on the development of Islamic law, see Wael B. Hallaq, *An Introduction to Islamic law* (Cambridge: Cambridge University Press, 2009); and Joseph Schacht, *An Introduction to Islamic Law* (Oxford: Clarendon Press, 1982). In addition, Donner's book *Narratives of Islamic Origins* is an excellent background text for understanding Muslim historical writings more broadly.

34. It is critical to note, however, that while the precedent established by Muhammad and the early caliphs was foundational, evidence suggests that other sources played a significant role in developing the juristic thinking on war. Donner notes the influence of the pre-Islamic culture of warring in Arabia, while Abdulaziz Sachedina argues that the very recent history of conquest affected juristic reasoning. See Donner, "Sources of Islamic Conceptions," in Kelsay and Johnson, *Just War and Jihad*, 31–69; and Sachedina, "Development of Jihad," in Kelsay and Johnson, *Cross, Crescent, and Sword*, 35–50.

35. For more detail on this point, see the "Translator's Introduction" in Khadduri, *Islamic Law of Nations*.

36. Khadduri, *War and Peace*, 1–18; and Kelsay, *Islam and War*, chap. 2, esp. pp. 29–36.

37. As noted by Richard C. Martin, the Islamic state is the "ineluctable conclusion" of Islamic ideas regarding proper piety, and a "Muslim polity, one capable of supporting and enforcing a life of walking in the Straight Path, is necessary and a duty for Muslims to establish, maintain, and extend" (96). See Martin, "Religious Foundations," in Kelsay and Johnson, *Just War and Jihad*, 91–117.

38. For a detailed discussion, see Kelsay, *Islam and War*, chap. 2, esp. 29–36;

Ibn Khaldun, *The Muqaddimah: An Introduction to History*, trans. Franz Rosenthal (Princeton: Princeton University Press, 1989), 45–48; and Khadduri, *War and Peace*, 1–18.

39. For specific and varied definitions of this term, see Khadduri, *War and Peace*, 155–61.

40. Ibid., 170–71.

41. Ibid., 64.

42. Khadduri, *Islamic Law of Nations*, 106–29, 136–42, 165–93.

43. Ibid., 158–94.

44. Ibid., 142–57.

45. Khadduri, *War and Peace*, 60–61, 94–95.

46. Ibid., 81–81, 94–95.

47. Hodgson, *Venture of Islam*, 1:12–61.

48. Khadduri, *Islamic Law of Nations*, 21–22.

49. See Abu'l-Hasan al-Mawardi, *al-Ahkam as-Sultaniyyah*, esp. chaps. 1, 2, and 3.

50. Ibrahim, *Al-Tabari's Book of Jihad*, 59.

51. Ibid., 19–24, 61–72.

52. For a book-length discussion of early debates over proper and legitimate Islamic leadership, as well as their current manifestations, see Lav, *Radical Islam*.

53. For an excellent book-length discussion of these intellectual trends, see Hourani, *Arabic Thought*.

54. The classic and still excellent source on the Muslim Brotherhood is Mitchell, *Society of the Muslim Brothers*. For updated discussions on the Muslim Brotherhood, see Lia, *Society of the Muslim Brothers*; Wickham, *Mobilizing Islam*; and Carrie Rosefsky Wickham, *The Muslim Brotherhood: Evolution of an Islamist Movement* (Princeton: Princeton University Press, 2013).

55. Sayyid Qutb, *Milestones* (Cedar Rapids: Mother Mosque Foundation), 7–8.

56. Thanks to Dr. Adam Gaiser, at Florida State University, for bringing this point to my attention.

CHAPTER THREE

Narratives
Al-Qaeda's Dual Nature

According to Lawrence Wright's account of Sayyid Qutb's last days, Gamal Abdel Nasser, then president of Egypt, began to worry that Qutb's execution would only serve to make Qutb and his ideas more popular in Egypt and hence more dangerous to Nasser's rule. He sent Anwar Sadat (who would succeed Nasser) to visit Qutb in prison, but Sadat could not convince Qutb to appeal his sentence. Nasser then sent Qutb's sister Hamida (to whom Qutb was very close) to see if she could change his mind. She pleaded with him, but he refused. "Write the words," he said. "My words will be stronger if they kill me."[1]

Qutb's statement was prophetic. His ideas, particularly those found in *Milestones*, were carried forward, developed, and radicalized by a series of al-Qaeda ideologues in the years after his death, creating a marginal but radical narrative that continues to drive al-Qaeda's strategic and tactical model. To demonstrate this point, this chapter presents the work of three major ideologues of armed jihad, each of whom made his own contribution to the theological reasoning and justifications underlying the al-Qaeda phenomenon in the contemporary world. It is critical to note that these ideologues referenced the historical narrative provided in chapter 2 both to make sense of contemporary Muslim ills and to determine how to move forward. In other words, this early history is meaning giving and action guiding, helping to provide both the diagnosis and the cure. For these thinkers, this history presented an example of a time when Muslims were living out the dictates of their religion properly and were therefore prosperous, successful, and powerful. They looked to this early Islamic history for guidance on how Muslims ought to structure their affairs and institutions, and they argued that if contemporary Muslims could follow the example of this period, then they too would prosper and succeed, successfully revitalizing themselves and their religion.

That said, in turning to this history, al-Qaeda's ideologues stressed five theological commitments that they argued ought to direct contemporary and future Muslims:

- an insistence that current conditions—that is, the lack of legitimate rulers and the degeneration and weakness of Muslims— necessitate and require armed resistance, as the use of force is the only way in which a proper Islamic state will be brought to fruition;
- an emphasis on armed jihad as the most critical duty undertaken by the faithful and, relatedly, as the most significant marker of an individual believer's sincerity and dedication to God and Islam;
- an assertion that current conditions trigger the individual authority for all Muslims to take up arms in defense of Islam, Muslims, and Muslim land;
- an insistence on a decentralized theater of war that eventually encompasses the entire world; and
- a dismissal of any serious distinctions between innocents and combatants.

While the first three are true of Islamic militancy more broadly, the last two points specifically characterize al-Qaeda as a distinct phenomenon.

This story is a gradual one, taking shape through the life and writing of its proponents and supporters. It begins with Muhammad abd-al-Salam Faraj, whose writing gives material life to Qutb's ideas as demonstrated in his justification for the assassination of Anwar Sadat (then president of Egypt) in 1981. It continues with Abdullah Azzam, a leading jihadi theoretician whose work on the jihad in Afghanistan against the Soviets turned Faraj's ideas into a Muslim-wide call. The story culminates in the work of Osama bin Laden, who, importantly, degraded any form of moral constraint found in the work of his predecessors and brought the diffuse, decentralized, and unrestrained model of jihad onto the global stage.

Muhammad abd-al-Salam Faraj: "The Neglected Duty"

The echoes of Qutb's thinking are clearly seen in a pamphlet written by Muhammad abd-al-Salam Faraj (1954–82) titled "al-Faridah al-Ghaibah ("The Neglected Duty"). Faraj was the leader of Tanzim al-Jihad (Islamic Organization), which was responsible for the assassination of Egyptian president

Anwar Sadat in October 1981.[2] The "Faridah" was published in December of that same year.

Faraj wrote the document to explain and justify on Islamic grounds his assassination of Sadat. For Faraj, killing Sadat was a religious duty, one that had to be undertaken given the grave situation that Egyptians (and Muslims more widely) were facing. Faraj, in this tract, also operationalized the ideas expressed by Qutb. Faraj interpreted them in such a way that, for him and the stream of militants that would be influenced by his thinking, the Muslims' current state—or *jahiliyya*, as Qutb described it—required that they rise up and use force to combat the sources of corruption and apostasy that had plagued their lands. Faraj's writing and his justification of Sadat's assassination, although rooted in Egypt and Egyptian concerns of the 1980s, related enormously influential ideas that would form the religious and intellectual foundation for the al-Qaeda phenomenon.

The principal contributions of the "Faridah" are twofold. The first is what I refer to as its "doctrine of apostasy," or Faraj's insistence that Muslims have a duty to remove "apostate" political rulers so that an Islamic state can be erected. The second is that this duty, in light of current conditions, is incumbent on every *individual* believer and, furthermore, supersedes all other obligations commanded by God (except the duty of belief).

Faraj, in this text, styles himself as a warner. He writes as someone who has come to awaken Muslims to their duty and to warn them of the looming consequences of their refusing to face the task. Muslims, he argues, must understand the gravity of the situation confronting them, for they have neglected to fulfill a primary commandment levied on them by God and are suffering for it as a consequence. This foundational commandment is the establishment of an *Islamic* state. This duty is clear in that Muslims both are subject to Islamic law and ought to emulate the example of Muhammad, who formed a religious-political community under his charge. Such requirements, Faraj continues, can be executed only under the direction of an Islamic state in which every Muslim is subject to God's laws.[3]

Furthermore, the Islamic state has not only been commanded but also ordained. Faraj cites a hadith in which Muhammad said, "God showed me all corners of the earth. I saw its East and its West, and (I saw) that my community will possess of it what He showed me from it."[4] God has promised, Faraj writes, to those who are faithful that God will make them successors to power and Islamic rule, and God will establish their success, their power, and that of their religion.[5] Muslims must take this message to heart. Insofar as the Islamic state has been both commanded and ordained by God as a requirement for proper Islamic political life, every Muslim is under the obligation to exert all possible effort to bring about the proper Islamic state, striving for its implementation by any means necessary.

Today, Faraj argues, Muslims are ruled by corrupt and tyrannical apostate rulers. Such regimes, while outwardly clinging to the precepts of Islam, are internally committed to the "tables of imperialism, be it Crusaderism, or Communism, or Zionism."[6] Referring to Egypt specifically, he writes, "The State (of Egypt in which we live today) is ruled by the Laws of Unbelief although the majority of its inhabitants are Muslim."[7] Of course, Faraj has to deal with an obvious contradiction to his argument—that is, the rulers he discusses, particularly the political leaders of Egypt, were in fact self-identified Muslims. Faraj is quick to note that their outward acts of piety are not true marks of faith. In other words, they are not demonstrations of the type of piety required for ruling a proper Islamic state. As he observes, "They carry nothing from Islam but their names, even though they pray and fast and claim . . . to be Muslim."[8] The true and proper mark of their legitimacy to rule, for Faraj, is determined by whether they rule through Islamic law.[9]

Labeling current Muslim rulers "apostates" is significant on Faraj's part. As noted in chapter 2, apostates, as opposed to non-Muslims, must be fought. This point then is a foundational part of Faraj's argument and his justifications for Sadat's assassination. Faraj goes to significant lengths to demonstrate that his position on apostate rulers is rooted in the Islamic tradition and validated through Muslim history. He writes, "It is a well-established rule of Islamic law that the punishment of an apostate will be heavier than the punishment of someone who is by origin an infidel (and has never been a Muslim)." He argues that the Maliki, Shafi, and Hanbali schools of law (major Sunni legal schools) all note that apostates are to be treated differently than non-Muslims (who have never been Muslims) in a number of ways. Apostates cannot inherit property, cannot enter into legally recognized marriages or a covenant of protection with Muslims. Moreover, these established authorities agree that apostates are not offered the right to pay a tax to maintain their new religion. In contrast to those who have never been Muslims, an apostate also can be killed even if he or she does not pose a threat to Muslims, "even if he is unable to (carry arms and) go to war."[10] This, Faraj writes, is indicative of the fact that apostasy is considered worse than "rebellion against the prescripts of a religion" by someone who has never been a Muslim.[11]

He uses these points to compare the contemporary situation of Muslims to those under the thirteenth-century Mongol invasion and rule. Because the Mongol rulers derived their laws based on the rulings of Genghis Khan, authoritative Muslim jurists (here Faraj cites quotations from Ibn Taymiyyah and Ibn Kathir) labeled them "apostates" and required insurrection against them until God's law was again fully implemented in the laws that ruled the Muslims.[12] This point is critical for Faraj, who maintains Muslims today are living under similar apostate rule. He argues, "The laws by which Muslims are ruled today are the laws of Unbelief" and are "codes of law that were made by infidels who then subjected the Muslims to these (codes)." He points to the clear injunction in Surah 5 of the Quran that states, "Whosoever does not rule (*yahkum*) by what God sent down, those are the Unbelievers (*kafirun*)."[13]

Like the Mongol rulers, Faraj asserts, today's apostate political rulers must be resisted through the use of force. As evidence, he discusses the example of the town of Taif (in modern-day Saudi Arabia), which Muhammad's forces captured in 631CE. Although the residents of Taif converted to Islam, they refused to give up the practice of usury. According to the traditional narrative, Muhammad argued that their refusal to stop this practice required him to fight them until they relented and abolished usury. If, Faraj writes, "these (people in the town of Ta'if) had to be fought (*yajib jihaduhum*) because they were at war with God and His Apostle (only because they continued to ask for the payment of usury agreed upon before the Muslim conquest of their town)," then "how much more (should the Muslims fight) those who omit (to carry out) many of the rites of Islam, or (perhaps) most of them, like the Mongols?"[14] Moreover, the "leading scholars of Islam" agree that those who profess to be Muslims yet do not carry out the "clear and reliably transmitted duties of Islam"—such as praying, fasting, undertaking the hajj pilgrimage, outlawing alcohol, and so on—must be fought on these issues until they abide by these precepts or, as Faraj puts it, "until the whole religion belongs to God."[15]

Using this reasoning, Faraj finds current Muslim rulers and regimes guilty of numerous transgressions, rebelling against Islam in ways that are egregious and pernicious, and he believes they must be fought. Today's rulers, Faraj argues, are not secessionists or rebels or revolutionaries or even Muslims who have lost their way; rather, they are apostates who have transgressed against the law of God. He writes, "These people recite the Quran but it does not go further than their throats (i.e., it does not enter their hearts). They go out of Islam the way an arrow goes out of the bow."[16]

This situation, he contends, leaves only one option—war. The apostate rulers and their regimes are inhibiting the emergence of the Islamic state. And insofar as the Islamic state is incumbent on all Muslims, they must fight these apostate regimes until they are destroyed, allowing the Islamic state to emerge from the ashes of their jihad. In fact, according to Faraj, the nefarious nature of these regimes transforms the jihad against what he terms the "near enemy" (the political rulers of Muslim states) into an immediate obligation of the highest order.[17] For Faraj, jihad against these apostate regimes is the only way to bring about the Islamic state. Furthermore, as he writes, "There is no doubt that the idols of this world can only be made to disappear through the power of the sword."[18]

In fact, any other means of obtaining the Islamic state are categorically dismissed in his thinking. For Faraj, "benevolent societies" (organizations that use a grassroots approach) will not bring about the Islamic state. Neither will the spread of Islamic education or increased devotion to Islam as demonstrated through charitable acts or good works. He rejects the suggestion that putting Muslims in positions of influence can bring the Islamic state to fruition. He also dismisses the idea that society requires a deeper knowledge of Islam and its principles. How, he asks, did the knowledge of the scholars of al-Azhar help them when Napoleon and his soldiers entered on horseback?[19] For Faraj other (nonviolent) forms of implementing change or exerting resistance will not be effective against the power of apostate rule. Not only does he deem such means as futile against these powerful regimes, but, furthermore, any means that do not resist and destroy the apostate states are working to support them and are therefore upholding their rule.[20]

The position of the "Faridah" on jihad as an *individual* duty is particularly significant. Faraj argues that in light of current circumstances, jihad is a duty that is incumbent on all Muslims. Pulling on Quranic texts and the example of Muhammad, as well as the juristic distinction between defensive and offensive war (discussed in chapter 2), Faraj claims that there are three situations in which jihad turns into an individual obligation. First, when Muslims are engaged in battle ("when two armies meet and their ranks are facing each other"), those engaged in battle are forbidden from fleeing, and "it becomes an individual duty to remain standing." Second, when "the infidels descend upon a country," its citizens then have an "individual duty" to fight and repel the invaders. Finally, "when the Imam calls upon a people to fight," they are required to heed that call.[21] For Faraj, the second situation is applicable to the contemporary period because the apostate regimes are living "right in the middle of them [Muslim lands]." Therefore, it is the individual duty of every Muslim to rise up in arms, expel the tyrannical regimes, and bring about the Islamic state that has been mandated by God.[22]

On this point, Faraj claims that the presence of an authority with the power to wage jihad—such as a caliph—is not required. Jihad, he argues, does not rely on the existence of the caliphate; furthermore, the absence of this institution is not a proper justification to prevent the jihad. He notes Muhammad's example of giving others the power of military command (as symbolized by the white banner). Faraj also references the following hadith attributed to Muhammad: "When three of you go out on a journey, then make one of them the commander (*amir*)."[23] Therefore, according to Muhammad's example, military command need not be the exclusive jurisdiction of the caliph. Faraj writes, "Whoever alleges that the (proper) leadership has been lost has no case, because the Muslims can (always) produce leaders from amongst themselves."[24] In times of the caliph's absence, such command may go to the best Muslim, as "if there is something lacking in the leadership, well, there is nothing that cannot be acquired. It is (simply) impossible that the leadership disappears (from among us)."[25] Therefore it is nonsensical, Faraj argues, to think that the Muslim community would have been denied the ability (in the sense of authority) to embark on war when it is necessary.

The "Faridah" very clearly decentralizes the authority to declare and initiate war, removing it from the grip of a single leader and into the hands of all Muslims. The jurists, though, had a different notion of defensive jihad in mind, one in which Muslim land was under immediate attack by those in the territory of war. In such a case, according to juristic construal, defense of Islamic lands becomes the immediate responsibility of all Muslims, and any individual believer may feel justified and permitted to take up arms in defense of the state without a caliph's having formally declared war. Faraj, however, claims this type of individual authority even in a context where an immediate threat, such as what the juristic thinkers imagined, does not exist. Rather, he extends the notion of an immediate threat to those brought on by heads of state and government institutions that he has deemed un-Islamic and therefore as impediments to the construction of the mandated Islamic state.

In this way, the "Faridah" takes the revivalist ideas found in Qutb's writings and develops them into the conceptual foundation that drives the trajectory of al-Qaeda thinking. As Faraj argues, Muslims are in a state of decline and weakness because they have neglected the primary duties of their religion. They have failed to uphold God's directives and neglected to implement God's foundational directive of the Islamic state. This state of affairs is intolerable, he maintains, as Muslims must live according to Islamic law. To do so thus requires an Islamic state, one that is governed by a true Muslim and only through the laws of God. Moreover, given the current conditions, with the enemies of Islam ruling Islamic lands, the duty to erect the Islamic state is immediate. Thus, all Muslims must take up arms and bring true Islamic rule into fruition. In light of these conditions, the only way that this state may be erected is through the use of force, with war against the apostate rulers and the forces of jahiliyya.

Importantly, though, and despite the decentralization of authority, the "Faridah" maintains a number of moral constraints on war found within the tradition, and this point is important to highlight insofar as they disappear by the time we reach the work of Osama bin Laden. In regard to proper conduct, the "Faridah" draws on the precedent of Muhammad as found in the hadiths and commentaries of the juristic tradition. In this way, Faraj develops a section on the importance of extending the invitation to Islam before attacking, arguing that this summons is an important and recommended part of jihad.[26] Of further interest is the restriction he places on noncombatants. With arguments similar to those of the juristic tradition, the "Faridah" claims that women, dependents, monks, and old men may not be killed directly; however, it does allow for attacking enemy armies or positions at night, even if the death of the noncombatant classes is unavoidable.[27] Last, the "Faridah" places checks on the use of force by containing the jihad to a war against the "near enemy," or the apostate regimes. In this way, the jihad is controlled and, just as important, limited insofar as it is to be fought specifically against tyrannical rulers impeding the emergence of the Islamic state.

Sheikh Abdullah Yusuf Azzam: "Join the Caravan" and "In Defense of Muslim Lands"

Well before Sadat's assassination and the publication of the "Faridah," however, another militant ideologue also spent time in Egypt, absorbing its post-Qutb intellectual atmosphere. That man was Abdullah Yusuf Azzam, a Palestinian and al-Azhar–trained cleric who, several years after the publication of the "Faridah," developed Faraj's notion of individual authority into a Muslim-wide call to jihad.[28] Faraj's thinking was focused on Egypt. His concern was to justify the killing of Sadat as a means of attaining the proper Islamic state. Azzam, however, was focused on the jihads in Afghanistan and Palestine, although in the years in which his influence was greatest, he had already turned himself directly toward the Afghan struggle. For Azzam, the Afghan jihad held more promise as it had the potential to ignite the type of global resistance that could reestablish true Islamic rule over all former lands of the historic Islamic empire.

In fact, Azzam is considered the primary ideologue of the Afghan jihad (the Soviet-Afghan War). The decade-long struggle of the Afghan mujahideen against the Soviet invasion saw Afghanistan also serving as part of the proxy war between the Soviets and the United States. Azzam, unlike

Faraj, was not particularly focused on the doctrine of apostasy and under-standably so, as he wrote in response to a different set of circumstances. Yet, for Azzam, like Faraj, the individual duty to jihad had been triggered because of the circumstances facing current Muslims. Rather than arguing that Muslims ought to take up arms against the apostate regimes in which they lived, though, Azzam called Muslims to jihad to defend Muslim lands and, in this particular case, to defend Afghanistan from the Soviet invasion. In this way, the individual call to jihad conceptualized by Faraj began to take a more global turn.

Azzam was born in the north Palestinian village of Silat al-Harithia in 1941. After the 1967 Arab-Israeli War, he fled to Jordan, where he became actively involved in Palestinian activism and militancy against the state of Is-rael. In 1966 he had obtained a degree in shariah from Damascus University in Syria and a master's degree from al-Azhar University in Cairo. He then began to lecture in the University of Jordan–Amman. In 1971 he went back to study at al-Azhar, on a scholarship, and obtained a PhD in *Usul al-fiqh* (principles of Islamic jurisprudence) in 1973. While at al-Azhar he became acquainted with Qutb's family.

From this point, his life events are unclear. The biography (not written by Azzam) that prefaces his well-known tract "Defence of Muslim Lands: The First Obligation after Iman" notes that in 1979, he moved to Pakistan to be closer to the Afghan jihad and worked as a teacher in the International Islamic University in Islamabad. Eventually he left this position to turn his full attention to Afghanistan.[29] A second biography (also not written by Az-zam) in his "Join the Caravan" does not mention the move to Peshawar, but it notes that his frustration with the Palestinian jihad, which he believed was not Islamic enough, led him to leave Palestine and to take a teaching position in Saudi Arabia at King Abdulaziz University in Jeddah. While there in 1980, he met a delegation of Afghan mujahideen who were performing the hajj (the annual pilgrimage that every physically and financially capable Muslim is required to undertake at least once in his or her lifetime). As he got to know them and learned more about the Afghan jihad, he was moved and won over to their cause, and eventually he turned all his energies to it.[30]

Once Azzam moved to Pakistan, he made several trips back to Jeddah, where he stayed in Osama bin Laden's guesthouse and held marketing and recruiting sessions for the Afghan jihad. The two men struck up a friend-ship and decided to pool their energies in support of the Arab fighters who were traveling to Afghanistan to fight the Soviets. Bin Laden took on the role of financier and fund-raiser. In 1984 he and Azzam created the Afghan Services Bureau (*Makhtab al-Khidamat*), an organization in Peshawar that sought to recruit non-Afghan (primarily Arab) mujahideen to fight along-side the Afghans. In this way, Azzam was not only the main architect of the political-religious dimensions of the Afghan jihad but also one of its most tireless supporters, traveling all over the world to recruit fighters and solicit financial assistance for the mujahideen. Through such efforts, his ideas took on heightened visibility and widespread acceptance among the communities supporting the Afghan jihad. Moreover, despite a later ideological split, his ideas were critically influential for the nascent militant community in Afghanistan, Pakistan, and Sudan in the late 1980s. Thus, Azzam's works left a deep ideological mark on figures such as bin Laden, Ayman al-Zawahiri, and Abu Musab al-Suri, and they remain a theoretical cornerstone of militant, radical thinking in contemporary Islam.

For Azzam, the current state of Muslims—subjugated and oppressed by others—was a direct consequence of their having abandoned jihad and the commandment to construct and maintain a state as directed by Islamic law. Azzam saw a critical connection between piety and the formation of an Islamic state. In his writings, he argues that Islam is the vessel of categorical truth, by way of which God has demonstrated his mercy to human beings. Human beings, then, are entrusted with its dissemination and its protection, as the "battle between truth and falsehood is for the reformation of mankind, that the truth may be dominant and the good propagated."[31] The battle for the Islamic state is thus a requirement on the faithful insofar as they have been charged with the task of supporting the battle for the reformation of human beings, and that occurs only through adherence to God's law. Therefore, he continues, the current state of weakness and decline is clearly the result of Muslims' refusing to obey a fundamental religious duty—that is, using force to maintain and defend Islam and ensuring the reality of the Islamic state.

According to Azzam, "Anybody who looks into the state of the Muslims today will find that their greatest misfortune is their abandonment of Jihad due to their . . . 'love of this world and hatred of death. . . .' Because of that, the tyrants have gained dominance over the Muslims in every aspect and in every land. The reason for this is that the Disbelievers only stand in awe of fighting."[32]

The Islamic state is the mechanism by which the correct vision of the good is brought into this world. Those who strive to adhere to what God commands are therefore obligated to bring the Islamic state into fruition. His insistence on this point leads him to argue that insofar as Muslims require the Islamic state and that, presumably, they have been commanded to strive toward its realization, the use of force *must* be used to construct, maintain, and defend it. Furthermore, considering the contemporary state of Muslims, the use of force to establish the Islamic state is a religious *duty* incumbent on all believers. In fact, the bulk of his most famous pieces *Join the Caravan* and *Defence of the Muslim Lands* are dedicated to defending this claim.

In both works, Azzam seeks to connect the individual duty to jihad to the Soviet-Afghan War. Defensive jihad, he argues, is a duty that is triggered when nonbelievers enter Muslim lands (or if a group of Muslims are captured or imprisoned). When this happens, he writes, the duty to protect Muslims and Muslim lands through jihad becomes *fard 'ayn*, or a duty imposed individually on all believers. If the Muslims closest to the point of attack cannot repel the invader, or they refuse to take up arms, then this duty moves outward to those nearest in proximity to the point of attack. If those Muslims are unable to repel the invaders, then this duty will spread outward "in the shape of a circle" to the next group of Muslims, and then outward again to the next, and the next, until the invaders have been repelled.[33] Moreover, defensive jihad does not require the standard types of "permissions," for the "children will march forth without the permission of the parents, the wife without the permission of her husband and the debtor without the permission of the creditor."[34] This is all, of course, to indicate both the importance and the immediacy of defensive jihad.

He provides excerpts from the Hanbali, Shafi, Hanafi, and Maliki legal schools as evidence for the compulsory defensive jihad, thus demonstrating a majority consensus on the point that the repulsion of non-Muslim forces is necessary. In fact, according to Azzam, it is necessary even if innocent Muslims are killed in the process.[35] He maintains the "protection of the remaining Muslims from Fitnah [strife, particularly of the intra-Muslim kind] and Shirk [idolatry], and the protection of the religion, 'Ard [land] and wealth are more of a priority than a small number of Muslim captives in the hands of the Kuffar [non-Muslims or unbelievers]."[36]

Furthermore, he writes, Muslim scholars agree that this duty becomes mandatory when "the enemy enters an Island or a land that was once part of the Islamic lands."[37] In this situation, he writes, "it is obligatory on the inhabitants of that place to go forth and face the enemy." Here, as Faraj did, Azzam references the same juristic doctrine of individual versus collective duties. He also writes that if the inhabitants of an invaded land cannot carry out that duty—or will *not* carry it out—then the obligation falls to those around them until this individual duty "encompasses the whole world." In addition, "the individually obligatory nature of Jihad remains in effect until the lands are purified from the pollution of the Disbelievers."[38]

Moreover, for Azzam, the duty of jihad is clearly proven by the example of Muhammad.

This is just as the Prophet (SAWS) has ordered the individual to help Muslims, whether or not he has been recruited for fighting. It is obligatory on every individual according to his capability and wealth, little or plenty, whether walking or riding. When the enemy proceeded towards the Muslims in the Battle of the Trench, Allah did not excuse anybody. The texts of the four juristic schools are explicit and definite in this respect, and leave no room for interpretation, ambiguity or uncertainty.[39]

Muhammad's example, according to Azzam, indicates that the authority of an imam or an emir was not necessary in the case of Afghanistan. Here, we see Azzam echoing Faraj's insistence that a caliph is not required to call Muslims to war. We "do not," he writes, "wait for the Caliphate to be restored." The caliphate "does not return through abstract theories, amassed knowledge and studying." Rather, he continues, only through the jihad may Muslims be restored, for "jihad is the right way to reform the divided authorities to the ultimate authority of the Caliphate." Insofar as the jihad is necessary, Muslims cannot linger on the sidelines, waiting for a leader. Rather, "the Mujahideen choose their Amir for jihad from amongst themselves. He organizes them and unifies their efforts and makes the strong support the weak."[40]

Azzam then quotes a *sahih* hadith (one considered sound or reliable) in which "Uqbah Bin Amar, who was amongst the to-be-mentioned party, said: 'The Prophet (saw) sent out a party and he chose from amongst us a swordsman (leader). When we returned I said: I have not seen the like of when the Prophet (saw) blamed us. The Prophet (saw) said: Are you unable that if I appoint a man and he fails to apply my order to replace him with one who applies my order?'"[41]

Here, Azzam argues, Muhammad had reprimanded the party for not choosing a leader, despite the fact that Muhammad had appointed an individual for this task. As Azzam reads this hadith, if the one chosen to lead by Muhammad himself can be replaced, then certainly in a situation such as the one Muslims are facing, they too may choose an emir to lead their jihad against forces of Muslim oppression.

Azzam is especially concerned to stress that the duty of jihad is not contextually contingent. It is not a commandment that God handed to the early Muslims in response to their specific circumstances; rather, the commandment retains its force until the caliphate has been established. Thus, it remains as true for Muslims today as it did during the time of Muhammad. As Azzam describes it, jihad is a "necessity accompanying the caravan which this religion guides."[42] This is why, he writes, "Jihad was a way of life for the

Pious Predecessors, and the Prophet was a master of the Mujahideen and a model for fortunate, inexperienced people. . . . The total number of military excursions which he accompanied was twenty-seven. He himself fought in nine of these."[43]

In much the same way as Faraj described it, Azzam argues that the duty of jihad is the preeminent duty for all believers. Given the foreign penetration of Muslim land, Azzam exhorts all Muslims to take up arms and join the fight against the Soviets in Afghanistan until these non-Muslim forces are repelled. Of course, while Faraj validated the merit of taking up arms against Egyptian apostate rulers and Azzam was interested in a specific and (at the time of his writing) ongoing battle in which he saw Muslims and Muslim lands threatened by non-Muslim forces, in their writings both Faraj and Azzam use the same argument and elevate jihad above all other duties (besides belief) in the life of the pious Muslim. For both men, the use of force to protect Islam from threat is a critical and immediate duty that should supersede all others—a duty that, Azzam writes, is the "peak" of Islam and the "most excellent form of worship."[44]

For Faraj and Azzam, other means of waging the jihad in defense of Islam are unacceptable and cannot replace the duty of jihad. This duty cannot be abandoned, nor fulfilled, by donating money or becoming more serious in one's other obligations before God. Jihad, they maintain, requires bodily participation in the armed conflict waged to defend Islam, Muslims, and Muslim land. For Azzam, this duty to expel non-Muslim forces from Muslim lands is obligatory, binding, and immediate on all Muslims, as *individuals*, until foreign forces have been expelled.

Azzam's greatest contribution to the narrative, however, was his ability to frame the Afghan jihad against the Soviets as a *Muslim* struggle. While the Afghan jihad certainly aimed to defend Afghan Muslims and their land from foreign aggression, ultimately, for Azzam, it was about defending Islam as a whole. Azzam saw Afghanistan as the base from which a broader revolution could be initiated—one that would eventually encompass all lands in which Islam historically held sway. Jihad, then, was critical and incumbent on the believer; no other method would serve to erect the Islamic state. According to Azzam,

Establishment of the Muslim community on an area of land is a necessity, as vital as water and air. This homeland will not come about without an organized Islamic movement which perseveres consciously and realistically upon Jihad, and which regards fighting as a decisive factor and as a protective covering.

The Islamic movement will not be able to establish the Islamic community except through a common, people's Jihad which has the Islamic
movement as its beating heart and deliberative mind.

It will be like the small spark which ignites a large keg of explosives,
for the Islamic movement brings about an eruption of the hidden capabilities of the Ummah, and a gushing forth of the springs of Good
stored up in its depth.[45]

For Azzam, the Afghan jihad was a watershed moment for contemporary
Muslim history. Through the Afghan jihad, he writes, the Muslim vanguard
will form an Islamic state, a base from which to start a large-scale revolution to reconquer all the lands that were once a part of the Islamic empire.
Thus, he argues, the significance of Afghanistan is its serving as the catalyst
for the larger uprising of Muslims that he (and Faraj and Qutb before him)
had imagined. These ambitions are demonstrated clearly when Azzam describes the importance and the priority of Afghanistan to the Muslim-wide
struggle. For example, he compares the jihad in Afghanistan with the jihad
in Palestine. While Palestine is the "heart of the Islamic world," he maintains
the majority of Muslims ought to devote their efforts to Afghanistan because
the struggle in Afghanistan is more *Islamic* and therefore more likely to lead
to the construction of a "true" Islamic state.[46]

Azzam understands the Afghan jihad as being more "Islamic" in that it
aims to institute a state ruled by shariah law. The Palestinian jihad, he writes,
has been co-opted by those who are interested in a political revolution that
is not based on a proper religious foundation. In other words, the Palestinian
jihad, and its leadership, is not motivated by the goal of instituting an Islamic
state. The situation was different, according to Azzam, in Afghanistan. For
example, he writes that the "Islamists" were the "first to take control of the
battles in Afghanistan" and still "refuse help from any Kaffir (non-Muslim)
country," while the Palestinians are motivated by a variety of political parties
(some of which are non-Islamist) and continue to accept aid from Western
powers.[47]

Azzam also argues that the Afghan jihad needs those who can help develop the specifically Islamic nature of the struggle that began against the
Soviets. The first generation of Afghan fighters was rooted in Islam; hence,
they understood the religious magnitude of the war. However, the first generation has "fallen in martyrdom," and now, many years into the war, a second
generation has taken up the cause. This second generation, though, is at a
disadvantage because these men have "not been fortunate enough to receive
the same share of upbringing and guidance, and have not come across a

stretched-out hand showing an interest in teaching and training them." They are in "dire need of somebody who can live amongst them and direct them toward Allah and teach them religious regulations."[48]

In fact, in the preface to the second edition of *Join the Caravan*, Azzam expresses his disappointment (and dismay) that most of those men who have joined the Afghan jihad are young and inexperienced. This situation, he writes, "has cast a great burden upon our shoulders."[49] He calls for more "mature propagators to Islam," those who can instruct in Quranic recitation, prayers, and other matters as related to the treatment of prisoners of war, as well as the distribution of booty—all places in which the mujahideen are lacking in appropriate Islamic knowledge.[50]

To make his points, Azzam, like Faraj, grounds himself in the traditional sources for Islamic discourse on the just use of force. In fact, all of Azzam's and Faraj's writings feature quotes from the Quran, collections of hadiths, and major Islamic jurists taking up the bulk of every page. For both thinkers, the religious nature of this struggle is paramount to understanding its importance and to discerning how Muslims should respond to the various challenges they discuss. Islamic history, symbols, doctrines, and law are the singular means for diagnosing the problem accurately and provide the only solutions that, according to Faraj and Azzam, will be successful. The lens of Islam is the only one that will take Muslims from a position of marginalization, subjugation, and oppression and that will reinvigorate them and their lands so that they may reach their former glory.

Importantly, of course, the historical materials that Azzam references also provide specific moral constraints on the just use of force in the Islamic tradition. In certain ways, Azzam's conceptualization of the jihad also preserves these limits. To begin, it is not unreasonable to construe the military struggle of the Afghan mujahideen as a defensive war. Thus, in noting the Islamic nature of their struggle as well as their desire to set up an Islamic state, Azzam can make reasonable arguments about why supporting the mujahideen is necessary. Furthermore, the Afghan jihad against the Soviets was confined to Afghanistan's borders, so Azzam called Muslims to Afghanistan, hoping that a mujahideen victory would transform the country into the type of Islamic state that would revitalize Muslims. Moreover, Azzam's jihad was restricted insofar as the theater of war remained in Afghanistan, though his wish to see Afghanistan become the launching point for a broader jihad begins to erode some of these limits.

This connection between the Afghan jihad and the Muslim-wide revolution that Azzam hoped to inspire reveals a difficulty in his thinking that is directly related to how he conceived of the individual authority to engage in jihad. For Azzam, the Afghan jihad marked a pivotal moment in Islamic history. The struggle of the mujahideen, he argued, was a symbolic battle for the soul of Muslims as well as a material and very real battle for the survival of the *ummah* (the global community of Muslims). It reflected the current religious and political conditions of the broader Muslim world, for a lack of piety and adherence to God's law had weakened the ummah, leaving Muslims unable to resist encroachment and subjugation by foreign (non-Muslim) powers. The only way for Muslims to restore their former power and glory was to take up arms and to ignite a revolution—beginning in Afghanistan and spanning the breadth of the Muslim world—to expel all foreign powers from Muslim territory. Winning the war against the Soviets, Azzam insisted, would transform Afghanistan into a spiritual and geographical base from which this global Muslim revolution could be waged. Moreover, winning in Afghanistan would drive this revolution to other parts of the world that were formerly under Muslim control, such as Spain, Kashmir, and the Philippines, so that these lands too could be liberated.

Perhaps Azzam's claim of a defensive war can be entertained within the specific context of the Afghan mujahideen, yet how such claims could be maintained outside the geographical boundaries of Afghanistan is unclear. Who might be considered a legitimate authority to lead such a war? How is the defensive jihad triggered in circumstances in which there are no immediate hostilities? While Azzam's ideas might be appropriated to the case of Afghanistan, it is difficult to see how even the most charitable interpretation of his conceptualization of jihad could be extrapolated to the type of revolution he envisioned.[51]

The writings of Osama bin Laden provide a solution to this problem. The Muslim-wide uprising Azzam had hoped for became the central feature of bin Laden's (and al-Qaeda's) thinking, though it did so only by categorically *dismissing* the moral constraints that the historical Islamic discourse provided on the just use of force and by producing a model of war that is indiscriminate and unrestricted in terms of both strategy and tactics.

Osama bin Laden

Osama bin Laden was born in Riyadh, Saudi Arabia, in 1957 to Mohammed bin Laden and his fourth wife, Alia. He was their only child. By the time Osama was born, his father was the owner of an extraordinarily successful construction business, the Saudi Binladin Group, which was responsible for a majority of the development projects in Saudi Arabia, including the restoration of the Grand Mosque in Mecca. Osama attended school in Jeddah and was a good student. He attended high school and university in Saudi Arabia, though it is unclear whether he completed a degree. In 1984 encouraged by Abdullah Azzam, bin Laden went to Afghanistan. When he returned to Jeddah he began to raise funds for the mujahideen, and as noted previously, he and Azzam joined forces.

By 1986 bin Laden had brought his wives and children to Peshawar and formed the group that would come to be known as al-Qaeda in 1988. When the Soviet-Afghan War ended in 1989, he returned to Jeddah with new ideas regarding the jihad. He approached the royal family with a plan to "liberate" Yemen from communist forces but was dismissed. Moreover, in 1990, when Iraq invaded Kuwait, bin Laden offered the services of his mujahideen to defend the Saudi kingdom. Once again, he was rebuffed. Eventually Saudi forces called in American troops. Bin Laden was enraged by this. His views were becoming problematic for the kingdom, and he was banished in 1992. He went to Sudan but was forced to leave in 1996, at which point he went to Afghanistan.

He turned his attention directly toward continuing the jihad that had been initiated in Afghanistan. The mujahideen's victory over the Soviets was a major boost to the development of the al-Qaeda phenomenon, as figures such as bin Laden viewed their victory as one of Muslims against non-Muslim forces. For bin Laden, that the mujahideen—a vanguard army of true Muslims fighting for the construction of a legitimate Islamic state—had prevailed against a much stronger non-Muslim power presaged the Islamic revolution. Motivated by the mujahideen's success, bin Laden believed that the Muslim-wide revolution could start, and Afghanistan would be the base from which this new war could be waged. In 1996 he declared:

> By the Grace of Allah, a safe base is now available in the high Hindukush Mountains in Khurasan; where—by the Grace of Allah—the largest infidel military force of the world was destroyed. And the myth of the super power was withered in front of the Mujahideen cries of Allahu Akbar (God is greater). Today we work from the same mountains to lift the iniquity that had been imposed on the Ummah by the Zionist-Crusader alliance, particularly after they have occupied the blessed land around Jerusalem, route of the journey of the Prophet . . . and the land of the two Holy Places.[52] We ask Allah to bestow us with victory, He is our Patron and He is the Most Capable.[53]

Yet bin Laden's vision for this revolution was different than that of his friend and partner Azzam. While Azzam sought to expel all foreign forces from lands formerly part of the caliphate and he and other figures, such as Faraj, wrote in support of a jihad against the "near enemy," bin Laden turned his sights to a different horizon. By the time bin Laden published his 1998 declaration of war against the United States, the focus of his diatribes had shifted from the Saudi Kingdom to the "Zionist-Crusader alliance"—a term he used to describe a series of forces (primarily those of the United States, Europe, and Israel) that were responsible for the subjugation and oppression of Muslims.

This important change in bin Laden's thinking is clear if we examine his epistles from 1996 and 1998. In his 1996 epistle, he focuses much more directly on the Saudi government. He enumerates a list of offenses on the part of the Saudi regime: practices of usury (prohibited in the Islamic tradition), cooperation with foreign governments (particularly the US government) in which Muslim resources have been exploited to the benefit of the West and to the detriment of Muslims, the co-option of media outlets by the Saudi government to hide the truth of its pernicious practices, the flagrant and ostentatious misuse of the regime's wealth and resources, the lack of social services (like gas and water) for ordinary Saudi citizens, and the replacement of shariah law with "man-made" (secular) law.[54]

As bin Laden argues, the occupation of the holy sites—at least in 1996—is the most devastating of the Saudi offenses. By "occupation," he means the presence of non-Muslim (American) troops who had been placed in Saudi Arabia during Operations Desert Shield and Desert Storm in the First Gulf War. Although he mentions the "massacre" of Muslims in other places—Tajikistan, Burma, Kashmir, the Philippines, and so on—he sees the "occupation" of Saudi Arabia as the most severe of these calamities. Important to understanding his thinking is that the term "occupation" held both material and symbolic significance. For bin Laden, the presence of non-Muslim forces in the land of the "two Holy Places" is a serious affront to their sanctity. Moreover, the troops' presence in Saudi Arabia also poses a symbolic offense for bin Laden that represents the depth of Muslim weakness, showing that Muslims can neither defend their own holy sites nor refuse the assistance of those non-Muslim forces that he sees as a main cause for the Muslims' feeble position in the first place. For bin Laden, the occupation of the heart and soul of Islam by non-Muslim forces demonstrates that Muslims have fallen to a state of weakness and peril unlike any other in their history. It is an unmistakable sign—both materially and symbolically—of Muslim oppression and weakness vis-à-vis the West.

For bin Laden, too, revitalization requires a proper Islamic state, for only through this institution would Muslims be able to remove the yoke of subjugation that non-Muslim forces have placed around their necks. Furthermore, he argues, the occupation of the holy sites is the direct product of the Saudis' neglect of Islamic law, which he sees as the source of Muslim strength. This neglect has led Muslims to a state of weakness, leaving them unable to protect their own land and holy places. This calamity, he argues, ought to clearly demonstrate to Muslims the gravity of what is at stake and the severity of the situation that they face. Important for bin Laden, the Saudi government's failure to rule Muslims appropriately was what brought this disaster on the Muslim community. Furthermore, the Saudis have allowed it to happen on their own doorstep. This inaction, he writes, has "torn off" the legitimacy of the Saudis and removed both their ability and their right to rule.[55] For bin Laden, however, these offenses, while certainly attributed to Saudi failing, are immediately tied to the "occupying American enemy," who is the principal reason for the plight and weakness of Muslims.[56] The Americans' occupation of the holy places is the product of an international and pernicious US foreign policy toward Muslims. Therefore, he writes, "efforts should be concentrated on destroying, fighting and killing the enemy [the Americans] until, by the Grace of Allah, it is completely defeated."[57]

Bin Laden, like Faraj and Azzam before him, insists that Muslim revitalization may be had only through the use of force. The situation has forced the hand of the faithful. To push the Americans out of Islamic land is the *most important* religious duty after faith or belief. Muslims must ignore the "minor" differences among themselves, he insists, so that they can unify their forces and take up arms against the non-Muslim occupation of Muslim lands.[58] He warns of the grave consequences of Muslim infighting, arguing that ridding the Muslim world of foreign occupation will require Muslims to work collectively. Otherwise, the consequences of internal divisions and dissent will only serve to weaken the Muslim cause even further.[59]

Interestingly, while he argues that the occupation of Saudi Arabia is an issue that critically concerns all Muslims, in the 1996 tract he ascribes the duty to wage jihad against US forces in Saudi Arabia primarily to Saudi "youths" (read: young men) and exhorts other Muslims both to offer material and emotional support and to boycott US goods. Likely bin Laden had the Afghan model in mind and was attempting to galvanize Saudi youths to a victory similar to the Afghans' against the Soviets. Moreover, he calls on the Saudis specifically in this tract because the responsibility to expel the invader (as we have seen in both chapter 2 and the preceding discussion) is first ascribed to those closest to the point of aggression or attack. In bin Laden's mind, Saudi Muslims held the first reins of jihad because they were geographically closest and, as such, had the individual duty to take up arms against the foreign occupying forces that had invaded their home and holy sanctuaries until they were ejected. He writes, "If the sons of the land of the two Holy Places feel and strongly believe that fighting (Jihad) against the Kuffar in every part of the world is absolutely essential; then they would be even more enthusiastic, more powerful and larger in number upon fighting on their own land—the place of their births—defending the greatest of their sanctities, the noble Ka'ba. . . . They know that the Muslims of the world will assist and help them to victory."[60]

This point is important to emphasize as it demonstrates a level of restraint in the early stages of bin Laden's thinking and writing. The jihad in Saudi Arabia, as construed through his 1996 epistle, focused on US military forces on Saudi Arabian soil. Drawing on the juristic tradition of jihad, bin Laden presumably ascribes the first level of responsibility to Saudis because they are closest to the area of "attack"; therefore, they are held responsible with attempting to expel American forces from their land. Furthermore, the jihad is limited to Saudi Arabia and, hence, constrained in an important way. While bin Laden mentions other places (like Somalia and Chechnya) that may also merit jihad against forces of oppression, in 1996 he limits himself primarily to ejecting foreign "occupying" forces from Saudi Arabia, an area with clear and discernible borders.

However, as we move forward to bin Laden's 1998 "Declaration of Jihad against Jews and Crusaders," this restraint is markedly absent. This document is significantly shorter (approximately 15 paragraphs) than the 1996 epistle (approximately 126 paragraphs). Furthermore, it was signed by a congregation of representatives of militant Islamist groups, including those in Egypt, Pakistan, and Bangladesh, thus demonstrating the vast theaters of interest and the expanding nature of the jihad that bin Laden describes. Moreover, rather than enumerating a detailed list of offenses and grievances, bin Laden simply makes the point that American aggression against Muslims continues. This is not to say that he was unconcerned with the American "aggression" outlined in the 1996 tract. Indeed, he very clearly indicates that US foreign policy plays a major role in the oppression and weakness of Muslims and that US forces must be fought and repelled. However, in the 1998 tract, bin Laden cites the Americans' continued presence in Saudi Arabia and observes they are being used to fight other Muslims (in Iraq) and to turn their attention away from Palestine. All of this remains a telltale sign that the United States is complicit in an ongoing war against Muslims and Islam. His ideas on this are worth quoting at length.

There is no one today that would dispute the following three facts . . . :

First, for more than seven years, America has occupied the lands of Islam in their holiest sites, the Arabian Peninsula, looting her bounties/ resources, dictating to her rulers and humiliating her people, terrorizing her neighbors and using her bases in the Peninsula to kill her people as well as her neighbors.

And if in the past there were those who disputed the reality of this occupation, now all the people of the Peninsula recognize it. And the best evidence of it is American persistence in the aggression against the people of Iraq that is proceeding from the Peninsula, even though its rulers—in their entirety—refuse the use of their land for this purpose. Yet, they are defeated (unable to resist).

Second, despite the great destruction inflicted on the Iraqi people at the hand of the Jewish-Crusader Alliance, and despite the terrible (great) numbers of killings, of which there has been over 1 million, despite all this, the Americans are trying to once again resume this horrific massacre. . . .

So here they come today to annihilate what is left of these people and to humiliate its Muslim neighbors.

Third, and even if the goals of the Americans in these wars are religious and economic, they also serve the Jewish state and its occupation of Jerusalem and her murder of the Muslims there. There is no better proof of this than their desire to destroy Iraq, the strongest Arab neighbor, and their attempt to fragment the states of this region, like Iraq, and Saudi Arabia, and Egypt, and the Sudan into weak states (دويلات ورقية) and through their weakness and fragmentation, to guarantee the survival of Israel to maintain the Crusader occupation of the Arabian Peninsula.

And all these offenses are a direct declaration of war against God, his messenger, and Muslims. And all the ulema–who have come before us and who will succeed us—throughout Islamic history have unanimously agreed without exception that the jihad is an individual duty (فرض عين) on the Muslim if the enemy demolishes/destroys Muslim countries. . . .

And based on that (the above), and in compliance with God's orders, we issue the following ruling (نفتي جميع المسلمين بالحكم التالي) to all Muslims:

The ruling to kill Americans—civilian and military—is an individual duty on every Muslim capable of this, in any country in which he is able to do it, so that the al-Aqsa Mosque and the Holy Mosque will be liberated from their grip, and that their armies will depart (تخرج) from all Muslim land, defeated and incapable of doing harm.[61]

This last statement, or "ruling,"—encompassed in a single, succinct paragraph—highlights the characterizing features of al-Qaeda's distinct understanding of jihad and its brand of militancy. All theological commitments discussed at the beginning of this chapter are present in bin Laden's 1996 and 1998 epistles. To begin, current conditions necessitate jihad. Like Faraj and Azzam, bin Laden argues that the current plight of Muslims will be relieved only through an armed confrontation with the source of oppression—primarily the United States. Additionally, jihad is the most critical duty that the faithful can undertake. Bin Laden also insists that given the oppression and subjugation faced by Muslims and in light of God's command to Muslims that they are ruled by God's law, the duty of jihad must take priority (after belief) in the lives of the faithful until such time as a true Islamic state is erected. Moreover, current conditions, which bin Laden describes as a war against Islam, trigger the religious duty of defensive war, thus granting every individual Muslim the authority to take up arms against the enemies of Islam. This is the case, he argues, even without a caliph or other legitimate authority.

Until this point, we see the influence of both Faraj and Azzam's thinking behind bin Laden's assertions of war. Like Faraj and Azzam, bin Laden is attempting to awaken Muslims to their plight of oppression, subjugation, and marginalization and to show them a solution—the use of force against the enemy (whether it be apostate regimes, the United States, or both) until such time as the proper Islamic state (with a legitimate Muslim ruler at its head) has been brought to fruition.

However, while bin Laden presumes the theological foundations established by the likes of Faraj and Azzam, his conceptualization of the jihad bypasses the limits they established. He thus steers away from both Faraj and Azzam insofar as his model of war categorically ignores the types of restrictions (however light) we see in his predecessors' work. He does so in two primary ways. To begin, al-Qaeda's theater of "war" is not contained in any way, and that has become a characterizing feature of al-Qaeda thinking. While both Faraj and Azzam gestured toward broader conceptualizations of jihad, both also indicated limits. Faraj discussed jihad in terms of Egyptian apostate rulers, and Azzam was primarily interested in galvanizing support for the mujahideen in the Soviet-Afghan War. For bin Laden, however, the individual duty to jihad is triggered and present in any country in which it is possible to wage it. Jihad, for bin Laden, is a war that may be pursued *anywhere* and *everywhere* that the forces of oppression are located.

Second, and also characteristic of al-Qaeda's brand of militancy, bin Laden's conceptualization of jihad is categorically *indiscriminate* without any method, attempt, desire, or even concern to differentiate between combatants and innocents.[62] This jihad is not described as a war waged against regular forces, a specific government, or American soldiers; rather, it is a total war within which every Muslim is required to take up arms and kill Americans—*civilians* and combatants alike. Certainly Faraj and Azzam both argued that in some circumstances the killing of civilians was legitimate and necessary given the realities of their jihad. Yet both discussed these issues in ways that indicated they were sensitive to the moral need to maintain distinctions between civilians and combatants. By the time of bin Laden's 1998 declaration, however, the tradition's theological requirements for discriminate war had collapsed entirely, insofar as bin Laden's thinking is concerned.

Conclusion

The dual nature of al-Qaeda's model of war is clear. Bin Laden grounded his thinking in the Islamic tradition's theological narrative on the proper use of force. His ideas about the proper political organization for an Islamic state, as well as his ideas about how to determine who is or who is not fit to rule, are premised on a specific reading of early Islamic history. Muslims, he argues in his writings, are weak because they are governed by leaders who do not rule by shariah law. Thus, they lack an Islamic state, or the source of Muslim power and achievement. Yet the al-Qaeda model, as articulated by bin Laden in the 1998 epistle, dismisses any and all moral constraints in terms of strategy and tactics. This is not, of course, to imply that Faraj's and Azzam's conceptualizations of jihad were in line with the Islamic tradition's ideas on proper war and moral limits. Yet, appreciating the full measure of al-Qaeda's thinking and its clear lack of restrictions requires us to note that earlier jihadi ideologues, whose thinking significantly influenced al-Qaeda, were more restrained.

The more important point, however, is the way that the al-Qaeda model of war makes a specific connection between theology and tactics and directs al-Qaeda thinking. We must understand the way that this narrative is used both to interpret the current environment and to provide direction, according to bin Laden, in rectifying the marginalization and oppression of Muslims. Of course, understanding al-Qaeda's model of jihad is an ambitious undertaking, especially considering the diffuse nature of this organization.[63]

With the inspirational nature of the al-Qaeda leadership, however, it appears natural to turn to one of these figures when attempting to distinguish the outlines and the particulars of the way that al-Qaeda has moved from religious justifications for jihad to determining strategy and tactics that are directed by this narrative. In this end, no one has made a more prolific, or comprehensive, articulation on this matter than has Mustafa Abd al-Qadir Setmariam Nasar, better known as Abu Musab al-Suri. It is to his work that we now turn.

Notes

1. Wright, *Looming Tower*, 36–37.
2. A historical background and an English translation of the "Faridah" are available in Jansen, *Neglected Duty*.
3. Ibid., 165.
4. Ibid., 162.
5. Ibid., 165.
6. Ibid., 169.
7. Ibid., 167.
8. Ibid., 169.
9. As evidence he quotes opinions from Abu Hanifa (699–767), Abu Yusuf (738–98), and Ibn Taymiyyah (1263–1328). He argues all of them agree that an Islamic state—or a territory that belongs to dar al-Islam—is one that is ruled by Islamic law.
10. Jansen, *Neglected Duty*, 169.
11. Ibid., 170.
12. Ibid., 167–68.
13. Ibid., 167.
14. Ibid., 171.
15. Ibid., 172.
16. Ibid., 179.
17. Ibid., 192, 172–79.
18. Ibid., 161.
19. Ibid., 190.
20. Ibid., 183–90.
21. Ibid., 199.
22. Ibid., 199–200.
23. Ibid., 203.
24. Ibid.
25. Ibid.
26. Ibid., 216. The "Faridah" quotes the hadith of Abul Husayn Muslim, as well as commentary on the hadith by al-Nawawi, in the attempt to provide evidence for the position. It states that an invitation to Islam before an attack is necessary in the

case where an invitation has not been extended in the past ("did not reach them"). In the case where the invitation did reach the enemy, the summons was recommended but not required.

27. Ibid., 217–18.

28. Note that parts of the materials on Azzam's biography were originally published in *The Oxford Encyclopedia of Islam and Politics*, edited by Emad El-Din Shahin, and has been reproduced by permission of Oxford University Press, http://www.oxfordreference.com/view/10.1093/acref:oiso/9780199739356.001.0001/acref-9780199739356-e-0108?rskey=uoqDPF&result=51. For permission to reuse this material, please visit http://global.oup.com/academic/rights.

29. Biographical note in Azzam, *Defence of the Muslim Lands*, 1–3.

30. Azzam, *Join the Caravan*, 8–9.

31. Azzam, *Defence of the Muslim Lands*, chap. 1, pp. 1–2.

32. Azzam, *Join the Caravan*, 19. The segment that is in quotation marks is from Azzam's use of Abu Dawud; see the translator's note 11.

33. Azzam, *Defence of the Muslim Lands*, chap. 1, p. 3.

34. Ibid., chap. 1, p. 3.

35. Here he also quotes Ibn Taymiyyah, who wrote, "If with the Kuffar there are pious people from the best of mankind and it is not possible to fight these Kuffar except by killing them, then they are to be killed as well. The leading scholars are in accord that if the Kuffar use Muslim captives as human shields, and there is fear for the rest of the Muslims if they are not fought, then it is permitted to shoot them aiming [at] the Kuffar." See ibid., chap. 1, p. 7.

36. Ibid.

37. Azzam, *Join the Caravan*, 27.

38. Ibid., 28–29.

39. Ibid., 42. Note that SAWS stands for *sallallahu alayhi wa salaam* (may God's prayers and peace be upon him), which is used to show respect for the Prophet.

40. Azzam, *Defence of the Muslim Lands*, chap. 4, p. 4.

41. Ibid.

42. Azzam, *Join the Caravan*, 25.

43. Ibid., 30.

44. Ibid., 39–40.

45. Ibid., 33–34.

46. Azzam, *Defence of the Muslim Lands*, chap. 2, p. 2.

47. Ibid.

48. Azzam, *Join the Caravan*, 41.

49. Ibid., 17.

50. Ibid., 20–23.

51. Of course, some might protest labeling Faraj and Azzam's conceptualizations of jihad as "limited," even with the preface that they are narrow in specific ways.

However, highlighting the areas where their ideas do adhere to certain moral constraints (even if loosely) is important so that al-Qaeda's dismissal of them is clear.

52. With "route of the journey," bin Laden is referring to the night journey of the prophet Muhammad, during which, according to the Quran and its interpretive tradition, Muhammad traveled by horse from Mecca to Jerusalem in one evening. "The land of the two Holy Places" is a reference to Saudi Arabia, which houses both the Sacred (or Grand) Mosque in Mecca and Muhammad's burial place in Medina.

53. Bin Laden, "Declaration of War," para. 9. An English translation is also available at https://en.wikisource.org/wiki/Osama_bin_Laden's_Declaration_of_War.

54. Ibid., para. 7. See also paragraphs 14, 15, 24, 29, 48, 49, and 50, among others.

55. Ibid., para. 29. See also paragraphs 14, 15, 24, 29, 48, 49, and 50, among others.

56. Ibid., para. 55.

57. Ibid.

58. Ibid., para. 39.

59. Ibid., paras. 39–46.

60. Ibid., para. 70.

61. Bin Laden et al. (World Islamic Front), "Jihad against the Jews and Crusaders." My translation.

62. Bin Laden justified the killing of American civilians by arguing that insofar as American citizens elect their representatives and support their government through taxes, they are complicit (and hence do not fit under the labels of "noncombatants" or "civilians") in those US policies that he perceived as attacks against Islam. See bin Laden's 2002 "Letter to America," *The Guardian*, November 24, 2001, http://www.theguardian.com/world/2002/nov/24/theobserver.

63. In testimony to the US Senate Foreign Relations Committee and based on a survey of al-Qaeda plots in the West beginning in August 1988, Marc Sageman reported that 54 percent of terrorist plots connected with al-Qaeda were "inspired" by al-Qaeda, meaning that they were "autonomous plots . . . with no connections whatsoever with any formal transnational terrorist organizations"; 25 percent were "al-Qaeda affiliated"; and 12 percent were "al-Qaeda controlled." While Sageman argued that this data demonstrates al-Qaeda's deflated strength (particularly since 2004), I maintain that the evidence in many ways proves otherwise and indicates al-Qaeda's continuing ability to incite violence around the world, even in situations where they are not directly involved. Furthermore, as Sageman's numbers indicate, 46 percent of terror operations for which he has collected information remain under direct or indirect al-Qaeda control. See Marc Sageman, "Confronting al-Qaeda: Understanding the Threat in Afghanistan and Beyond," Testimony, Senate Foreign Relations Committee, October 7, 2009, http://www.foreign.senate.gov/imo/media/doc/SagemanTestimony091007p1.pdf. See also Bergen, *Holy War, Inc.*, specifically chap. 8.

Tactics
Al-Suri and al-Qaeda's Model of War

On March 11, 2004, Spain was rocked by a series of coordinated attacks against the commuter train system in Madrid. The blasts left 191 dead and 1,800 wounded. Out of the rubble, Abu Musab al-Suri, a young, red-haired, and fair-skinned young man, rose from relative anonymity and into the international spotlight as the possible mastermind behind the attacks.[1] Al-Suri had been an important figure in radical Islamist circles well before Madrid. He had spent time in Syria, Iraq, Egypt, Afghanistan, Pakistan, Spain, and London and was closely involved in each of their respective militant movements. Shortly after the events in Madrid, the United States offered a $5 million reward for information leading to his arrest, serving to elevate his importance to the jihadi community. In response, al-Suri launched a personal website containing links to audio and video files of his lectures, as well as most of his written works.[2]

Details on his capture and whereabouts thereafter are murky. According to several reports, Pakistani police captured him during a raid in Quetta in November 2005.[3] He was then taken to a US detention facility and eventually transported to Syria (where he was a wanted man) and imprisoned. The most recent rumors of his release circulated in 2012; however, statements on al-Suri's whereabouts by al-Qaeda spokesman Adam Yahiye Gadahn (1978–2015) and Ayman al-Zawahiri in 2014 suggested that he was still in prison.[4]

His importance, though, is not traced to a specific operation or a spectacular terrorist attack. Nor was he the leader of an internationally known jihadi group. In fact, al-Suri was never able to amass a significant following before his imprisonment. Instead, his importance to the al-Qaeda phenomenon stems from the influence of his writing. Though he had years of military training, al-Suri is, at heart, a theoretician who sought to provide a comprehensive tactical and strategic framework for a global jihad. He spent the better part of his adult life writing, lecturing, and recording his ideas on jihadi military strategy, focusing on the question of how it ought to evolve in the post-9/11 environment.

While al-Suri never reached levels of notoriety enjoyed by figures such as bin Laden, al-Zawahiri, and Abu Bakr al-Baghdadi, the community of academics and analysts interested in the al-Qaeda phenomenon have taken note of al-Suri's importance. Two book-length studies exist to date. The first is a biography by Brynjar Lia that details the events of al-Suri's life and his influence. It also includes translations of key excerpts from his most influential work, *The Global Islamic Resistance Call*. Thanks to Lia's research, the outlines of a shadowy and elusive figure have come to light. The second is a condensed and highly readable translation of the *Call* edited by Jim Lacey that provides an excellent overview of al-Suri's thinking. Both of these works have aided our understanding of al-Suri's life and aims significantly, and I draw on them in this chapter.

As noted in both Lia's and Lacey's work, al-Suri did not understand himself as a religious thinker, as "politics and strategy, not religious doctrines, remained his focus."[5] It is true al-Suri's *Call* is focused on constructing a new model for jihad. Although his writing is focused heavily on tactics and strategy, for al-Suri, understanding the religious justification for this "call"—that is, primarily understanding the necessity of jihad and of individual Muslim participation in the "resistance"—is foundational. For this reason, I draw attention to the way his theological beliefs and commitments serve to root his highly influential conceptualization of the jihad.

The jihad, he argues, must be based on and founded in a set of theological ideas that direct the use of force. It is al-Suri's ability to translate and connect the ideas discussed by Qutb, Faraj, Azzam, and bin Laden into a model of war that has directed major developments in jihadi tactics and strategy. Through the work of al-Suri, the theological narrative of the jihad—initiated by Qutb, operationalized by Faraj, developed by Azzam into a Muslim-wide struggle, and then expanded to a global war by bin Laden—is transformed into a diffuse, decentralized, and indiscriminate model of war.

Based on my translation of the relevant parts of chapter 2 of al-Suri's treatise, I demonstrate that the foundation of his strategic and tactical model is his understanding of the religious duty of individual jihad. Al-Suri constructs a model of war that has directed and presaged two major tactical developments in the al-Qaeda phenomenon—the growing line of lone-wolf terrorist attacks and the rise of ISIS. In this way, his work demonstrates the connection between theological thinking, strategy, and tactics that characterize the al-Qaeda phenomenon.

Abu Musab al-Suri

Al-Suri was born in Aleppo, Syria, in October 1958. At the age of eighteen he enrolled at the University of Aleppo's engineering department. Tensions at the time were brewing between the ruling Alawite minority (led by the newly installed military dictator, Gen. Hafaz al-Assad) and the Islamist streams in Syria over a variety of social and political issues. By the end of the 1970s, these tensions erupted into violent protests and assassination attempts against Syrian officials. Al-Suri claimed to have had a religious awakening during this period and, in 1980, left his studies to join an armed Syrian jihadi group called the Combatant Vanguard.[6]

Government crackdowns on the Islamist elements in Syria forced al-Suri to flee to Jordan in 1981. While there he joined the Syrian Muslim Brotherhood, which, at the time, was attempting to regroup. By the end of that year, he was sent to Iraq and subsequently to Egypt in order to receive military training. By 1982 he had served as an instructor in the Muslim Brotherhood's military training camps in both Iraq and Jordan; however, the military failures of the Brotherhood, coupled with ideological differences, led al-Suri to resign from the group's ranks (despite his recent promotion as a military commander). To be more specific, he was outraged by the leadership's willingness to compromise with secular (nationalist and communist) regimes, such as the Syrian and Iraqi ruling parties. These compromises led al-Suri to claim that the Muslim Brotherhood was not fully devoted to the religious cause. He believed that a military campaign could not succeed without the theological and ideological base that would allow for its success.[7] As a result, he decided to abandon the military struggle and devote himself to obtaining a religious education.

He tried, unsuccessfully, to attain theological credentials from Medina's Islamic University in 1982 (he blamed his failure on Muslim Brotherhood sympathizers and claimed they were impeding his way).[8] From Saudi Arabia, al-Suri relocated to France in 1983, enrolled at a university there, and once again took up engineering (Lia states that the specific university is unknown). Despite his studies, he continued his involvement with Syrian jihadi groups, eventually abandoning his pursuit of an engineering degree altogether to devote himself more fully to the Syrian jihad. While living in France, he traveled to Syria in 1983 and 1984 and attempted to reignite the jihad there. After both efforts failed, he moved to Amman, Jordan; enrolled in a branch of Beirut University; and started taking correspondence courses in history (eventually getting a bachelor of arts degree in 1991). He moved to Spain in 1985 and lived there until 1990. Although he resided in Spain, he spent significant periods between 1987 and 1992 traveling back and forth to Afghanistan.

He traveled to Peshawar in 1987, hoping to join the Afghan jihad and to foment support for the struggling Syrian jihad. That same year, he met Abdullah Azzam, who by then was running the Afghan Services Bureau that he had started with bin Laden. Under the influence of Azzam, al-Suri claimed that he came to understand the *Muslim-wide* nature of the duty of jihad. For al-Suri, the jihad was no longer just about Syria or about reinvigorating the struggle there; rather, it was about initiating jihad and liberating and defending Islamic lands wherever possible.[9]

Al-Suri successfully climbed the ranks at the Peshawar and Afghani camps.[10] He became a well-known military instructor and lecturer. He claims to have met bin Laden in 1988 and joined al-Qaeda when it was formed that same year.[11] He was eventually sent to al-Qaeda's Farouqi camp, a training ground established to produce high-level leaders and commanders. Furthermore, during this period, al-Suri began to devote himself heavily to his intellectual pursuits and began to see his role evolving from a military instructor toward that of an intellectual or an ideologue. This evolution in his thinking was stirred by the failure of the Syrian jihad and what he believed was the inadequacy of military training alone.[12] During his experience in Afghanistan, he came to appreciate the importance of theological education, insisting that this element was the superior one in training Muslims for the jihad. The military component, he argued, could not be properly initiated without understanding the "principles, ideas, and foundations [for jihad]. . . . This is what distinguishes a knowledgeable mujahid from a warrior who may turn into a Godless brigand."[13] All this was interrupted, however, by a Pakistani crackdown on the Peshawar camp, forcing those in the Afghan-Arab community to flee.

Al-Suri fled in 1991 to Spain, where he remained until 1994, and then he lived in London until 1997. While in London, he became involved in the Algerian jihad and served as the editor of *Al-Ansar* (The partisans), a major publication for news of the Algerian jihad. The period between 1992 and 1996 was one of intense travel for al-Suri. He traveled to Afghanistan, Sudan, and Britain, as well as back and forth to Spain, often to work for the jihadi movement and to meet with al-Qaeda's leadership. During this period in London, he also served (allegedly) as bin Laden's media adviser, organizing interviews between bin Laden and Western journalists.[14] Pressure exerted by the British anti-terror police led him to relocate to Afghanistan in 1997, following the Taliban's seizure of Kabul and the return of al-Qaeda's leadership to Afghanistan. By this time, al-Suri had also moved his family there.

For al-Suri, the Afghan jihad was symbolic of a new era, one in which the forces of Islam had defeated a Western power and, he insisted, could do so again in other places where Muslims were fighting against foreign forces or corrupt and tyrannical rulers. Al-Suri considered the Islamic emirate in Afghanistan the springboard from which the jihad would pour out into the rest of the world.[15] Notably, the Taliban's commitment to ruling through shariah law was what earned al-Suri's allegiance and loyalty. The state of Afghanistan (under Taliban rule) was, for al-Suri, the first proper Islamic state in modern history, for it was the first state of its kind to be based exclusively on Islamic law and to have a leadership that was committed to living out that law in ways that al-Suri found sincere and impassioned. While having their shortcomings, the Taliban were engaged in a great project, and unlike other apostate rulers of current Muslim states, they were committed to a true (as al-Suri understood it) interpretation of Islamic law and what it entailed of the believer.[16] They had managed to establish "the first Islamic Emirate ruled by the *Sharia* of Allah, (SWT) in Afghanistan and thus the birth of the first *Dar Al Islam* since the fall of the Islamic caliphate."[17]

For this reason, Afghanistan, as an Islamic state, was a victory of Muslims as a whole. It was, for al-Suri, a triumph of great measure as "the Ummah of Islam" had defeated the "Ummah of unbelief" (Soviet Union), which was "one of the mightiest forces of atheism and evil in the modern era." This victory, he continues, ought to be perceived as a watershed moment in Islamic history, illuminating Muslims to their true abilities and revitalizing their sense of confidence. He describes it as a "major shift in contemporary human history and the future in general," for the victory of the Taliban has served to restore "the spirit of hope, and life in the body of the Ummah of Islam."[18] For this reason, Afghanistan had become the space from which a larger jihad could be waged. It was, in al-Suri's words, a "springboard for the liberation of all lands."[19]

Importantly, al-Suri claimed that he broke ties with bin Laden in 1992. The two men, according to most accounts, had split over differences of opinion regarding the Taliban and bin Laden's refusal to abide by a set of restrictions that they had levied on him in return for his residence in Afghanistan. Despite the Taliban's request, bin Laden continued to give interviews to foreign media, consequently drawing unwelcome attention to the Taliban. Al-Suri also took issue with the way bin Laden had announced the creation of the World Islamic Front for Jihad against Jews and Crusaders, again without permission from the Taliban. In short, al-Suri thought that bin Laden's actions were dismissive of the Taliban's importance to the jihadi movement and put the stability of the Taliban at risk. Given Afghanistan's importance as the base for jihad, he argued, bin Laden's actions were jeopardizing the jihadi cause. Consequently, al-Suri pledged his allegiance to Mullah Mohammed Omar (head of the Taliban) in 2000 and devoted himself to various activities that he hoped would aid the growing jihadi movement. While in Afghanistan he established a media center and a training camp near Kabul. He also worked directly with the Taliban's Ministry of Defense, helped publish the Taliban paper, and continued to write on the various issues that occupied his interest.

However, all of al-Suri's activities in Afghanistan were interrupted in 2001 by the post-9/11 US invasion, which destroyed his training camp. Al-Suri and the remainder of the Arab-Afghan community fled Kabul. He became a fugitive on the run. He claims to have spent this time (2002–05) in isolation, devoted to his writing, and eventually produced *The Global Islamic Resistance Call*, a 1,600-page treatise on jihad.

The Global Islamic Resistance Call

Although the text is widely understood as a tactical model, this is a limited view of the nature and purpose of the *Call*. Al-Suri provides a diagnosis of the major ills confronting Muslims in his text and prescribes a comprehensive remedy to lift them out of their position of weakness and degeneration. For al-Suri, both the diagnosis and the remedy are revealed through the lens of the historical jihad tradition, and he was intent on pressing the obligatory nature of the duty of jihad in particular. This required that the reader understand the *theological* significance and necessity of this resistance movement. Though he spent the vast majority of his work outlining strategy and tactics, those discussions and ideas were meaningful if and only if Muslims first understood the importance and urgency of the jihad he described.

The immediacy of the threat is the result of what he terms the "New World Order" (النظام العالمي الجديد).[20] This term describes an international environment in which the Islamic ummah is subjugated by the "American-led Crusader-Jewish will," including the United States, Israel, current apostate heads of Muslim-majority countries, the ulema (clerical class in Islam), the Muslim Brotherhood, and Islamic democratic movements.[21] It has placed Muslims in a position of marginalization and weakness, in which the people, their land, and their resources are being capitalized and exploited. In the New World Order, Muslims' ills, according to al-Suri, are traced back to three foundational issues.

The first is the absence of proper religious practice among the majority of Muslims. According to al-Suri, this case is true in both private and public life. Muslim nations, he argues, have failed to properly implement God's laws in public institutions and have chosen to organize through secular models of political and social organization. As a consequence, Muslim societies are failing to abide by the laws that God has decreed and are living in contradiction to the laws of God. Furthermore, secular institutions have penetrated the Muslim world, bringing what al-Suri argues is the moral depravation and decadence of Western society. A majority of Muslims, he believes, have only superficial loyalties to their religion and, for the most part, have abandoned God in their decision to take on Western ways of living that have steered Muslims away from proper Islamic piety.[22]

Second, the abandonment of religion has led to a state of weakness and decline of Muslim societies as demonstrated by their military deficiency and economic depravity. For al-Suri, the occupation of the three holy sites is the most visceral symbol of the shortcomings of the Muslim world: the Great Mosque in Mecca, the Prophet's Mosque in Medina, and the Al-Aqsa Mosque in Jerusalem. The presence of foreign troops in Saudi Arabia and the continuing "occupation" of Jerusalem, al-Suri argues, are testaments to Muslim impotence. The lack of adherence to God's law and the continuing loyalties to foreign systems of government and influence have left the Muslim world crippled in its abilities to resist foreign encroachment. As additional evidence, al-Suri points to the widespread poverty among Muslims. In light of the material riches of the Muslim world—oil in particular—its economic depravity is further evidence of Muslim weakness. Foreign powers (led by the United States, Europe, and Russia), in league with corrupt Arab governments, have manipulated the oil markets and robbed the Muslim people of the wealth of their very own resources.[23]

This point leads to al-Suri's third concern. The state of Muslims today is a result of concerted efforts to dominate the region by the United States and Europe, in partnership with various governments that are more interested in maintaining their power than they are in promoting the liberation of Islam. For example, al-Suri argues that since its inception Saudi Arabia has been a client and puppet government of the British and the United States, leading the Saudis to make foreign policy decisions that are contrary to the best interests of the Muslim people. American influence and pressure, he argues, led Saudi Arabia to allow the US military on its soil during the First Gulf War and to continue making overtures toward the state of Israel.[24] This occupation, he contends, is now total—spanning all Muslim lands in one form or another. It cannot be denied.

In his section called "The Situation of Muslims Today," al-Suri notes, "It has become widely accepted as a commonsensical fact, that the entirety of our lands, from border to border, is occupied either directly by the enemies or by their apostate deputies. And this is through a heavy military presence of the Crusaders, who spread their bases throughout the land, coupled with complete economic occupation that is achieved through economic monopoly control."[25]

Significantly, according to al-Suri, this program on the part of the West—and specifically the United States—has magnified in scope since September 11. The wars in Iraq and Afghanistan, he argues, have become the new entry points for the comprehensive occupation of the Muslim world—an occupation led by the United States but buttressed by an international environment in which US allies are allowed to continue their aggression against Islam. He writes,

> And here is America today reoccupying the Muslim world from anew in the clear light of day. It has occupied Afghanistan directly. It has spread its control to Pakistan and central Asia. And here is the occupation of Iraq. It has placed hundreds of thousands of soldiers in the Arabian Peninsula and Turkey and the southern Levant as well as in Egypt and the Horn of Africa and North Africa . . . and here is Bush announcing that he will direct onto Muslim lands a "crusade" and he is joined by the European NATO [North Atlantic Treaty Organization] allies and in addition to the main ally (Israel) who occupies Palestine, and is preparing to demolish the sacred mosque and expel the rest of the Muslims there.[26]

Here we see al-Suri's framework emerging while he attempts to make sense of current conditions encumbering the Muslim world. Al-Suri argues that Muslims cannot regain their former strength until they are able to implement God's decrees, the foremost of which is the proper execution of God's law. For al-Suri, this cannot happen under the New World Order when foreign, oppressive regimes are subjugating the Muslim world, and apostate governments are supporting its pernicious policies. The Muslim world must rise up and wage the jihad. Muslims must resist the occupation of their land so that they might bring the world into alignment with God's will and ultimately regain their strength and position.

This is the purpose of the *Call*—to instruct and direct a large-scale resistance within the Muslim world and to liberate it from the occupation of Western forces. According to al-Suri, in an international environment defined by the New World Order, establishing the appropriate strategy for this resistance requires formulating new tactics that respond to these realities, and the majority of his writing and thinking is devoted to this task. Yet, *foundational* to al-Suri's thinking is a religious commitment to the notion of individual jihad. His understanding of individual war in the path of God is the very heart and soul of his tactical and strategic model for jihad.

On the Individual Duty to Jihad

Al-Suri insisted that training for the jihad must include understanding the religious foundations of the struggle not only so that the person undertaking the jihad may understand the meaning of the resistance but also so that appropriate means or tactics of engaging in the jihad were clear. In chapter 2 of his *Call,* al-Suri explicates his understanding of the relevance of shariah law to the current situation of Muslims. In particular, al-Suri describes the immediacy, urgency, and therefore obligatory nature of participating in the jihad for all able Muslims. There are five circumstances that trigger the specific shariah rulings for individual jihad:

> First: The lands of Islam today are under direct or indirect occupation from the enemies. . . . Second, the governments of the lands of Islam today are such that they are apostates and infidels. They have changed the laws and their rulings with other than what God has revealed. Their loyalty is to the infidels, and they have betrayed God and His messenger and the believers. Third: The revolt against the ruler that is in retreat against Islam or is an apostate is a collective obligation of all Muslims. Fourth, the rulings of the Islamic Shariah have definitively determined that those who cooperate with the apostates are apostates and unbelievers, and must be combated. Fifth: The rulings of the Shariah have determined the necessity of combating those who assault the faith, honor, or assets of Muslims.[27]

Al-Suri's justifications mirror those of Faraj, Azzam, and bin Laden. For al-Suri too the current situation of Muslims, as he understands it, is defined by the foreign occupation and apostate rule. Moreover, the situation is dire, threatening Muslims and their religion and ensuring that they remain weak and oppressed. These circumstances, and the threat they pose to Muslims and Islam, are not only deeply offensive but also categorically unacceptable. As noted by Qutb, Faraj, Azzam, bin Laden, and now al-Suri, Muslims must live under Islamic law as organized through the institution of an Islamic state. The Shariah, al-Suri argues, is specific regarding the responsibilities of Muslims in the face of such circumstances. In other words, for al-Suri,

Muslims must understand the theological significance of their current status so that they might also understand, in turn, the commandment to jihad
imposed on them by Islamic law.

"In short," he writes, "the Shariah has determined the jihad is an individual
duty (فرض عين) on every Muslim in a situation of this kind today (under the
current circumstances)." Moreover, he continues, "the shariah's proof on this,
it is as clear as the light of day" that "the jihad is an individual duty today on
all the Muslims from all places."[28] For al-Suri, it is clear, and unobjectionable
from the position of shariah law, that the current circumstances of Muslims
require them to rise up and engage in a jihad against the forces of oppression,
the New World Order. This jihad is a defensive one, imposed on the Muslim
nation as a result of foreign occupation and influence. As the Muslim world
is under attack and subject to immediate danger, the defensive jihad is the
religious and individual duty of the Islamic nation. The individual Muslim,
he argues, is obligated to participate in the jihad. In this situation, where the
life of the tradition is at stake, the duty to fight is mandated, and every Muslim is under an immediate obligation to resist the occupiers. He notes, "And
this is the truth: a collective resistance to this foreign infidel occupation, and
the apostate forces collaborating with it, and crushing the chests of Muslims,
is a required duty (فرض واجب) by the Islamic shariah, and it is a truth that is
commonsensical."[29]

Al-Suri goes to significant lengths to establish a theological foundation for
the individual duty of jihad. Clearly textual evidence—from the Quran, the
hadiths, and various commentaries on both by Islamic jurists—is important
to establishing his case. He quotes extensively from Abdullah Azzam's work
on this point, relying heavily in some parts on his understanding of the textual sources and their position on defensive jihad as an individual Muslim
obligation.

> Then spoke the late Sheikh [Azzam] . . . on the case of infidels in the
> land of Muslims. And he said: "In this situation, those who have pre-
> ceded and succeeded us, and the jurists of the four legal schools, and
> the narrators, and the expositors in the entirety of the Muslim age
> without exception, agreed that the jihad in these circumstances is
> clearly an individual duty on those whose lands are being attacked by
> infidels and also those who are their allies."[30]

It is natural that al-Suri would turn to Azzam's exposition of these ideas.
Azzam was a trained cleric whose opinions held weight in light of his formal
education, a credential that al-Suri lacked. Moreover, militant circles highly

respect and repeatedly cite Azzam's authority on the theological aspects of jihad. Al-Suri uses Azzam's work to demonstrate that the current circumstances are exactly those that trigger the obligatory duty to jihad and require Muslims to take up arms. Important for al-Suri (still referencing Azzam's work), this duty is such that the standard permissions—from parents or spouses, for example—are not required. *Individual* jihad, as a special category of war, is an urgent matter and thus requires immediate participation "wherein the son will rise up without the permission of his father, and the wife without the permission of her husband, and the debtor without the permission of his creditor."[31]

Moreover, al-Suri continues, this obligation—while first falling to those closest to the areas of attack—continues to move outward to others until the duty to expel foreign forces from Muslim lands has been met. "And if there are not people of this land [that is under attack], or if they fall short, or if they are idle, the individual duty transfers in a circular form, onto the closest, and then to the next most closest. And if they are not sufficient, or if they fall short, it is effective on those who come after them, and those following, until the individual duty prevails throughout the land."[32]

Al-Suri then references Azzam's discussion substantiating the individual duty to jihad in the circumstances outlined from the Hanafi, Maliki, Shafi, and Hanbali schools of Islamic law. He also relies on Azzam's allegorical reasoning when using other circumstances in which the early Muslims were called to fight. For example, he quotes Quran 49:9 (also quoted by Azzam): "As stated by God, great and almighty: 'If two parties among the Believers fall into a quarrel, make ye peace between them: but if one of them transgresses beyond bounds against the other then fight ye (all) against the one that transgresses until it complies with the command of god; but if it complies then make peace between them with justice and be fair: for God loves those who are fair (and just)."[33]

Moreover, quoting Quran 5:33, "on the issue of banditry, stated the almighty: 'the punishment of those who wage war against God and His Apostle, and strive with might and main for mischief through the land is: execution and crucifixion, or the cutting off of hands and feet from opposite sides or exile from the land: that is their disgrace in this world, and as a heavy punishment is theirs in the hereafter."[34]

If, al-Suri reasons, the use of force is commanded against those who "intimidate the Islamic nation and who spread corruption among the earth and abuse people's money and property," then how can it not also be the case that Muslims are obligated to "fight the infidel nations that corrupt the people, their religion, and their money and property"? If it is a religious duty to combat bandits, then is it not, he argues, a religious obligation to fight "infidels"? Moreover, he continues, is it not "more likely that this is so?"[35]

Al-Suri then applies these rulings to the current situation of Muslims as he understands it.

> This is some of the evidence and justification for a universal call to arms: if the infidel enters the land of the Muslims, to expel the enemy is the most important obligation after the faith. . . . There is no Muslim country today that is not occupied by infidels, by the Jews as demonstrated in the country of Palestine, and parts of the Levant, or by the Crusaders, the lands of Bosnia and the Balkans, and Chechnya and the Caucasus. . . . And the Muslim republics in Central Asia and the Philippines, among others. Or by Pagans, as in the case of Kashmir, which is occupied by Hindus, and East Turkistan and parts of South East Asia that are occupied by the Chinese, among others.[36]

Al-Suri also echoes bin Laden's occupation with Saudi Arabia as a visceral symbol of Muslim weakness. He writes,

> As for the rest of the Muslim and Arab countries, including the heart of Islam and its Ka'aba and the Mosque of the Prophet. These are occupied indirectly through the sanction of the Crusaders and the Jews, by the apostate rulers, and their allies who put their armies in the service of the infidels. Led by America and her master Israel and their crusader alliance and their crusader allies, who have filled the country's military bases—both by air and by sea—resulting in a modern-day occupation.[37]

The effects of this, he argues, are incontestable: God's law has been disabled, while Muslim rulers capitulate to "infidel" rule and influence and try to silence those who are attempting to call the attention of Muslims to their plight.[38] For these reasons, the applicable shariah rulings are clear. In particular, he argues, circumstances are such that individual jihad is obligatory and that the believers must rise up and converge against the infidels. All Muslims, given the dire and all-pervasive nature of this threat, must understand that they are individually called to wage a Muslim-wide resistance.

This resistance—and the individual duty at its core—ought not be encumbered by the lack of a proper leader. According to al-Suri, the Muslim world does not have a single leader who is fit for, or who is capable of, initiating this resistance and the call to arms.

And there is not on the whole face of the earth today a single Imam who is legitimate. Rather, what is available are those who wage war [or rebel] against God and his prophet in lands of corruption. And they all support the infidels, the Jews, the Crusaders, and the Pagans. . . . And there is not a legitimate Imam to call the people to arms for the jihad. . . . So has the jihad, in the absence of a legitimate ruler, been abandoned?[39]

It is impossible to think that this is the case. How can it be, he argues, when corruption and apostasy are the lay of the land, that there is no one to repel the aggressor? He contends, "The truth is that God has enjoined all his believers in the entire world."[40] While the official clerical class—linked to the state—has lost its gall and disputes the truth of the necessity of jihad, he asserts, there are others in every Muslim country who are "advocates for guidance," who are faithfully illuming Muslims to their true condition, and therefore who are faithfully leading the jihad.[41] Moreover, he continues, even if such figures were absent, it "remains to say that in regard to this obligation, the Islamic nation is one."[42]

What he means by this is that the obligation to "expel the attacker" is a Muslim-wide obligation. Muslims, he argues, must refuse to acknowledge the "borders drawn by the crusaders between our nation" and reject the synthetic and forced notions of nationality that accompany them. Muslims must understand that the obligation to resist is one that falls on all Muslims, on the entire ummah. Thus, all Muslims are called and "required . . . to respond to the call of their religion and to arms to expel the attacker."[43]

This notion of individual jihad—construed by al-Suri as the religious duty of *all* Muslims *wherever* they may be to rise up and wage the resistance—is the cornerstone of his tactical model. To this end, al-Suri's unique contribution is his ability to operationalize the theological narrative described in the works of Qutb, Faraj, Azzam, and bin Laden into a model of jihad that, arguably, has initiated major developments in the tactics and overall strategy of the al-Qaeda phenomenon. In this way, al-Suri's work demonstrates the characterizing feature of the al-Qaeda phenomenon—the connection between theology, on the one hand, and strategy and tactics, on the other.

Al-Suri's Model for Jihad

Al-Suri's concern was to construct a model of jihad capable of responding to an environment characterized by a deep power asymmetry between the Muslim world and the West. His strength as a systematic thinker is brought out well in this effort. He provides a historical analysis of jihadi operations (beginning in the 1960s) to articulate an operational framework for the new environment. He categorizes his analysis into three schools and analyzes their strengths and weaknesses.

The first is the "school of secret military organizations," referring to regional, secret, and hierarchical organizations aimed at overthrowing local governments in places such as Morocco in the 1960s (Harakat-al-Dawlah al-Islam [Moroccan Youth Organization]), Algeria in the 1970s (Tanzim al-Shabibah al-Maghribiyyah [Islamic State Movement]), and Egypt in the 1990s (Al-Jihad). According to al-Suri, this method of jihad has failed on all accounts. It did not succeed militarily as it was unable to topple the current regimes and replace them with an Islamic state. The secret organizations failed in terms of security in that they were "exposed and disbanded, and the attempts to build them were aborted." They were unable to foment mass support and resistance among the people; thus, they did not lead them to jihad. They also faltered in educating their members on "ideology, doctrine, program, security[,] . . . politics and military experience." Such shortcomings led not only to their collapse or their disbanding by the regime but also to their failure to "realize the general goals of the project."[44]

The second school is that of "open fronts and overt confrontations" in the pre–September 11 world. Here, al-Suri refers to places where open hostilities between the regime and the organization prevailed. Al-Suri mentions Afghanistan, Bosnia, and Chechnya as examples of open fronts where the jihad was waged outright. According to his analysis, the open front organizations enjoyed significantly greater military, security, agitation, and education successes. In regard to the military aspect, these open fronts were able to defeat a major world power—the Soviets—on the part of the Afghans and were able to "alter the balance of power in the Serbian genocide war" on the part of the Bosnian mujahideen.[45] Moreover, he writes, the organizations' successes were also fruitful in terms of fomenting support. "The Islamic nation with its hundreds of millions rose to support and advocate them, and her devoted sons joined the Fronts. The shaykhs and elders prayed to God for the Mujahidun's victory, and rich Muslims and poor Muslims alike donated their money and supported the jihad."[46] Success in terms of education was modest, for they were hampered by being in combat; but educational training was possible and "conducted in a partial manner by some people."[47] Yet, despite all these victories, the open fronts were unable to bring about the Islamic state (except for the short-lived example of Afghanistan). For these reasons, al-Suri deems this particular school or method only generally successful.

Third is the "school of individual jihad and small cells." This particular program had significant military success in carrying out a series of operations that initiated responses by the "local and international intelligence apparatus" and putting it in a "state of confusion." Moreover, even if the individual operators were arrested, it did not necessarily lead to the collapse of the larger jihadi group, for these operations were independent and not linked to any particular organization. Such operations also had "great agitation success" in their ability to transform and galvanize new recruits. These terrorist operations turned individuals into "symbols of a nation . . . and a generation of youth dedicated to the Resistance followed their example."[48] Their failures, however, were in their inability either to bring about the Islamic state or to transform this particular tactic into systematic strategy and method.

Noting these schools and their history of failures and successes, al-Suri argues that in the post–September 11 environment, those leading the resistance must understand their history. In particular, he contends, the "old ways" of secret, regional, and hierarchical jihadi organizations are clearly no longer possible. Pointing to examples such as Egypt, Syria, and Algeria, he asserts that government intelligence and anti-terror initiatives make such hierarchical models too easy to find, dismantle, and destroy. In addition, the West's—specifically US—military superiority has made these models ineffective and untenable. "Times have changed," and for this reason, those who wage the jihad must "design a method of confrontation" that is "in accordance with the standards of the present time."[49] Noting this need, al-Suri constructs a strategic and tactical model of war that builds on the strengths and attempts to ameliorate the weaknesses of the two more successful methods—individual terrorism jihad and jihad at the open fronts.

The first, individual terrorism jihad, is to be conducted by highly decentralized cells, consisting of one to ten individuals who participate in an exceedingly disconnected method of training and recruitment. Members are never aware of one another's identities; therefore, if they are caught, then they cannot pose a security risk to other members of the cell. Only one member knows the identities of all who belong. Their operations include "light guerrilla warfare, civilian terror, and secret methods." In this individual method of jihad, the individual executes a constant stream of operations conducted wherever the individual may be and in such a way that he or she poses no security risks to others or to other operations currently under way. Focusing on a theory of "system, not secret organization," al-Suri argues that organizational links between members must be minimized to those of "beliefs, a system of action, a common name, and a common goal"—that is, resistance against the West.[50]

Al-Suri attempts to capitalize on the unique strengths of this method and to do so in a way where the incidents are not separated from an overarching strategy. The point is to incite these types of terrorist practices so that individual terrorism is a focused method of jihad for the entire Islamic ummah. This approach, he insists, not only will decentralize the resistance (making it exceptionally difficult to combat) but, if instituted into an overarching method, will also expand its reach and allow Muslims, wherever they may be, to participate in this global resistance and fight the power of the United States. In particular, it gives those who cannot travel to the open fronts the chance to participate fully and in such a way that they help the global resistance make significant progress. Thus, "any Muslim, who wants to participate in jihad and the Resistance, can participate in this battle against America in his country, or anywhere, which is perhaps hundreds of times more effective than what he is able to do if he arrived at the open area of confrontation."[51] Decentralizing the strategy and tactics in this way, al-Suri argues, "opens the possibility to participate for thousands, say hundreds of thousands or millions, of Muslims sympathizing with jihad and with their Islamic Nation's causes."[52] Other methods, particularly those of the secret organizations and the open fronts, are much more restricted in their abilities because they cannot absorb all those who wish to join. This individual jihad method, however, incorporates all. Moreover, it allows these individuals to be released from the risk of joining secret organizations, which are highly prone to security breaches.[53]

The second method of jihad is that of the open fronts. This type of jihad, according to al-Suri, is much more limited as success in open fronts requires a specific set of conditions. Some of these conditions are related to space, borders, terrain, and natural supplies as well as the support of the indigenous population. Therefore, according to al-Suri, participation in the open front jihad affords fewer opportunities and is available only in unique geographical and historical moments.[54] However, the open fronts must be taken advantage of when the opportunity is afforded to Muslims. They represent a further step in the confrontation with the West, for the open fronts will lead to the liberation of Muslim lands and construction of the Islamic state.[55]

It is critically important to note that, for al-Suri, these two methods—individual jihad and jihad of the open fronts—work together. Those participating in individual operations may benefit from those engaged in the open fronts in a variety of ways. To begin, they may immigrate to the open fronts for training. Those in the open fronts may be recruited for individual jihadi operations, or they may provide asylum for those who are on the run.[56] While the open fronts are not, at the time of his writing, in a position to overpower the United States, individual terrorist operations will help agitate others in such a way that they will strengthen the jihads in current open fronts and lead to the initiation of others. "Thus," he writes, "this is the opposite of the trailing theory one had in jihadi circles during the last two decades, which was based upon calling the Islamic Nation to the camps." Rather, he continues, "in our Resistance Call, the training theory is based upon moving the camps inside the Islamic Nation."[57]

How is this global movement to happen? It will be accomplished by multiplying the theaters in which jihad is waged. Al-Suri claims that prioritizing targets is determined by two factors—wherever the enemy is afforded the most damage and wherever a target might have the effect of galvanizing the Muslim spirit of resistance.[58] For al-Suri, then, the top priority is to strike at Western interests wherever possible. For example, his list is topped with the "countries of the Arab Peninsula, the Levant, Egypt, and Iraq" as they have a Western military presence and oil. He then lists North Africa, Turkey, Pakistan, Central Asia, the "rest of the Islamic World," and then "the American and Allied Interests in third world countries," all the while highlighting Western interests.[59] "The goal," he writes, "of the operations of the Resistance and the Individual Terrorism Jihad is to inflict as many human and material losses as possible upon the interests of American and her allies" so that they "feel that the Resistance has transformed into a phenomenon of popular uprising against them."[60] As for specific targets, US cultural, political, and economic interests once again top al-Suri's list: missionary centers, diplomatic institutions, military bases, tourist companies, and so on.[61] That said, he does not leave out political figures, security leaders, military bases, and various political and security buildings as well as media personalities.[62]

In addressing the killing of women, children, the elderly, and other noncombatants, his thoughts on this are worth quoting at length:

> To summarize the issue: Whoever is useful for the unbelievers or others should be killed—whether he is an old man, a monk, or a crippled person. The assembly of Muslim scholars agreed that whatever is useful for Muslims and harmful to the infidels during war or when preparing for it is permissible whether it means killing a human being or an animal or destroying buildings. War means the start and finish of eliminating disorder and spreading the call to raise Allah's religion.
>
> Killing Communist Women in Afghanistan—as for the communist women in Afghanistan, they should be killed whether they participated in the war, provided advice, did not participate, whether they separated or mixed, or whether they were one or a group, because they have beliefs against Islam and they harm Islam and Muslims.

Using Guns, Planes, Mortars, and Rockets in Shelling—We indicated that fighting for Islam is intended to eliminate the hurdles that obstruct its call and to destroy the political regimes that prevent Islam from reaching the people. If we can deliver this without killing or fighting, then this is what Muslims wish. However, if this cannot be accomplished, then all barriers should be removed by any means possible. And if we cannot reach the tyrants that rule the earth unless we kill humans and demolish installations, then we should do it! Because we have been forced to do this.[63]

While al-Suri does mention that places of worship ought to be avoided and that citizens from countries not affiliated with the New World Order ought not be harmed, such points seem meaningless in terms of the preceding statement. When it comes to al-Suri's (and al-Qaeda's) defensive jihad against the United States, killing innocents is considered a necessary and legitimate part of conducting the jihad.

The Influence of His Model

The most significant aspect of al-Suri's model is its influence. To begin, his work has been featured on a wide variety of jihadi websites, receiving significant amounts of attention.[64] His work has also benefited tremendously from its publication in Anwar al-Awlaki's *Inspire* magazine and the influence of al-Awlaki himself. The most compelling evidence of al-Suri's influence, however, is the rise of lone-wolf jihadi operations, or terrorist attacks attempted (successfully and unsuccessfully) by individuals who lacked formal affiliation with a specific terrorist group.

A 2008 report by the US Senate Committee on Homeland Security and Governmental Affairs demonstrates that al-Suri's hopes have materialized. It argues that the United States is facing an increasing threat from lone-wolf jihadis in language that recalls al-Suri's insistence that the jihad be released from the confines of training camps and secret organizations so that operations may be conducted with greater geographical reach. As noted by the report's authors, Joseph Lieberman and Susan Collins, "Radicalization is no longer *confined to the training camps in Afghanistan or other locations far from our shores*; it is also occurring right here in the United States" (emphasis mine).[65] Quoting Robert Mueller, then director of the Federal Bureau of Investigation (FBI), the report argues that the United States faces threats from "homegrown extremists in the United States" who are "self-radicalized." While they are not "formally affiliated with a foreign terrorist group," they remain a threat in that they "are inspired by those groups' messages of violence, often through the internet," making them "particularly difficult to detect."[66]

Moreover, al-Suri's writing helps situate ISIS and its "caliphate" within the al-Qaeda phenomenon. His *Call* presaged and helps to explain the rise of ISIS.[67] As he notes, Muslims are called—and granted the individual authority—to engage in individual jihadi operations wherever they might be. This option, he argues, would alleviate the hardships and difficulties of traveling to the open fronts. Yet, the open fronts, for al-Suri, are still the ultimate goal. Individual operations were to be used in the hope of agitating the masses and creating the type of international environment that would encourage the development and success of open fronts as the birthplaces of Islamic states and, eventually, the caliphate.

Al-Suri's Model Takes Life

Part 1: Lone-Wolf Jihad

In particular, the publication of excerpts from the *Call*, in al-Qaeda's English-language online publication *Inspire*, testifies to the importance of al-Suri's strategic and tactical thinking among al-Qaeda's ranks. *Inspire* published these excerpts in issues 1, 2, 4, 5, and 6.[68] Importantly, *Inspire* is the creation of Anwar al-Awlaki, the Yemeni-American cleric who, along with *Inspire* editor Samir ibn Zafar Khan, was killed in a 2011 US drone strike. Al-Awlaki's work focused on inciting young Muslims—especially in the United States—to jihad.[69] He was clearly galvanized by al-Suri's model of individual jihad and hoped to make al-Suri's ideas easily accessible and widely available through their publication in *Inspire* magazine. Moreover, al-Awlaki, or his teaching, has been linked to the radicalization of a number of high-profile, lone jihadi attacks, including those of Faizal Shahzad (Times Square bombing), Nidal Malik Hasan (Fort Hood shooting), and possibly the Tsarnaev brothers (Boston Marathon bombing).

In this way, then, al-Awlaki is a direct link between al-Suri's conceptualization of the individual duty to jihad and the actions of these men. The point here is to demonstrate how al-Suri's ideas have moved beyond his writings and into the world through those (like al-Awlaki) who saw their potential in decentralizing the jihad. It is true that the path to radicalization is an individual one.[70] This was certainly the case for Shahzad, Hasan, and the Tsarnaev brothers (from what we know). Important for our purposes, though, all four were inspired by an understanding of the duty to individual jihad—well described in al-Suri's *Call*—that urged individuals to join the resistance by engaging in local and indiscriminate acts of terror.[71] Narrating their stories reveals both the power and influence of al-Suri's ideas and his tactical and strategic model, which allowed ordinary individuals to commit extraordinary acts of terror. The lives and stories of these men are diverse, differing in circumstances, means, and challenges. Yet all of them were so motivated by the al-Qaeda narrative and by al-Suri's ideas of individual jihad that their religious convictions led them to leave what were, by most accounts, comfortable lives in exchange for jihad.

Faisal Shahzad, Times Square Bomber

Faisal Shahzad was born into a prominent and wealthy Pakistani family in June 1979.[72] His father climbed the ranks of the Pakistan Air Force, with his career taking Shahzad and his family to England and Saudi Arabia. By the time Faisal was twelve years old, his father had been transferred from Jeddah, Saudi Arabia, to Quetta, Pakistan, and then to Rawalpindi. As noted in several media accounts, as the son of a high-ranking military officer, Shahzad grew up in relative privilege and comfort, surrounded by servants, chauffeurs, and armed guards. He spent his high school years in Karachi, in southwest Pakistan, where his family had settled by that time. After high school, he enrolled in Greenwich University (also in Karachi) and attended business school. Once he finished his degree, he applied for a student visa so that he could study in the United States. He emigrated on January 16, 1999, to attend the University of Bridgeport and graduated with a bachelor's degree in computer applications and information systems.

Shahzad then took a job with Elizabeth Arden in Stamford, Connecticut, as an analyst and eventually enrolled in night courses at the University of Bridgeport business school. In July 2004 he bought a house in Shelton and later that year married Huma Mian, a twenty-three-year-old Pakistani-American woman (also from a prominent Pakistani family) who had recently graduated from the University of Colorado with a degree in accounting. By June 2006 Shahzad had accepted a new job as an analyst at the financial marketing firm Affinion Group in Norwalk and shortly afterward finished his master's degree. He and his wife were expecting the first of their two children.

Shahzad seemed to be living a happy and active life, hosting barbecues in the backyard, and had friendly interactions with neighbors. Friends and family, however, did remark that his religious life had become more intense. He stopped drinking and had started observing the required Islamic daily prayers—a development that was not particularly welcome by either his wife or his family, especially his father, who found his son's behavior troubling. He also reportedly had become vocal about his opposition to US foreign policy shortly after September 11. He felt discriminated against and insulted as an immigrant, arguing that he was treated differently because of his Pakistani roots. He sent emails to friends expressing that he found mistreatment of Muslims in the United States and abroad excessively troubling. He also suggested that peaceful means of dealing with these issues were not always effective. These sentiments took a more urgent turn during a 2008 visit to Pakistan when he asked his father for permission to fight in Afghanistan. His father refused.

In April 2009 Shahzad became an American citizen. Shortly after, he quit his job. On June 2 he called his wife from John F. Kennedy International Airport to tell her that he was leaving for Pakistan. Shahzad was in Pakistan for five months, eventually disappearing from his parents' home and never returning. During that time he was allegedly trained in explosives by Tehrik-i-Taliban, a Pakistani Taliban group. He returned to the United States on February 3 on a one-way ticket. He then rented a small apartment and, most likely, began to initiate the details of what would be the foiled Times Square terrorist attack. He maintained contact with elements in Pakistan as demonstrated by twelve phone calls that were made to his prepaid cell phone during that period. On April 24 he purchased a Nissan Pathfinder for $1,300 in cash. He also purchased fertilizer and fireworks in order to make the bomb.

On May 1, 2010, Shahzad attempted to detonate a car bomb in Times Square, but it failed to explode. Smoke from the Pathfinder alerted passersby, who called the New York City Police Department. The bomb was dismantled before it caused any damage. Shahzad was arrested approximately fifty-three hours after the failed attempt. The police traced the Pathfinder back to Shahzad through its previous owner, who had Shahzad's prepaid cell phone number. They arrested him while he was sitting in his seat on a flight to Dubai. Shahzad waived his Miranda rights and pleaded guilty of all counts. The judge sentenced him to life in prison.

He described to authorities how he learned to build a bomb from Tehrik-i-Taliban. The group also released a video shortly after the botched attempt, claiming responsibility and warning that it was the first of many attacks yet to come from suicide bombers hidden in the United States. Despite Shahzad's admissions, the full details of his radicalization are unclear. Friends, neighbors, and acquaintances described Shahzad as a "nice guy" and as someone who doted on his two children. Why Shahzad decided to build and detonate a bomb in one of the busiest parts of New York City is uncertain. According to reports, Shahzad, while in custody, told authorities that he was moved, at least in part, by Anwar al-Awlaki's calls to jihad.[73] There is, though, a remarkable affinity between al-Suri's model and Shahzad's story. Shahzad was, by all accounts, a relatively unremarkable person who had no formal training in bomb making or any other kind of violent tactic; however, he was able to travel to Pakistan, receive training in explosives, return to the United States, and build a bomb.

The attempt was a failure, with Shahzad even accidentally leaving the keys to his apartment in the abandoned Pathfinder. That Shahzad was convinced that he should try to carry out what could have been a devastating attack in the heart of New York City, however, is a testament to how al-Suri's ideas have been taken to heart by the very people—ordinary individuals with no past training or formal affiliations to any group—al-Suri has sought to reach. The duty to wage jihad, he has argued, is religiously incumbent on all Muslims wherever they may be, and in assuming this duty, ordinary individuals turn into lone-wolf jihadis.

Nidal Malik Hasan, Fort Hood Shooter

Nidal Malik Hasan was born in Arlington, Virginia, on September 8, 1970, to Palestinian parents who had emigrated from the West Bank in the 1960s.[74] They eventually took their family of three boys to Roanoke, where they started and ran several family businesses, including a restaurant and a convenience store. Hasan attended Virginia Tech, majoring in biochemistry, and graduated with honors in 1995. He enlisted in the US Army after graduating and entered an officer's basic training program at Fort Sam Houston, Texas. After being commissioned in 1997, he attended the Uniformed Services University of Health Sciences in Maryland. During this time, he lost both his father and mother, who passed in 1998 and 2001, respectively. He graduated in 2003, conducting his internship and residency in psychiatry at Walter Reed Army Medical Center, and had a two-year fellowship in preventive and disaster psychiatry. He also earned a master's degree in public health. He was promoted to major after completing his fellowship and was transferred to Fort Hood shortly thereafter.

Hasan began turning toward religion after his parents' deaths, which he took hard. Moreover, during his years in medical school and his fellowship, he became increasingly more vocal regarding his opposition to the wars in Iraq and Afghanistan. He began to talk about his difficulty in reconciling his identity as a Muslim with that of an American army officer fighting other Muslims. He seemed terrified of deployment and often complained of the harassment he received from others in the military because of his religion.

Such feelings led him to look into an early discharge from the army, but he was told that obtaining such a discharge would be next to impossible.

Hasan's feelings of discrimination, and his difficulty in reconciling his Muslim identity with his job in the military, materialized in ways that brought him to the attention of his fellow officers and superiors. A 2011 special report by the US Senate Committee on Homeland Security and Governmental Affairs documents some of these events, providing a complicated picture of Hasan. According to the report, Hasan "openly questioned whether he could engage in combat against other Muslims." In the last month of his residency, he was supposed to make a "scholarly presentation on psychiatric issues" as a requirement for graduation but ended up giving an "off-topic lecture on violent Islamist extremism." His presentation "consisted almost entirely of references to the Koran, without a single mention of a medical or psychiatric term." His presentation also included "extremist interpretations of the Koran as supporting grave physical harm and killing of non-Muslims," even suggesting that "revenge might be a defense for the terrorist attacks of September 11, 2001." Moreover, according to the report, Hasan stated in this presentation, "One of the risks of having Muslim-Americans in the military was the possibility of fratricidal murder of fellow service members."[75]

In August 2007 Hasan gave another "off-topic presentation on a violent extremist subject," though he was stopped only a few minutes into it after classmates protested. The title was, "Is the War on Terror a War on Islam? An Islamic Perspective." According to the Senate report, Hasan argued that US military operations in the war on terrorism constituted a war against Islam.[76]

On November 4, 2009, Hasan gave away a number of his personal belongings to his neighbor, including bookshelves, clothing, a microwave, his alarm clock, and a copy of the Quran. The next morning he attended early prayers, and around noon, he walked into a processing center at Fort Hood. According to media accounts, Hasan sat down at a table and put his head down for a few minutes in prayer. He stood up and opened fire, targeting only officers in uniform. Hasan killed thirteen and wounded more than thirty others, chasing some wounded soldiers out of the building with repeated fire. He eventually went down from shots fired by two members of the civilian police force at Fort Hood. As a result, he is paralyzed from the waist down.

Ample evidence suggests al-Awlaki played a role in facilitating Hasan's turn to violence. In 2008 Hasan began to communicate with al-Awlaki through email.[77] They exchanged approximately eighteen to twenty messages. Hasan, unlike Shahzad, had immediate access to weapons and did not require training in explosives or in gaining access to materials. But like

Shahzad, Hasan also was relatively unremarkable; those who knew him described him as an ordinary guy and even as quiet and gentle.

What these descriptions did not note, however, was that Hasan was driven by a narrative of religious duty and obligation that he believed required certain actions on his part. Hasan continued to insist on the necessity and the legitimacy of what he did. From his wheelchair, in court, he declared,

> Panel members, good morning. On the morning of November 5, 2009, 13 US soldiers were killed and many more injured. The evidence will clearly show that I am the shooter.
>
> The bodies found that day show that war is an ugly thing. Death, destruction and devastation are felt from both sides, from friend and foe.
>
> The evidence will show I was on the wrong side. The evidence will also show that I then switched sides. The evidence will show we Mujahideen are imperfect soldiers trying to establish a perfect religion in the land of the supreme God.[78]

Heeding al-Suri's tactical model, Hasan was able to follow his call to jihad—and to do so smack in the middle of one of the US military's largest installations. He did not need to visit a training camp or to affiliate himself with a jihadi organization or cell. All he needed was the conviction that he was called—required and obligated—to use indiscriminate force to do what he believed God had commanded.

The Tsarnaev Brothers, Boston Marathon Bombers

Tamerlan Tsarnaev and Dzhokhar "Jahar" Tsarnaev came from a first-generation family of Chechen immigrants, who sought political asylum in the United States.[79] Their family history was troubled and marked by discontent and challenging circumstances. Their father, Anzor, and his family were victims of Stalin's displacement program of minorities. Their mother, Zubeidat, was from a family of Avars in Dagestan. Anzor and Zubeidat met in Novosibirsk, Russia, fell in love, and were married. In 1986 Tamerlan was born. In the early 1990s, the family moved Tamerlan and his two sisters, Ailina and Bella, to Chechnya, which had declared independence from Russia in 1991. Their youngest son, Jahar (Dzhokhar), was born in 1993. In 1994 they moved to Kyrgyzstan to escape the violent war still raging in Chechnya.

Anzor and Zubeidat moved their family to the United States a few months after 9/11. The reasons for their move are unclear, as each gave conflicting explanations to friends and neighbors. Anzor claimed that while in Kyrgyzstan, he worked on cars and for a district prosecutor's office in Bishkek, though there is no record of him working there. It is possible he had an unpaid internship and, using the ID card from the prosecutor's office that he would have obtained, participated in "shuttle trading"—that is, transporting tobacco from the south to buyers in other parts of the Soviet Union. Such work often involves criminal networks, and possibly threats from such networks impelled the Tsarnaevs to move. Anzor, however, maintained that his family had suffered oppression because of their Chechen heritage. At one point, Anzor reportedly told his psychiatrist that he had been captured and tortured by Russian troops during the war in Chechnya. Zubeidat once confided in a friend that they had moved because Anzor had tried to persecute members of the mob, and as a result, they had captured and tortured him for a week.

The family's early years in the United States were relatively stable. In Massachusetts both parents had steady work, and the children did well in public schools. Tamerlan, in particular, showed promise as a boxer, winning enough local matches to develop a reputation as a skilled fighter. In 2004 he won the novice title in his weight division of the Greater Lowell Golden Gloves Competition. He was the golden child in the family, whose dreams of a successful and prosperous life in the United States were hanging on the hope that he would eventually make it to the Olympics. Jahar, too, was well liked in school, made decent grades, and wrestled on his high school's team.

Then things turned. In 2009 Tamerlan lost the National Golden Gloves Tournament of Champions. The following year he was blocked from participating because of a recent rule change prohibiting noncitizens from boxing in this tournament. Although he had enrolled in community college, his attendance was spotty, and it was clear he was not going to finish. The Tsarnaev sisters had both married and quickly divorced, thereafter moving back home with their young children. Meanwhile, Anzor's health had deteriorated; he was plagued by chronic headaches and stomach pain. As he was unable to work, the family went on government assistance. Jahar, by all accounts, was still active and well liked in school, yet he was lost in the family. His family did not attend any of his wrestling matches or his high school graduation.

By this time, Zubeidat urged her children to turn to their faith as they dealt with the string of hardships and disappointments they faced in the United States. Tamerlan and Jahar took an interest in Islam but were not as religiously observant as their mother was. Tamerlan started dating a woman named Katherine Russell, a communications major attending Suffolk University, after they were introduced at a nightclub. She became pregnant, converted to Islam, and married Tamerlan in June 2010. Shortly afterward their daughter, Zahira, was born. Katie worked to support the family as a home healthcare worker, while Tamerlan stayed at home with their daughter. Friends and acquaintances noted that Tamerlan spent a great deal of time on the Internet, browsing websites associated with Muslim militants in the Caucasus region. Around this same time, on a tip from Russian authorities, the FBI investigated Tamerlan and Zubeidat for possible ties to jihadi organizations. The case was closed shortly after it began.

In 2011 Anzor and Zubeidat ended their marriage, and they returned to Dagestan. In 2012 Tamerlan also went to Dagestan, saying that he was going to visit family. This trip has caused significant speculation. Interviews with Tamerlan's friends and family in Dagestan indicate that he was interested in learning more about his faith. Other accounts suspect that he met with members of the failed Chechen insurgency who had moved to Dagestan and that they helped him plan the Boston Marathon bombing. Whatever happened, Tamerlan had visibly changed when he returned to the United States. He had grown a thick beard and wore dark clothes and a white prayer cap. He also became more vocal in his protests of US foreign policy and what he perceived to be the Americans' unjust treatment of Muslims.

Jahar attended the University of Massachusetts–Dartmouth. While as a high school student he had shown moderate signs of promise, he did not do well in college and was placed on academic probation. He also started a lucrative business dealing marijuana on campus. Jahar developed a close-knit circle of friends who described him as a leader and as someone who was generous to others in times of need. But he was also secretive: On the brink of expulsion, he lied to his friends and told them that he was transferring to a different university.

By the spring of 2013, apparently the brothers were forming a plan. Information on the details of this period and the reasons why they decided to target the Boston Marathon are lacking. Theories regarding the brothers' radicalization vary widely, and their individual contributions to the plot are unclear. Investigators did find downloads of Anwar al-Awlaki's work, however, and articles from *Inspire* magazine on their computer, including "How to Make a Bomb in the Kitchen of Your Mom." According to reports, Jahar later told investigators that he had been inspired by al-Awlaki.

On April 15, 2013, at approximately 2:49 p.m., two pressure cooker bombs exploded nearly simultaneously at the Boston Marathon finish line on Boylston Street. The bombs killed three people and injured more than two hundred. By April 18, investigators released surveillance photos of the suspects, who were identified that day as Tamerlan Tsarnaev and Jahar Tsarnaev.

Friends and family members all expressed shock and dis[...] to imagine that the brothers had hatched and carried out the [...]

Shortly after they were identified, the brothers killed a ca[...] man at the Massachusetts Institute of Technology, supposedly beca[...] wanted his gun. They carjacked a Mercedes and, while on the run, ent[...] into a gunfight with police in Watertown, Massachusetts. Tamerlan was shot. As he struggled with police, Jahar drove the car straight toward them. The policemen fled, but Tamerlan was run over and killed. Jahar escaped but was found later that day hiding in a boat in a resident's backyard. He was shot, taken into custody, and charged with thirty counts, including using a weapon of mass destruction to kill or injure and murdering the police officer, Sean Collier. Tsarnaev was found guilty on all charges on April 15, 2013, and sentenced to death shortly thereafter.

The two major journalistic accounts of the Tsarnaev brothers are from Masha Gessen and the *Boston Globe* (both of which were consulted to construct the preceding account). Their reporting presents different theories for why the brothers bombed the Boston Marathon. Gessen presents a picture of an immigrant story gone wrong, a life in which the Tsarnaevs were faced with hardship at every turn. The *Boston Globe* paints a picture of Tamerlan as mentally ill, citing several friends and acquaintances who witnessed either him or one of his family members mentioning that he heard voices in his head and that his body was inhabited by two people. These sources also discussed the immense challenges that the Tsarnaevs had faced as immigrants, commenting that ten years after arriving in the United States the family simply imploded as a result of dysfunction and hardship.

Both accounts contest the idea that the Boston Marathon bombing was orchestrated or aided by a foreign terrorist organization. Both reports—though they paint different pictures—present the Tsarnaev brothers as lone actors, who, for various reasons, had decided to vent their anger at US foreign policy and the treatment of Muslims through a terror attack. If these accounts are correct, the Tsarnaev brothers represent the extraordinary strength of al-Suri's model, with them deciding to plan and execute a terror attack, or radicalizing, through the Internet and acting on their own convictions. For reasons yet unknown, Tamerlan and Jahar came to believe that they were required to respond through indiscriminate violence to their perceived oppression and subjugation of Muslims. They were able to put those convictions to actions with relative ease. They were two ordinary men—clearly without extraordinary means—who were motivated by, and successfully responded to, the conceptualization of individual jihad in al-Suri's call.

_ate

with the figure of Abu Musab al-Zarqawi,
:os of terrorist attacks, hostage executions,
to the violently sectarian nature of post-
a troubled youth. He was a heavy drinker
_n the law. In his early twenties, however, around
_figious awakening and joined the Afghan mujahi-
_ie Soviets. He returned to Jordan in 1993, and along
mentor and friend, the famous jihadi cleric Abu Muham-
mad a_ _si, was involved in a series of unsuccessful terrorist operations.
Both were eventually arrested and incarcerated in a Jordanian prison. Al-
Zarqawi was released in 1999 and participated in the foiled Millennium Plot.
He escaped arrest and fled to Afghanistan, where he met Osama bin Laden.

In Afghanistan al-Zarqawi set up his own training camp. Although he had
a relationship with bin Laden, he refused to acknowledge him as his emir or
to give him his *bayah* (an oath of allegiance and loyalty). Despite an eventual
alliance between them, the relationship between al-Zarqawi and bin Laden
remained tumultuous. Al-Zarqawi went to Iraq after the US invasion in 2003,
seeing Iraq as a new, fertile ground for the jihad. Between 2003 and his death
in 2006, al-Zarqawi and his group, Jamaat al-Tawhid wal-Jihad (Organization
of Monotheism and Jihad), were responsible for a series of violent attacks
against UN installations, civilians, Shia mosques and holy sites, diplomats,
embassies, and hotels. In 2004 al-Zarqawi gave his bayah to bin Laden and,
in exchange, was named as the emir of an organization called Tanzim Qadat
al-Jihad fi Bilad al-Rafidayn (Al-Qaeda in the Land of Two Rivers), better
known as Al-Qaeda in Iraq (AQI). He was eventually killed by a US military
strike in 2006.

After al-Zarqawi's death, al-Zawahiri called on AQI to take the opportunity and form an Islamic state in Iraq. A few months later, a coalition of
jihadist groups in Iraq formed a group known as the Mujahideen Shurah
Council and announced the formation of the Islamic State of Iraq. They appointed Abu Omar al-Baghdadi as its head. Now under the leadership of Abu
Hamzah al-Muhajir, AQI gave its pledge to al-Baghdadi, signaling its participation in the new umbrella group. The Mujahideen Shurah Council formed
around the same time as the US military's surge in Iraq and the period now
referred to as the "Sunni Awakening" in which a number of Iraqi Sunni tribes
and former insurgents joined US-led efforts to extricate al-Qaeda–affiliated
forces from their neighborhoods. By 2008 the surge had proved successful,
initiating a period of relative calm in Iraq that was bolstered by the adminis-

tration of the newly appointed Shia prime minister, Nouri al-Maliki. Despite early promise, though, al-Maliki's administration began to unravel as it faced charges of nepotism and corruption. This, coupled with the withdrawal of US troops in 2011, initiated a new period of sectarian violence in Iraq.

In 2010 Abu Omar al-Baghdadi was killed, and the new leader, Abu Bakr al-Baghdadi, took his place. The second al-Baghdadi had spent years at Camp Bucca, a US internment facility in Iraq. By the time he had left prison, he had formed the alliances that would eventually fill the top levels of leadership in ISIS. After leaving Camp Bucca, the second al-Baghdadi and his men attacked a series of prisons and freed those who, eventually, would enter the ranks of ISIS. Moreover, in light of the civil war raging in neighboring Syria, the second al-Baghdadi sent deputies there to set up their own groups. One of al-Baghdadi's men established a jihadi organization called Jabhat al-Nusrah, which quickly proved to be one of the most capable insurgent groups in the Syrian civil war. On April 9, 2013, al-Baghdadi announced the merger of Jabhat al-Nusrah and his organization and named the group the Islamic State in Iraq and the Levant (ISIL or ISIS). Al-Nusrah, however, had plans of its own and rejected the merger, pledging its allegiance to al-Zawahiri's al-Qaeda.

By February 2014 al-Zawahiri had disavowed ISIS. By this time, however, ISIS had attacked two major cities in Iraq, capturing Mosul and shortly afterward taking Tikrit. Galvanized by their newfound conquests, ISIS spokesman al-Adnani announced that ISIS had declared a caliphate, named al-Baghdadi as its caliph, and changed its name simply to the Islamic State.

The significance of ISIS, and its declaration of the Islamic State, is monumental to the religious narrative that drives the al-Qaeda phenomenon. As it has repeated over and over again through its propaganda machine, ISIS has succeeded in doing what no other group in the al-Qaeda phenomenon has managed: to accrue significant amounts of territory under its control, to exert its vision of Islamic law, and to declare the caliphate. Of course, most Muslims reject ISIS and find their claims to represent the Islamic ummah (a group numbering upward of 1.6 billion people) to be preposterous. As discussed previously, thinkers such as Faraj, Azzam, bin Laden, and al-Suri would likely have rejected a number of the Islamic State's practices. But from the position of those in the al-Qaeda phenomenon, ISIS's success in erecting the Islamic state was epic. As noted in chapter 2, the theological narrative that drives the al-Qaeda phenomenon is rooted in the idea that an Islamic state is an incumbent requirement that Muslims have neglected.

Despite this success, however, ISIS has been deeply criticized by a number of significant figures in the jihadi movement, including Ayman al-Zawahiri, Abu Qatada al Filistini, and Abu Muhammad al-Maqdisi. The latter two helped issue a fatwa compelling Muslims to resist the aggression of ISIS.[81] Others contested both al-Baghdadi's suitability as the caliph and the legitimacy of the group's spontaneous declaration of the caliphate. In response, ISIS has defended al-Baghdadi's suitability for the position. Moreover, as noted in its English-language magazine *Dabiq*, the group is intensely focused on demonstrating the power, authority, and legitimacy of the "state" it claims to rule and govern. Story after story, feature after feature (now totaling fourteen volumes) provides descriptions of successful battles and the "liberation" of territory, of tribes giving their allegiance to ISIS, and exhortations to join the ranks or to give allegiance from afar—all in an attempt to establish the proper theological underpinnings of the Islamic State. A significant amount of the magazine's content provides theological justifications both for the necessity of the Islamic State and, now that it has materialized, of the incumbent duty of Muslims in giving their allegiance to it.

The establishment of the caliphate, according to *Dabiq*, has initiated a new era, one in which Muslim subjugation and oppression will undoubtedly end. It promises to regenerate Muslims' strength and power as it restores to Muslims the proper methods of life and political organization—ruled and determined by Islamic law—that will allow them to regain their source of strength.[82] The caliphate will usher in the day when "the Muslim will walk everywhere as master, having honor, being revered, with his head raised high and his dignity preserved." Muslims, *Dabiq* argues, "have a statement to make that will cause the world to hear and understand the meaning of terrorism, and boots that will trample the idol of nationalism, destroy the idol of democracy, and uncover its deviant nature" while demonstrating the legitimacy of the Islamic State and its rule.[83]

The restoration of the caliphate, however, not only promises certain victories but also entails certain responsibilities on the part of the believer. Now that the caliphate has been restored, Muslims are obligated to come to its support and to give their allegiance to the Islamic State. While living in other places was acceptable when a true Islamic state did not exist, now that the caliphate has been restored, and now that Muslims have the option to live under Islamic law through a proper Islamic state, they must do so. There is no, as ISIS puts it, "gray zone" on this issue. The world is now divided into two clear camps—the camp of belief and the camp of apostates and unbelievers. The materialization of the Islamic State has created this reality. ISIS claims the camp of righteousness is available, and it is the only camp that Muslims can join.[84] All Muslims, *Dabiq* argues, must pledge their allegiance to the Islamic State by performing hijrah (immigration) to the Islamic state, or by pledging their allegiance to the Islamic State and al-Baghdadi in an open and public way (they suggest recording this pledge and posting it online), or by performing individual jihadi operations in its name to help further its strength and power.[85]

Notably, the relationship that al-Suri establishes between individual jihadi operations and the open fronts remains a part of ISIS's strategy. *Dabiq* is particularly interested in featuring stories of those who have fought in the name of ISIS in their own countries through lone-wolf operations. Issue 6 of *Dabiq*, for example, featured the story of Man Haron Monis in Sydney, Australia. He was "a Muslim who resolved to join the mujahidin of the Islamic state in their war against the crusader coalition." Monis, however, did not accomplish this by "undertaking the journey to the lands of the Khilafah and fighting side-by-side with his brothers" but "by acting alone and striking the kuffar where it would hurt them most—in their own lands and on the very streets that they presumptively walk in safety." *Dabiq* continues, "It didn't take much; he got hold of a gun and stormed a café taking everyone inside hostage. Yet in doing so, he prompted mass panic, brought terror to the entire nation, and triggered an evacuation of parts of Sydney's central business district. The blessings in his efforts were apparent at the very outset."[86]

ISIS, seeing an open front, waged war against all elements in its way to establish the Islamic state. The group continues to advocate for individual operations wherever they may be and to help the Islamic State in its goal of weakening US opposition and expanding the geographical boundaries of the Islamic state.

While ISIS certainly presents us with something new, the ideas that drive ISIS are linked to the theological narrative that drives the al-Qaeda phenomenon. ISIS understands its caliphate as the culmination of the militant Islamist struggle that is described in the work of Qutb, Faraj, Azzam, and bin Laden, and that is given tactical and strategic direction by al-Suri. The overarching goal of al-Suri's work in the *Call* was to urge Muslims to undertake jihadi operations that would prepare the ground for the rise of an Islamic state. The history of ISIS follows al-Suri's story, for its leadership, stemming from the group Al-Qaeda in Iraq (or Al-Qaeda in the Land of Two Rivers), recognized what al-Suri would have referred to as an "opportunity" to erect an Islamic state and, eventually, the caliphate. The power vacuums in both Iraq and Syria, the depletion of US resources and stamina in fighting in the region, and the capture of territory by ISIS—all were ideal circumstances in which to declare the Islamic state that al-Qaeda ideologues had been pursuing. Of course, the al-Qaeda group led by al-Zawahiri has distanced itself from ISIS, yet the ideas that ISIS relies on are a clear part of the al-Qaeda phenomenon and the narrative that drives it.

Conclusion

The stories of Shahzad, Hasan, and the Tsarnaev Brothers, coupled with that of ISIS, demonstrate the power of al-Suri's model of jihad. They also are a testament to the heart of al-Suri's thinking, which connects religious belief and action in the world. For al-Suri, Muslims live in a state of political, social, and economic weakness and decline because they have failed to uphold a primary obligation—rule by shariah law through an Islamic state. Muslims must therefore use force to fight the forces of tyranny and oppression so that they may once again live under proper Islamic rule. Moreover, current conditions, in which Muslims are governed by apostate rulers who are backed by the United States and Europe, have triggered the type of environment that, according to al-Suri, requires Muslims to heed their individual duty to rise up in arms until proper Muslim rule has been restored. The jihad must expand and decentralize. Otherwise, al-Suri argues, it cannot succeed in light of the power imbalances between Muslims and the West that he believes defined the New World Order. In this way, Muslims must engage in a decentralized and diffuse form of war, legitimated by their individual duty to jihad, until the ground has been readied and the open fronts may succeed. He wrote the *Call* to explain both the necessity and the means for a global revolution that would restore Muslim rule. Both jihadi operations and open front campaigns are to work together to collapse infidel rule and to erect a true Islamic state.

For al-Suri and the ideologues who came before him, proper Islamic piety requires that Muslims understand their duty to wage an indiscriminate war until such time as proper Muslim rule can be restored.[87] For this reason I argue that ISIS represents a climax in the story of the al-Qaeda phenomenon. The Islamic State has managed to do what all others have failed to achieve (or, by their own admissions, have postponed doing): By erecting the caliphate—the heart of their claims to legitimacy—as they insist, they have restored "proper" Islamic rule. Of course, though, their claims are challenged by a spectrum of clerics and personalities who contest their authority and legitimacy. Being able to make the claim that one's position is authentically Islamic in the relevant and necessary ways is a significant point, for it demonstrates the power of legitimacy in this narrative. In making its claims to the caliphate, ISIS has shown both its greatest strength and its greatest liability, for such claims have not only given ISIS potency but also made it more vulnerable as respected personalities have bucked its authority and legitimacy.

In this way, al-Suri's model and the repeated efforts by ISIS to construct a recognized caliphate bring us to a critical juncture that must be examined. If we are to conceptualize the al-Qaeda phenomenon through the religious narrative that gives it meaning and direction, then this narrative must be confronted in any response to al-Qaeda.

Notes

1. Cruickshank and Ali, "Abu Musab Al-Suri," 1–14. Cruickshank and Ali argue that reports claiming al-Suri's operational involvement in these attacks are inaccurate. The al-Qaeda connection to the Madrid bombings has not been definitively established. It is not clear whether al-Suri was directly involved in the training, funding, and organizing of the men who undertook the attack or whether the men acted on their own but were "al-Qaeda inspired." See Paul Hamilos, "The Worst Islamist Attack in European History," *Guardian*, October 31, 2007; and Sean O'Neill, "Spain Furious as U.S. Blocks Access to Madrid Bombing 'Chief,'" *Times* (London), February 15, 2007.

2. Brynjar Lia dates the publication of *The Global Islamic Resistance Call* to January 2005, while Paul Cruickshank, Mohammad Hage Ali, and Jim Lacey date its publication on jihadi websites to late 2004.

3. Cruickshank and Ali, "Abu Musab Al-Suri," 1; Lia, *Architect of Global Jihad*, 1; and Lacey, *Terrorist's Call*, viii.

4. Steven Stalinsky, "The Release of Top al-Qaeda Military Strategist/Ideologue Abu Mus'ab al-Suri from Syrian Prison: A Looming Threat," The Middle East Media Research Institute (MEMRI), Report No. 796, February 8, 2012, http://www.memri.org/report/en/0/0/0/0/0/0/6068.htm; Bill Roggio, "Al Qaeda's American Propagandist Notes Death of Terror Group's Representative in Syria," *Long War Journal*, March 30, 2014, http://www.longwarjournal.org/archives/2014/03/al_qaedas_american_p.php; and Thomas Joscelyn, "Zawahiri Eulogizes al Qaeda's Slain Syrian Representative," *Long War Journal*, April 4, 2014, http://www.longwarjournal.org/archives/2014/04/zawahiri_eulogizes_a.php.

5. Lia, *Architect of Global Jihad*, 263.

6. Ibid., 35–39; and Cruickshank and Ali, "Abu Musab Al-Suri," 3.

7. Lia, *Architect of Global Jihad*, 40–48.

8. Ibid., 48–50.

9. Ibid., 72–75; and Cruickshank and Ali, "Abu Musab Al Suri," 3.

10. See Cruickshank and Ali, "Abu Musab Al-Suri," 4–5.

11. His exact relationship with bin Laden and al-Qaeda is contentious. He claims to have been among bin Laden's inner circle and to have served as his media adviser until he stopped working for him in 1992, but other sources (specifically Lia's

interviews with prominent Islamic figures who were in touch with al-Suri during this period) dispute his assertions. Al-Suri did not cut ties with al-Qaeda or with bin Laden after 1992, for Lia's evidence showed he continued to meet with leading al-Qaeda figures and attempted to influence their strategies and tactics.

12. Lia, *Architect of Global Jihad*, 87.

13. 'Umar 'Abd al-Hakim (Abu Musab al-Suri), "The Islamic Jihadi Revolution in Syria, Part I, pg. 10," cited in Lia, *Architect of Global Jihad*, 86.

14. He was depicted as "Karim Omar" in Mark Huband's *Warriors of the Prophet: The Struggle for Islam* (Boulder, CO: Westview Press, 1999) and as "Ali" in Bergen's *Holy War, Inc.*

15. Lia, *Architect of Global Jihad*, 230–46.

16. See, for example, Abd-al-Hakim (al-Suri), *Afghanistan, the Taliban*. Note that Azzam made similar claims in his writings on Afghanistan, arguing that despite the perceived "backwardness" of the Taliban's interpretation of Islam and their practices, their sincerity and desire to live under the rule of Islam ought to supersede any critical statements about their status as Muslims.

17. Al-Hakim (As Suri), "Muslims in Central Asia." Italics in original. SWT stands for *subhana wa tala* (the sacred and the mighty), which is used to show respect for the Prophet.

18. Ibid.

19. Ibid. Afghanistan's success, he argued, was especially significant in light of its geographic position. Central Asia, he maintained, would be the base of the future jihad. In "Muslims in Central Asia," al-Suri provides information related to topography, population size, demographics, and the resources of this area. He also notes that its people (significant population of Muslims), its location (isolated yet importantly linked to key areas such as the Persian Gulf, East Asia, and China), and its natural resources make it an excellent place for the Muslim-wide revolution to grow, develop, and eventually move outward.

20. Al-Suri, *Global Islamic Resistance Call*, 52. My translation.

21. Lacey, *Terrorists's Call*, 13–18.

22. While al-Suri is particularly focused on the contemporary issues, he mentions that this process of decline (due to foreign dominance) was initiated with the fall of the Abbasid Caliphate, and it continued uninterrupted until the present date. The process halted during the Ottoman Caliphate when the Muslim world once again experienced a period of strength and regeneration. See ibid., 30–47.

23. Ibid.

24. Ibid., 30–32.

25. Al-Suri, *Global Islamic Resistance Call*, 138. My translation.

26. Ibid.

27. Ibid., 137. My translation.

28. Ibid.

29. Ibid.

30. Ibid., 139. My translation.

31. Ibid.

32. Ibid.

33. Ibid., 141. My translation. All translations of the Quran come from the Yusuf Ali translation.

34. Ibid.

35. Ibid.

36. Ibid., 141–42. My translation.

37. Ibid., 142. My translation.

38. Ibid.

39. Ibid., 142–43. My translation.

40. Ibid., 143. My translation.

41. Ibid.

42. Ibid.

43. Ibid.

44. Lia, *Architect of Global Jihad*, 349–55.

45. Ibid., 360.

46. Ibid., 361.

47. Ibid., 362.

48. Ibid., 366.

49. Ibid., 359.

50. Ibid., 422–23.

51. Ibid., 370.

52. Ibid., 419.

53. Ibid.

54. See his analysis of Afghanistan, Chechnya, and Bosnia in ibid., 374–82.

55. Ibid., 373.

56. Ibid., 436–37.

57. Ibid., 477.

58. Ibid., 393.

59. Ibid., 394–95.

60. Ibid., 396.

61. Ibid., 397.

62. Ibid., 411.

63. Lacey, *Terrorist's Call*, 178–79.

64. See the introduction in Lia, *Architect of Global Jihad*.

65. Lieberman and Collins, "Violent Islamist Extremism," 1.

66. Ibid., 3.

67. Relatedly, William McCants argues that al-Suri was convinced of the specifically apocalyptic narrative that ISIS puts forward (though al-Suri was writing well before ISIS's declaration of a caliphate). See McCants, *ISIS Apocalypse*, 51–52.

68. Moreover, *Inspire* has continued to publish articles calling for individual jihad and "open source" jihad (terrorist operations that are undertaken with everyday weapons). The authors provide information on how ordinary individuals who lack training in explosives can still plan and execute successful terrorist plots in their own countries, thus cutting out the need for external support from any kind of organization and the need to travel for instructions or training. The magazine affords the opportunity and religious justification for how ordinary individuals (with or without access to training and weapons) can participate in the jihad by undertaking terrorist attacks in their own home nations, consequently further escalating, decentralizing, and radicalizing the jihad. For example, in the summer issue of 2010, *Inspire* published an article titled "How to Make a Bomb in the Kitchen of Your Mom" with instructions for making a bomb out of everyday materials.

69. See, for example, al-Awlaki's online article, "44 Ways to Support Jihad," Victorious Media, http://ebooks.worldofislam.info/ebooks/Jihad/Anwar_Al_Awlaki_-_44_Ways_To_Support_Jihad.pdf.

70. For an excellent and novel illustration of this point, see Ballen, *Terrorists in Love*.

71. The reader may want to raise the points that Hasan targeted only soldiers in uniform and that such acts are relatively discriminate for "imperfect soldiers" (see Hasan's quote in the section on his life). I suspect that Hasan's actions were the result of his military training, where a military uniform distinguishes combatants (soldiers) from civilians. I imagine too that targeting those in uniform had the perverse effect of easing his conscience, allowing him to believe that such targeting was a more justified act. That being the case, though, it is hard to understand how the events that transpired—an American serviceman opened fire on his fellow soldiers in uniform—can be described as a "discriminate" use of force. While it may be the case that killing only those in uniform is more discriminate than opening fire on all, how one considers fellow soldiers as legitimate targets (regardless of whether one has understood himself to have "switched sides") is unclear. I would have to agree with the report of the US Senate's Committee on Homeland Security and Governmental Affairs that described the Fort Hood shooting as a terror attack on US soil. See Lieberman and Collins, "Ticking Time Bomb," 7.

72. I relied on the following journalistic accounts to construct the details of Shahzad's story: "Times Square Suspect Had Explosives Training, Documents Say," CNN, May 4, 2010, http://www.cnn.com/2010/CRIME/05/04/new.york.car.bomb/; Benjamin Weiser and Colin Moynihan, "Guilty Plea in Times Square Bomb Plot," *New York Times*, June 22, 2010, http://www.nytimes.com/2010/06/22/nyregion

/22terror.html?_r=0; William K. Rashbaum and Al Baker, "Smoking Car to an Arrest in 53 Hours," *New York Times*, May 4, 2010, http://mobile.nytimes.com/2010/05/05 /nyregion/05tictoc.html; Mark Mazzetti, Sabrina Tavernise, and Jack Healy, "Suspect, Charged, Said to Admit to Role in Plot," *New York Times*, May 4, 2010, http:// mobile.nytimes.com/2010/05/05/nyregion/05bomb.html; James Barron and Michael S. Schmidt, "From Suburban Father to a Terrorism Suspect," *New York Times*, May 4, 2010, http://www.nytimes.com/2010/05/05/nyregion/05profile.html?page wanted=all; and especially Andrea Elliott, Sabrina Tavernise, and Anna Barnard, "For Times Sq. Suspect, Long Roots of Discontent," *New York Times*, May 15, 2010, http:// www.nytimes.com/2010/05/16/nyregion/16suspect.html.

73. See, for example, Yochi J. Dreazen and Even Perez, "Suspect Cites Radical Imam's Writings," *Wall Street Journal*, May 6, 2010, http://www.wsj.com/articles /SB10001424052748704370704575228150116907566.

74. I relied on the following journalistic accounts to construct the details of Hasan's story: Nick Allen, "'I Am the Shooter': US Army Major Nidal Hasan Declares as He Faces Court Marital over Fort Hood Massacre," *Telegraph*, August 6, 2013, http://www.telegraph.co.uk/news/worldnews/northamerica/usa/10226875/I-am -the-shooter-US-army-major-Nidal-Hasan-declares-as-he-faces-court-martial -over-Fort-Hood-massacre.html; Josh Rubin and Matt Smith, "'I Am the Shooter,' Nidal Hasan Tells Fort Hood Court Martial," CNN, August 6, 2013, http://www.cnn .com/2013/08/06/justice/hasan-court-martial/; James C. McKinley Jr., "Major Held in Fort Hood Rampage Is Charged with 13 Counts of Murder," *New York Times*, November 12, 2009, http://www.nytimes.com/2009/11/13/us/13inquire.html; "Profile: Major Nidal Malik Hasan," BBC News, November 12, 2009, http://news.bbc.co.uk/2 /hi/8345944.stm; James Dao, "Suspect Was 'Mortified' about Deployment," *New York Times*, November 5, 2009, http://www.nytimes.com/2009/11/06/us/06suspect.html; Jeff Brady, "Portrait Emerges of Hasan as Troubled Man," *All Things Considered*, NPR, November 11, 2009, http://www.npr.org/templates/story/story.php?storyId= 120317524; and especially James C. McKinley Jr. and James Dao, "Fort Hood Gunman Gave Signals before His Rampage," *New York Times*, November 8, 2009, http://www .nytimes.com/2009/11/09/us/09reconstruct.html?pagewanted=all.

75. Lieberman and Collins, "Ticking Time Bomb," 28–29.

76. Ibid., 29.

77. Ibid., 35. Note that al-Awlaki is not listed by name in this report. His name was redacted in the report made available to the public.

78. See Allen, "'I Am the Shooter'"; and Rubin and Smith, "'I Am the Shooter.'"

79. I relied on the following journalistic accounts to construct the details of the Tsarnaev brothers' story: Gessen, *The Brothers*; and Jacobs, Fillipov, and Wen, "Fall of the House of Tsarnaev."

80. To describe the history of ISIS's formation, I relied on the following accounts:

Stern and Berger, *ISIS*; Weiss and Hassan, *ISIS*; and Aaron Y. Zelin, "The Islamic State: A Video Introduction," Washington Institute for Near East Policy, February 16, 2015, https://www.youtube.com/watch?v=oIm76e1vMv0.

81. Text of the fatwa (English) is available at http://www.bilalabdulkareem.com /scholars-isis/. See also Thomas Joscelyn, "Pro–Al Qaeda Saudi Cleric Calls on ISIS Members to Defect," *Long War Journal*, February 3, 2014, http://www.longwarjournal .org/archives/2014/02/pro-al_qaeda_saudi_c.php.

82. "The Concept of Imamah Is from the Millah of Ibrahm," *Dabiq* 1 (June 2014): 24–27, http://media.clarionproject.org/files/09-2014/isis-isil-islamic-state -magazine-Issue-1-the-return-of-khilafah.pdf.

83. "Islamic State Reports," *Dabiq* 1 (June 2014): 8, http://media.clarionproject.org /files/09-2014/isis-isil-islamic-state-magazine-Issue-1-the-return-of-khilafah.pdf.

84. "Khilafah Declared," *Dabiq* 1 (June 2014): 10–11, http://media.clarionproject .org/files/09-2014/isis-isil-islamic-state-magazine-Issue-1-the-return-of-khilafah .pdf.

85. "Hijrah from Hypocrisy to Sincerity," *Dabiq* 3 (August 2014): esp. 25–35, http://media.clarionproject.org/files/09-2014/isis-isil-islamic-state-magazine-Issue -3-the-call-to-hijrah.pdf. This article is dedicated to undertaking hijrah to the Islamic state.

86. "Foreword," *Dabiq* 6 (December 2014): 3, http://media.clarionproject.org/files /islamic-state/isis-isil-islamic-state-magazine-issue-6-al-qaeda-of-waziristan.pdf.

87. For an expanded argument on this point, see John Kelsay, "Muslim Discourse about Jihad and the Counter-Narratives Project," *Soundings* 98, no. 4 (2015): 449–59.

CHAPTER FIVE

Counter-narratives

Moderate Muslim Voices and
a Debate within the Tradition

In moving forward we need to pay attention to the pragmatic consequences of al-Qaeda's theological underpinnings, the ideas that give al-Qaeda meaning and direction. In addition to a military response, the struggle against al-Qaeda must counter the interpretation of Islam that has led its ideologues to argue that the use of indiscriminate force and terrorism is both justified and necessary to revitalize the religion and to restore the Muslim people. In this way, combating al-Qaeda requires directly engaging the theological arguments it uses to understand the contemporary environment and, by extension, to determine the proper military course that it (and the Muslim world) should follow.

A number of prominent Muslim thinkers who have tackled issues of radicalism, militancy, and extremism in Islam have assumed this task and put forward interpretations of the textural tradition on matters related to shariah, the Islamic caliphate, and religious tolerance and pluralism. Their arguments demonstrate common themes and concerns, which, taken together, may be loosely referred to as the "moderate" interpretation; this presents itself as a direct alternative to the militant interpretation espoused by al-Qaeda. The qualifier "moderate" is not meant to indicate that "moderate Islam" is different from "orthodox" or "mainstream" Islam (qualifiers that are equally problematic); rather, it is used to make the point that all the thinkers discussed in this chapter are contesting al-Qaeda's *militancy* and *radicalism* directly.

Even though I reference individual thinkers as evidence for the ideas that I am explaining, presenting the arguments of the moderate thinkers as a "position" more clearly demonstrates an intellectual debate within the Islamic tradition on issues of militancy. And while I present it as a position to help provide organization and clarity to the variety of ideas discussed, the reader will quickly note that such arguments are being made from a wide cross-section of Muslim thinkers. The point here is not to minimize the differences between them but to show the points of a position within the tradition that denounces al-Qaeda's interpretation of what Islam requires of the believer.[1]

It is important to note that the thinkers discussed in this chapter are writing within the context of what Khaled Abou El Fadl has called a "crisis of authority" in Islam. According to Abou El Fadl, contemporary changes to the traditional training and institutions of the ulema, or the juridical class, have impeded the scholars' authority to interpret the textual tradition. Consequently, this authority is increasingly claimed by members of a rising professional class who have argued for the right to interpret Islamic law without the customary credentials or training, leading to interpretations of the textual sources that are at odds with the ethical and moral principles of Islam. Abou El Fadl's chief concern is the rise of fringe elements that are arguing for literal and static interpretations of the texts. This, he argues, directly contradicts a tradition that has historically demonstrated, and allowed for, plurality. Such changes in authority have led to what he terms a "puritan" stream in Islam that misconstrues the Islamic tradition and critically conflicts with the tradition's commitments to peace and justice.

Taking this into account, we can explicate the common denominators of their respective positions. To begin, the moderate position is characterized by a distinct hermeneutical approach whose main elements are twofold. First, while militant thinkers argue that history is authoritative and categorically normative for Muslim self-understanding, the moderate position argues that history ought to have a more limited (though still critically influential) scope of authority. In the attempt to determine how the Islamic tradition can provide guidance on changing and contemporary conditions, the legal rulings and institutional arrangements of the past ought to be examined and consulted but not treated as static and universal models that must be emulated in all their particularity. Second, the moderate position grants a prominent role to human agency and human reason in the hermeneutical process. While the militant position maintains that readings of the text are not open to discussion or dissenting viewpoints, the moderate position emphasizes the role of human reason as part and parcel of any interpretive act. According to the moderates, while interpretation is bound by the textual tradition—and by divine law as understood in a specific way—it remains a function of human thinking and historical circumstances. Therefore, Muslims in new circumstances can and *ought to* reexamine the textual sources to determine new rulings.

This last point splits the thinkers discussed in this chapter into two camps. The first includes figures such as Abdulaziz Sachedina, Bassam Tibi, Abdullahi An-Na'im, and Abou El Fadl. John Kelsay has aptly called these scholars the "Muslim democrats."[2] They argue that any attempt to apply Islamic injunctions to contemporary conditions must face squarely the realities imposed by an international order organized under a system of nation-states. In this order, Muslim countries share equal membership with non-Muslim countries, and juridical decisions of the past must be reexamined in order to shed light on how Muslims might position themselves within the international system. While the militant position rejects the contemporary international order, the moderate position argues that the Islamic textual tradition contains the necessary tools through which Muslims can be, and ought to be, full participants.

As evidence, these moderate thinkers offer readings of the Quran and the traditions of Muhammad (hadiths) that demonstrate an emphasis on religious liberty and peaceful coexistence with other religious traditions. They reject the idea that the Islamic state is necessary or incumbent on the believer and insist that an injunction to build an Islamic state (as put forward by militant elements) is a modern construction; moreover, they argue, it lacks a substantial basis in the texts. Instead, they contend that true and unfettered religious expression, as demanded by their interpretation of the textual tradition, *prohibits* the construction of a state that imposes shariah law.

The critical question, however, is to what extent this interpretation is capable of discrediting al-Qaeda and the militant stream it represents. In other words, to what extent does the work of the Muslim democrats contest the authority and legitimacy of the al-Qaeda narrative and those who may lend it support or may be encouraged to join its ranks? Their position disputes a relatively established understanding of history and its normative claims within the Muslim world. Therefore, the attempt to oppose the militant interpretations of al-Qaeda must also include figures that maintain the traditional emphasis of the role of history in Islamic hermeneutics and jurisprudence.

This brings us to our second camp of moderate thinkers, or as I refer to them, the moderate "traditionalists." It includes Salman bin Fahd bin Abdullah al-Ouda, Sayyed Imam al-Sharif (more commonly known as Dr. Fadl), and Yusuf al-Qaradawi. All three figures have critiqued al-Qaeda and its militancy directly. Of course, they are, by no means, the only traditionalists to have critically examined al-Qaeda or its brand of Islamic militancy. Numerous important and influential clerics have offered public judgments of al-Qaeda.[3] The work of al-Ouda, al-Sharif, and al-Qaradawi, however, offers a clear and, perhaps most important, widely disseminated critique of militancy in Islam and prohibits the militant solutions to Muslim problems that al-Qaeda thinkers put forward. Moreover, their opinions carry significant weight because at one time or another prominent figures in al-Qaeda have praised and lauded them.

For example, bin Laden's 1996 epistle praised al-Ouda by name for his criticism of the Saudi government, but after September 11 al-Ouda wrote a highly publicized "open letter" to bin Laden, chastising al-Qaeda and the widespread destruction it has caused among Muslim societies. Al-Sharif is a former jihadi theoretician whose work achieved importance in the militant community. Al-Qaradawi, a highly influential Muslim cleric with a large following, has been exceptionally successful in disseminating his ideas and particularly his critique of certain forms of jihad. In this way, the work of these figures demonstrates not only the marked diversity of the moderate position and the spectrum of opinions that exists regarding the appropriate relationships between Islam and that state, but, perhaps most important, also the various ways that traditionalist thinkers are a part of this conversation.

The last point is particularly significant for thinking about responding to the al-Qaeda phenomenon. Al-Qaeda thinkers see themselves as the vanguard of Islam and insist that theirs is the only "true" or "authentic" expression of what God requires of the believer. They not only cite authoritative sources as evidence for their claims but also argue that to deny their specific interpretation of these texts is to deny the texts themselves. For them, Islam as it was practiced closest to the time of Muhammad is the most authentic form.[4] While not clinging either to Islam as it was practiced in the time of Muhammad or to static interpretations of the Quran as tightly as the militants, figures such as al-Ouda, al-Sharif, and al-Qaradawi are formidable opponents to al-Qaeda thinkers because they hold traditional understandings of how Muslims ought to reference their important texts and Islamic history when providing guidance for contemporary issues and problems. This point lends the traditional thinkers more widespread appeal.

Al-Ouda, al-Sharif, and al-Qaradawi are also concerned with the erosion of the ulema's authority and the ways that this development has led to misinterpretations of Islam. For this reason, they argue that those who seek to understand and apply the Shariah must consult the experts, jurists who have been trained in the complex task of interpreting this textual tradition. In contrast to El Fadl, Sachedina, Tibi, and An-Na'im, the traditionalist moderate thinkers argue that the implementation of Islamic law is a necessary element of a just Islamic polity, yet, at the same time, they say the militant streams have misinterpreted what those texts require and have led their followers astray. Not only do militants then suffer from a lack of insight into the true and proper teachings of Islam but they also fail to understand the realities of contemporary Muslim societies. The traditionalist moderates contend that while the ends sought by the militants have a foundational basis in the Islamic tradition, their *means* are unacceptable and must be challenged.

Abou El Fadl and the Crisis of Authority

Islam, like other religious traditions, has historically been interested in questions of right and wrong, good and evil, justice and injustice. Furthermore, it has invested in examining how such determinations may be used to guide the individual and the community toward a good and proper way of living. While the Islamic tradition has developed several modes for examining such questions, the most prominent—in both duration and influence—is shariah law.

As discussed in chapter 3, traditionally, the determination of shariah law involved a process where the normative sources of authority—the Quran and the traditions of Muhammad and the early community—were referenced to determine how they might guide the believer in resolving a specific question. This process led to the development of multiple hermeneutical methods as well as the ulema, a class of scholars comprising jurists and specialists in Islamic law. Through a rigorous process of training in institutions specifically dedicated to the task, the ulema represents the primary class of society that is engaged in the production and interpretation of Islamic law. While the existence of multiple schools of law has ensured a plurality of opinions and rulings, the authority to engage in Islamic jurisprudence has been retained in the hands of this class of specialists. Thus, the questions of who had the authority to determine shariah and how it was to be done were subject to a relatively clear set of guidelines and limits.

As Abou El Fadl explains, by the mid-twentieth century, the authority and method of this system were in question. Through a series of social, political, and economic reforms instituted into the Muslim world, the foundational system of the traditional methods of shariah authority eroded. To begin, the role of shariah gradually narrowed as Western-based legal systems replaced them. The Ottoman Empire's adoption of Western codes and systems of administration had a determinate effect on the role of the Shariah in Islamic society in general and became the model for the Muslim world in the twentieth century. The Ottomans, in the attempt to implement European administrative models, codified certain aspects of the Hanafi school. This codification process consequently transformed the shariah, whose production traditionally entailed fluid processes of legal reasoning into positive law.[5]

Furthermore, the institutions that had trained and produced the clerical class were closed or nationalized and were subject to the authority of the state. Abou El Fadl also notes that changes to the curriculum in these institutions had serious consequences. The training of students shifted, limiting their ability to "provide intellectual leadership," and focused on preparing them to take on much more limited roles, "such as leading prayers in mosques, delivering Friday sermons, and at most, serving as judges in personal law courts."[6] The curriculum was no longer geared toward the material of legal jurisprudence and theory; consequently, the ulema were no longer effectively trained as legal experts in the same sense as they had been in the past.[7]

Increased literacy rates also effected these changes to the authority of the ulema. Greater levels of literacy meant that a wider spectrum of Muslims had access to the textual foundations of shariah law. The cumulative effect of these changes was such that the legitimacy and prestige of the ulema were called into question, opening the door for an emerging professional class to claim the right to interpret the textual tradition. As Abou El Fadl writes, "The vacuum in authority meant not so much that no one could authoritatively speak for Islam, but that virtually every Muslim with a modest knowledge of the Qur'an and the traditions of the Prophet was suddenly considered qualified to speak for the Islamic tradition and shariah law—even Muslims unfamiliar with the precedents and accomplishments of past generations."[8]

Some of the moderate thinkers consider this to be a positive change. For example, An-Na'im maintains that the corrosion of the ulema's authority has opened the door for individual Muslims to participate in the process of interpretation and, in this way, to determine the present and future application of Islamic law in the international order as well as in matters of public concern. Other intellectuals, however, offer more qualified assessments. As Abou El Fadl argues, the vacuum of authority has allowed for the rise of what he terms "puritanical" streams within Islam—that is, groups that are uncompromising in their beliefs and that are willing to resort to militant means to impose them not only on other Muslims but also on those outside the Muslim fold. In responding to the puritan stream, he asserts, Muslims today must understand that they are in the midst of a decisively formative moment in the history of their tradition.

The Moderate Position

Structuring the divide between the moderate and the militant positions are disagreements regarding the proper approach to the textual tradition. The foundational roots of this divide are the marked divergences on the correct methods of interpretation and, by extension, the appropriate means of applying the wisdom and guidance contained in the normative sources to contemporary issues and problems. Both militant and moderate arguments attempt to give form to the divine will by seeking out the guidance and injunctions provided in the normative sources. And while both the moderate and militant positions consider the knowledge and counsel contained therein as eternal, the question of how such instruction is affected or influenced by history is the cardinal factor that differentiates their respective understandings of Islam and its contemporary applications.

As noted in chapter 4, the militants argue that the application of shariah law into all matters of state and society is necessary for the strength and flourishing of Muslim communities. As evidence, they reference the example of the prophet Muhammad and the early Islamic polity, holding that Muhammad's example establishes that Islam should rule all facets of the life of the believer. This requires, they argue, constructing political mechanisms dedicated to instituting shariah law—God's law—into political life. Furthermore, the militant understanding of history is such that the mechanisms established by the earliest Muslims have a normative claim on the present. As chapter 4 explains, in light of their proximity to Muhammad—the ultimate interpretive authority of the tradition—the earliest Muslims are thought to have understood and expressed God's mandates most fully and most perfectly. Therefore, the ways in which early Muslims arranged their political communities and their social and civic institutions are considered the ultimate models through which God's law should be given form on earth. In short, for the militants, those social and political models that the early Muslim communities established have critical and enduring purchase on contemporary conditions. History, for the militants, must be referenced in negotiating and settling contemporary issues, as these historical precedents carry normative weight.

The moderate position understands the role and authority of historical models and precedents in a different way. Before discussing this point, it is important to stress that while the moderates' positions emphasize the role of human reason in the process of constructing shariah law, their ideas remain rooted in the textual tradition. The moderate thinkers discussed here maintain that the values and commitments of the tradition require one to reference the authoritative sources—the Quran and the hadiths. In doing so, determining Islamic values is performed within certain parameters. However, unlike the militants, the moderates reason that the guidance contained in the authoritative sources may be expressed in a variety of ways. The proper expression of these values is not contingent on, nor fully contained within, the forms they took in the past. Thus, while the moderates contend that the guidance contained in the normative sources remains relevant to the present, such guidance may change in regard to the challenges and conditions of the contemporary period. Therefore, while moderate thinkers reference and investigate the institutions and political mechanisms of the earliest Muslims, these models—in all their specifics and particularities—are understood as historically contingent and thus not as categorically binding on Muslim communities of today. The past is referenced for guidance but not for categorical authority and unquestioned imitation. Rather, the moderates, in their approach to the past, seek to "remember it, retrace its path, interpret it, reconstruct it, and make it relevant to the present."[9]

So Clear

The Muslim Democrats

The first camp of moderate thinkers, the Muslim democrats, begin from these points. For example, Tibi writes that Islam is a "pure system of symbols offering a model for reality." He states that this system of symbols may be thought of as an "Islamic canon" that is "binding on all Muslims." As determined by time and place, this pure system of symbols produces actual existing symbols.[10] While Tibi does not provide an elaborate discussion detailing what is contained within the "Islamic canon," he does note that the core of Islamic beliefs includes "submission to God and unconditional recognition of his messenger (*rasul*) Muhammad as arbitrator. Since that time it has also entailed acknowledgment of the Qur'an as the ultimate, definitive word of God, and the Sunnah (tradition) of The Prophet and Messenger of God."[11] However, beyond this, Tibi argues, the existing symbols are derived ones, brought into existence through a process of human construction.[12] The interpretation and construction of shariah law, then, cannot ignore social change.

The moderates claim that shariah is neither fixed nor immutable; rather, it is an evolving human construct produced through the efforts of human beings as they attempt to understand and apply God's will. To clarify this point, Abou El Fadl maintains that the moderate position distinguishes between shariah and *fiqh*: Shariah is the eternal law of God, but fiqh is the human law that is a product of a human struggle to realize the eternal law. Shariah is inaccessible in its full and perfect form to human beings. While Muslims are required to strive to fulfill the law, he continues, "it is arrogant and offensive to claim that human beings could be certain that they have successfully comprehended eternal law." Therefore, fiqh is "subject to error, alternation,

shariah as an evolving construct

development, and nullification" through the continual (and fallible) efforts of human beings to appropriately effect God's will.[13]

This understanding of the law creates a deep and wide space for the role of human agency in the hermeneutical method. To make this point, An-Na'im argues that since the divine will is not fully accessible, human reason has always been a necessary part of the interpretive process. Human beings, under their requirement to strive to understand the eternal law, are a primary and directive element in the process of its construction. He notes that Islamic scholars developed the methodological processes of determining Islamic law (*Usul al-fiqh*). In this way, both the interpretive tools that are applied as well as the decisions regarding *who* may interpret the law are a product of human reasoning and reflection. Therefore, he determines, while the texts that Muslims reference cannot change, the history of the interpretive tradition, as a *human* tradition, demonstrates "there is nothing to prevent the formation of a fresh consensus around new interpretive techniques or innovative interpretations of the Qur'an and Sunna, which would become a part of Shari'a, just as the existing methodologies and interpretations came to be a part of it in the first place."[14] Why, he asks, should a process clearly driven by human reasoning and reflection preclude successive consideration?

As noted previously, the Muslim democrats also attest that the application of Islamic tradition squarely faces the realities of contemporary political conditions. As An-Na'im notes,

> Any and all proposed possibilities of change or development must therefore begin with the reality that European colonialism and its aftermath have drastically transformed the basis and nature of political and social organization within and among territorial states where all Muslims live today. A return to precolonial ideas and systems is simply not an option, and any change and adaption of the present system can be realized only through the concepts and institutions of this local and global postcolonial reality.[15]

For this reason, the Muslim democrats categorically reject the militants' insistence that the Islamic state is necessary. The Muslim democrats argue that the demand for a state that imposes shariah law through political institutions is untenable given the modern system of international relations. The notion of an Islamic political state, particularly as imagined by the militants, would include shariah rulings on women, non-Muslims, and other classes of individuals that, the Muslim democrats point out, are not only objectionable but also unthinkable in a public international order where Muslim states are interacting as participating members. Furthermore, their participation in this order, at the very minimum, implies a commitment to values of equality and liberty that, according to these thinkers, an Islamic state does not provide.

In addition, the moderate democrats assert that an Islamic state that imposes shariah law flies directly in the face of Islam's commitment to religious liberty, pluralism, and peaceful coexistence with other traditions. These values, they argue, are enjoined on believers by God. These commitments not only allow but also direct Muslims to be full participants in the current international order. An-Na'im maintains that a secular state, or one that is religiously neutral, is critically important to contemporary Islam. While Muslims are required to observe the eternal law as a matter of fulfilling their responsibility to God, such observance may be done freely, and therefore properly, only under circumstances in which the state does not enforce its own understanding of Islamic law. In light of the constructed nature of shariah and the primary role of human interpretation that is qualified by time and place, An-Na'im states that any attempt to determine the content of shariah is subject to change and individual reflection. Therefore, true religious piety, done with honesty and conviction, cannot be a product of the state's claims to propagate and enforce its own understandings of religious law. True compliance cannot be coerced by government mechanisms and the power of the state that enforces them.

An-Na'im's argument is based on what moderate thinkers contend is the Quran's and the hadiths' commitment to freedom of religion and conscience. As Sachedina writes, "Without recognition of freedom of religion, it is impossible to conceive of religious commitment as a freely negotiated human-divine relationship that fosters individual accountability for one's acceptance or rejection of faith in God, commitment to pursue an ethical life, and willingness to be judged accordingly."[16]

As Sachedina outlines, within the Islamic tradition, the acceptance of faith and the pursuit of the ideal life are made possible through an innate human capacity that directs the human being to the good. This innate capacity (*fitra*) is part of individual human nature as designed by God. This innate spiritual disposition imbued in human nature is further assisted by prophetic revelation; therefore, fitra grants human beings the ability to see and understand the proper path determined by God's universal guidance. However, despite human beings' having been divinely engineered with natural capacities that incline them toward the good, Sachedina argues that the Quran is clear: Accepting or rejecting God's revelation and submitting to God's will are an individual's choice.

Sachedina writes that such verses imply human responsibilities for being led astray and, thus, for accepting or rejecting the divine will and the requisite duties. The concept of fitra, then, ought to breathe new life into the Quranic verse, "No compulsion is there in religion."[17] If the role of revelation is to provide guidance, such an idea presupposes that both faith as well as the acts that flow from it are the result of a deliberate act made possible only by a sincere, individual, and unfettered submission to God. Such an act of submission, Sachedina argues, cannot be coerced or enforced; indeed, it can evolve only from personal reflection and intentional decision-making. Faith, he notes, "is freely and directly negotiated between God and the human being and cannot be compelled."[18]

With this understanding of individual religious liberty, Sachedina proclaims, the Quran's commitment to religious pluralism and peaceful coexistence are clear. He argues that a reading of the authoritative texts that removes the historical and political contingencies of the juristic tradition demonstrates that Islam, as expressed by the Quran and the Sunnah, was not only aware of the existence of other traditions but also sought to manage such interactions in a way where they were perhaps subjected to a critical lens but were not "rejected as false." The Quran, he avers, is committed to religious liberty, pluralism, and peaceful coexistence with other religious traditions.

This commitment, he continues, has been obscured by a relatively established yet controversial juridical method known as abrogation (*naskh*). In the attempt to determine Islamic law and to reconcile verses within the Quran that were seemingly contradictory, the classical jurists argued that the principle of abrogation determined that later verses in the Quran supplanted earlier verses. In response to a change in circumstances or conditions, a later verse was thought to have superseded one that was revealed previously. Sachedina, however, argues that it occurred as the result of political and social circumstances in which jurists demanded unquestioning acceptance to the new faith and the political orders established by the early caliphs. A proper understanding of the Quran that is removed from the principle of naskh, he explains, demonstrates a clear commitment to religious liberty, toleration, and justice.[19]

As evidence, Sachedina provides various texts from the Quran that admonish Muslims to build a just political order while remaining committed to notions of pluralism, particularly the freedom of human conscience and the ability to negotiate one's own spiritual destiny. For example, he references the following:

We have revealed to thee as We have revealed to Noah, and the Prophets after him, and We revealed to Abraham, Ishmael, Isaac, Jacob, and
the Tribes, Jesus and Job, Jonah and Aaron and Solomon, and We gave
to David Psalms, and Messengers We have already told thee of before . . . Messengers bearing good tidings, and warning, so that humankind might have no argument against God, after the Messengers . . .
(Q 4:163)[20]

Say: We believe in God, and that which has been sent down to us,
and sent down on Abraham and Ishmael, Isaac and Jacob, and the
Tribes, and in that which was given to Moses and Jesus, and the Prophets, of their Lord; we make no distinctions between any of them, and
to Him we surrender. (Q 3:84)[21]

Then in recognizing the common ground that Muslims share with the
People of the Book, Sachedina argues that Islam neither denies other religious traditions of salvation nor claims sole proprietorship over divine
guidance. Rather, the Quran recognizes the existence, particularities, and
intrinsic value of other traditions. Only by appealing to the controversial
hermeneutical tool of naskh, he insists, may the Quran's inclinations toward
pluralism be denied.

Abou El Fadl, in the same line of thinking, writes that the Quran "not
only accepts, but even expects, the reality of difference and diversity within
human society." As evidence, he discusses the following verse:

O Humankind, God has created you from male and female and made
you into diverse nations and tribes so that you may come to know each
other. Verily, the most honored of you in the sight of God is he who is
the most righteous (Q 49:13).

This verse, he argues, not only affirms diversity as a purposeful and intentional component of God's providence but also demonstrates the overall
inclination of the Quran toward coexistence and cooperation. The command
of human beings to "know each other," he writes, "places an obligation on
Muslims and non-Muslims alike" to negotiate their interactions in a way
that takes note of and accords respect and recognition toward difference and
plurality. Human beings, then, must "work together in pursuit of goodness."[22]

This has serious implications for militants' understanding of war and enmity. Abou El Fadl notes, "The net effect of the moderates' Qur'anic analysis
is that, contrary to the puritans, they do not believe that God intends or
desires that Muslims dominate non-Muslims." While Muslims are indeed

advocated to call people to Islam "in kindness," the moderate position argues that in light of a divinely created order of plurality, "people will never
all follow one faith."[23]

Furthermore, Abou El Fadl argues that the juristic division of the world
into two realms (dar al-harb and dar al-Islam) is a product of historical circumstances. This state of permanent war was a result of the then prevailing
norms of international relations. He writes that "unless there was affirmative
agreement to the contrary, every nation or empire in existence assumed itself to be in a belligerent relationship with the rest of the world." While this
division was formative for the Islamic law of nations, however, it is not supported in the textual sources. As he asserts, "Both sources do mention that
all Muslims should think of themselves as a single people belonging to one
nation, but they do not divide the world into two abodes, and they do not
say that Muslims should be in a perpetual state of war with non-Muslims."[24]
As a product of Islamic history, contingent on time and place, he argues
that the divisive system no longer has relevance. While it may have served a
purpose in a particular historical moment, it no longer reflects the current
international order, and, furthermore, its implementation today would lead
to "disastrous consequences."[25]

A Critical Issue

Responses to the work of the moderate thinkers have focused on at least two
issues. First, the authority of moderate thinkers, specifically regarding the
ability of their arguments to gain a foothold in the Muslim world, is called
into question. Second, the moderate position is charged with not ascribing
enough weight to the effects of colonialism on the emergence of Islamic
militancy. For example, Stanley Kurtz, writing directly in response to Abou
El Fadl, contends that while Abou El Fadl's position is admirable, the appeal
of such reform, and the chance that it will be adopted, will be limited to
"those who have already accepted modernity, chiefly assimilated and highly
educated Muslims in the United States, as well as the relatively small number
of highly modernized Muslims in the Middle East itself."[26] Kurtz then argues
that wide-scale adoption of the type of reform called for by Abou El Fadl,
and presumably like-minded others, requires foundational social changes.

Kurtz's argument gestures toward a critical issue in the moderate position. The moderate thinkers rely on a hermeneutical method that limits the
normative claims of history. For example, An-Na'im states that the "conflation" model of an Islamic state—one that combines religious and political
authority—is not replicable; given that the prophet Muhammad established

the Islamic state, it cannot be duplicated successfully in Islamic political history. He argues that the attempt by subsequent caliphs to conflate religious and political leadership resulted in wars of insurrection and serious political and civil strife in the early periods of Islam (he notes the Riddah Wars as examples). The Prophet's combination of religious and political authority was unique, and other Muslims cannot reproduce what he achieved. As the vast majority of Muslims do not accept the possibility of prophecy after Muhammad, any attempt to reproduce a model of the state premised on the conflation model is unmerited and lacking the necessary foundations for success.[27]

While An-Na'im makes an excellent point, his critique of the conflation model does not erase the rule of Abu Bakr, Umar, Uthman, and Ali and the achievements of Islamic civilization under the Umayyads and the Abbasids from the Muslim imagination. This history continues to have a significant hold on Muslim self-understanding. Abou El Fadl himself maintains that reasoning has proceeded since the seventh century through consensus. The common belief among Muslims both that the normative texts are authentic and authoritative and that the interpretive methods applied are, in fact, legitimate has carried forward the process of shariah reasoning. While the Muslim democrats are thinking historically, they are also confronting traditional interpretations of the texts that appeal to history in a different manner.

It is difficult to know whether this understanding of history is an impediment to the widespread acceptance of the moderate thinkers. The point is worth pursuing, though, as it directs us to the fact that the militant position is also being contested by more "traditional" thinkers in the Muslim world, or by those who insist on the normative claims of history that those thinkers who were discussed earlier have contested to varying degrees.

As the traditionalists and their work are less accessible to an English-speaking audience (al-Qaradawi is an exception since a number of his works have been translated into English), next I provide explications of their critique of al-Qaeda and my translations of their work when necessary.

The "Traditionalists"

The traditionalist thinkers, like the Muslim democrats, also argue that Islamic history and the textual sources must be investigated to understand how they lay claim on Muslim life today. Unlike the Muslim democrats, however, the traditionalists have more conventional ideas regarding the role of Islam in society and tend to argue that Muslim revitalization requires the incorporation of Islamic ideas and commitments into social and political life.

Unlike the militants, however, the following scholars assert that understanding how this ought to be done in contemporary society requires serious and specialized training in understanding the text. Lacking this type of training, they insist, has led militants astray and to espouse extreme and radical positions. Yusuf al-Qaradawi's work, in particular, helps clarify these claims.

Yusuf al-Qaradawi

Yusuf al-Qaradawi is concerned with the manifestation of extremism in Islam, especially as it has taken hold among young Muslims. However, he does want to make clear differentiations between those who, in their desire to please God, have committed themselves to a conservative interpretation of an issue and those who manifest signs of extremism. The former, he argues, insofar as their intention is to please God and to live out their understanding of the proper Islamic life, ought not be treated as extremists. Al-Qaradawi here makes a point that ought to be highlighted: He wishes to stress that "conservative" or "traditional" expressions of religiosity in Islam do not equate to militancy, extremism, or radicalism; rather, Muslims who adhere to conservative ideas are living out the dictates of their religion as they understand them. This point becomes important in the conclusion, particularly when we discuss US attempts to deal with al-Qaeda's militant theology. Suffice it to say here, though, that al-Qaradawi emphasizes the importance of attempting to differentiate between militancy and conservative expressions of Islam.

He points to the fact that the Islamic legal school has always had a plurality of interpretations on a variety of issues, all of which fall on a spectrum. Adhering to the rigid end of the interpretive stream is to live out the dictates of the divine will as understood by a particular type of interpretation of the texts. This is *not* extremism. Al-Qaradawi argues that extremism has other identifying characteristics. The first is a type of bigotry and intolerance that deprives a person of "clarity of vision regarding the interests of other human beings, the purposes of the shariah, or the circumstances of the age."[28] The second is a commitment to excessiveness and the continual imposition on others to do likewise. Next is the overburdening of others—both Muslims and non-Muslims—in the way that the extremist zeal is applied and forced onto other people. A fourth characteristic involves the excessively harsh treatment of others, especially in the extremist's attempts to call others to Islam or to impose his or her understanding or interpretation of the tradition.[29] The clearest distinguishing factor of extremism, he argues, is when "a single group deprives all people of the right to safety and protection, and instead sanctions their killing and the confiscation of their lives and property.

This, of course, occurs when an extremist holds all people—except those in his group—to be *kuffar* [those who have rejected the faith]."[30]

For al-Qaradawi, then, extremism is a manifestation of rigidity and excess displayed by those who refuse to acknowledge the tradition's history of juristic plurality and multiplicity of interpretation. While he writes that the causes of extremism are multiple and complex, he focuses on two that he believes are critically important for both understanding and treating extremism in Islam.

To begin, he declares that the extremist elements have identified a significant point: Muslim countries have failed to properly apply the Shariah and have replaced it with "imported systems and alien ideologies." Present-day Muslim societies are characterized by chaos and inner contradictions, all due to the rejection of Islam. The extremist elements have witnessed the clear disparities between the wealthy and the poor, and they live under corrupt governments whose legislation transgresses the values embodied in Islam. The extremist elements also watch the same governments stand by submissively as the Muslim world is attacked by the powers of "Zionism, Christian, Marxist, [and] Pagan" forces that not only destroy the geographic territory of Islam but also erode the moral fabric of society. In response, the extremist elements have become frustrated. Unable to bring real change, they have resorted to violence.[31]

Second, the turn toward extremism has been exacerbated by interpretations of the textual tradition that lack proper insight. Like the moderate thinkers discussed earlier, al-Qaradawi is also concerned with the erosion of the ulema's authority in the tradition. He too maintains that it has led to misguided interpretations. On this point he is worth quoting at length. He writes,

> Many of them [the extremists] have never been taught by reliable Muslim ulama specialized in the field. Rather, they have received semi-knowledge directly from books and newspapers without any opportunity for revision or discussion which could test the learner's understanding and analyze the depth of his knowledge . . . their reading, understanding, and deduction may well be wrong or deficient . . .[32]
>
> . . . A person may presume—and sometimes genuinely believe—that he knows all there is to know; that he is a scholar, a *faqih*. But actually he has no more than a hodgepodge of undigested and unassimilated "knowledge" which neither enhances insight nor clarifies vision. A person possessing such "knowledge" concentrates on marginal and trivial issues only, and thereby fails to see the relationship between

the parts which form the whole (and the whole itself) or between the categorical and the fundamental texts vis-à-vis the allegorical ones.[33]

An authoritative and proficient understanding of the textual tradition, al-Qaradawi argues, demonstrates that Islam, while open to multiple inter-pretations, clearly rejects extremism and *enjoins* a path of moderation on the believer.[34] As evidence, he cites a variety of hadiths demonstrating that the Prophet condemned any form of zealotry in Islam. Muhammad, he affirms, was disinclined toward excess, as it overburdens the individual and is "too disagreeable for ordinary human nature to endure or tolerate."[35]

Al-Qaradawi appears to favor one hadith especially. He declares that the Prophet not only condemned others for prolonging the duration of prayer (and, in the process, overburdening them) but also, when he led the prayer, was often inclined to shorten it to refrain from overburdening others.[36] Thus, while the individual Muslim may choose to take on the more burdensome task of longer prayer on his or her own, he or she may not overburden others by claiming that it is necessary and incumbent on all Muslims to engage in lengthy prayer. As al-Qaradawi argues, clearly when Muhammad was faced with two choices, he "always chose the easiest, unless it was a sin."[37]

This reading of the example of Muhammad is supported by what al-Qaradawi says is the Islamic tradition's underlying approach to religious change and development: God's actions in the world (including God's deal-ings with humankind) demonstrate that change occurs in stages. "Grada-tion," asserts al-Qaradawi, is God's preferred approach. Whether in relation to the creation of the universe or the transition from paganism to mono-theism, God's work reveals a clear preference toward gradual change. As al-Qaradawi writes, God's design and action in the world show that "every-thing has an appointed term during which it reaches ripeness and maturity. This applies to the material as well as the moral. Nothing should be har-vested before its appointed time."[38]

While al-Qaradawi concedes that the call for an Islamic state among the militant elements of Islam is appropriate as determined by the dictates of the tradition, he states the extremist elements have resorted to means that are contrary to the inherent teachings and values of Islam. Their demands on other Muslims exceed Muhammad's injunctions for temperance and bal-ance, and they overburden those believers who are not able to adhere to the rigid interpretations of the militant streams. While al-Qaradawi sympathizes with the extremists' call for the injection of shariah rulings into all areas of Muslim society, he takes serious objection to using extreme and militant measures for the realization of an Islamic state.[39]

For al-Qaradawi, the imposition of an Islamic state, particularly through militant means, is premature and will impose undue demands on a society that is not yet ready. While he does believe that establishing an Islamic state, one that "applies shariah and strives to unite all Muslims under the banner of Islam," is a duty of all Muslims, he also argues that Muslim society is not ready for the Islamic state. Much work remains to be done, including getting Muslims on board. He describes this task as the need to "unite all efforts, to remove all obstacles, to convince the suspecting minds of the nobility of the cause, to bring up Islamically oriented youngsters, and to prepare local as well as international public opinion to accept their ideology and the state." This effort, al-Qaradawi writes, requires "time and, indeed, perseverance." For this reason, he calls on the extremist elements to revise their approach given the Quran's emphasis on gradation. They ought to focus on the type of activity that will prepare the ground for the Islamic state as opposed to forcing it on a society that, at the current moment, would be overburdened by its implementation.[40] Moreover, he argues, the extremist elements ought to realign themselves with a proper understanding of what God has required of them. The extremist elements must return to and respect the juridical class that specializes in providing the interpretation of the shariah; these interpretations, through their balance, exhibit a serious and learned engagement with the authoritative texts.[41] Even the "Rightly Guided Caliphs," he reminds us, respected the expertise and specialization of a learned class and often consulted "their learned Companions when confronted with critical issues."[42]

Salman bin Fahd bin Abdullah al-Ouda

Salman bin Fahd bin Abdullah al-Ouda, better known as Salman al-Ouda, is a Saudi-born and Saudi-based Islamic cleric and writer. He directs the Arabic editions of *Islam Today* and, through his work, has become a popular media personality. His critiques of al-Qaeda and of Osama bin Laden, in particular, have garnered a wide audience in the Middle East. Not only does al-Ouda have a tremendous following and status—listed as number 16 on the 2014–15 "Muslim 500"—but he also is a high-profile critic of the Saudi regime.[43] Notably, bin Laden mentions al-Ouda by name in his 1996 epistle, arguing that al-Ouda's arrest and imprisonment by the Saudi regime in 1994 was a signal of the regime's intransigence and refusal to accept a critique from those who could help guide it toward the right path.

Although al-Ouda still vocalized support for the Saudi regime, he and a group of other clerics criticized the Saudi royal family for its lack of participation and consultation with the country's Islamic scholars on matters related to the relationship between Saudi law and its adherence to shariah law. He was part of two major petitions to the Saudi regime in the early 1990s, asking for the establishment of a consultative council or other mechanism to ensure clerical (religious) oversight of media-, law-, and other government-related affairs. Al-Ouda was imprisoned by the Saudis from 1994 until 1999 and emerged with a changed perspective. Although one would think that his having reformed some of his positions after being imprisoned would hurt his credibility, his public works and attempts to reach ordinary Muslims through lectures, media, and the Internet have made him a respected and influential figure.

In an ironic turn of events, on September 14, 2007—approximately a decade after bin Laden named him in his 1996 epistle—al-Ouda publicly denounced al-Qaeda's actions and bin Laden by reading an "open letter" (رسالة مفتوحة) addressed to bin Laden on MBC, a popular Middle East television network. In this letter, addressed to "my brother Osama," al-Ouda describes the destruction of lives and property that al-Qaeda has caused as a lamentable and unnecessary result of its futile attempt to bring the world toward its goals of Muslim revitalization. The letter begins by asking bin Laden, "How much blood has been spilled? How many innocents, and children, and the elderly, and the infirm, and women have been killed or displaced or expelled in al-Qaeda's name?"[44]

He describes the consequences of al-Qaeda's tactics and notes the damage and suffering it has caused in Iraq and Afghanistan, thus undermining their chances for stability and for their citizens to have a normal life. He also details the destructive nature that al-Qaeda's ideas of apostasy have had on families and the unity of Muslims. Who, al-Ouda writes,

> is responsible, [I ask of you] my brother Osama, for promoting ideas of excommunication and bombings, and killing that have spread inside the whole family unit that has torn families apart and has led to sons calling their fathers infidels? Who is responsible for fostering a culture of violence and murder that has led people to shed the blood of their relatives in cold blood, rather than nurturing the spirit of love and tranquility that a Muslim family is supposed to have?
>
> Who is responsible for the young men who leave their mothers weeping, husbands who abandon their wives, whose small children wake up every day asking when Daddy is coming home? What answer can be given, when that father may very well be dead, or missing with no one knowing his fate? . . .

. . . My heart pains me when I think of the number of young people who had so much potential—who would have made such great and original contributions to society, who had so much to offer that was constructive and positive—who have been turned into living bombs.

Further, al-Ouda argues, the image of Islam in the world today has been marred, to the great detriment of Muslims and the religion. He writes,

The image of Islam today, my brother Osama bin Laden, is not at its best, as people throughout the world are saying that Islam kills those who do not submit to this religion, and they are also saying that the Salafis kill those among the Muslims who do not adhere to their views.

Importantly, al-Ouda critiques al-Qaeda's actions on Islamic grounds, pointing out that the killing of innocents—a primary tactic in al-Qaeda's model of war—is categorically prohibited and that resorting to force should be done only when all other options have been exhausted. He reminds bin Laden that, contrary to al-Qaeda's stance on the necessity and religious obligation of jihad, Muhammad detested war.

In reality, our Prophet (peace be upon him) refused to kill the treacherous hypocrites in his midst, even though God had revealed to him who they were and informed him that they were destined for the deepest depths of hell. For this, he gave the following reason: "I will not have people saying that Muhammad kills his companions."

Moreover, he continues, the events of September 11 and al-Qaeda's actions since that day constitute the murder of innocents, leaving blood on the hands of Osama and those within his fray. He urges bin Laden to consider alternative actions that, according to al-Ouda, are not only permissible but also encouraged within Islam and successful in moving toward Muslim revitalization. In contrast to the three thousand innocent lives lost on September 11, he writes,

Muslim preachers—who remain unknown and unheralded—have succeeded in guiding hundreds of thousands of people to Islam, people who have ever since been guided by the light of faith and whose hearts are filled with the love of God. Is not the difference between one who kills and one who guides obvious?[45]

Sayyed Imam al-Sharif, "Dr. Fadl"

Sayyed Imam al-Sharif, better known as Dr. Fadl, was a prominent figure in the jihadi community whose public profile only increased after his 2008 condemnation of bin Laden, al-Zawahiri, al-Qaeda, and other elements fighting the jihad in their home countries against apostate rulers. Dr. Fadl's notoriety stems from the fact that he was an ardent supporter of the militant cause, at least until he was imprisoned by Egyptian authorities. While in prison he had a change of heart about using violence to establish an Islamic state. Once considered a luminary thinker by those in militant circles, including al-Zawahiri and bin Laden, and a major religious guide for al-Qaeda, his condemnation of the tactics of al-Qaeda and like-minded groups reverberated in the jihadi community. His relationship with al-Qaeda and al-Zawahiri, in particular, is significant to the weight of his critique. As he made the details of his biography and relationship with al-Qaeda available in a recent newspaper interview, I provide them here.

Al-Sharif was born approximately seventy miles south of Cairo, in the Egyptian governorate of Beni Suef in August 1950. He grew up in a pious Muslim family, tracing its lineage on both sides to Muhammad. He showed significant academic promise throughout his life and was enrolled in a school for exceptional students in his teen years in Cairo. He then attended the Faculty of Medicine at Cairo University and, by his own account, graduated at the top of his class in 1974. He then went on to specialize in surgery. Although he had memorized the Quran at an early age and spent significant time in personal study of shariah law, al-Sharif is not a trained Islamic cleric.[46] However, his standing in the jihadi community was significant owing both to his publications on jihad and to his time in the Afghan jihad.

While he claims neither to have been a member of the Muslim Brotherhood in Egypt nor to have associated with any of its members, al-Sharif states that his "interest in Islam as a general system" began in 1965 after the government cracked down on the group and executed Qutb for plotting the assassination of Nasser in 1966 (see chapter 2). These events moved al-Sharif from an individual who was observant in his religious practice to one who began to understand Islam and shariah law as a comprehensive system that ought to direct all aspects of Muslim life (including politics). He notes that in high school he began to study the books of shariah law, and through this "scientific method of study," coupled with the aid of a few trained clerics, he learned to approach the shariah systematically.[47] Despite his growing belief that implementing shariah law was the path to revitalizing Egypt, al-Sharif maintains that he did not join any of the Islamist groups proliferating at the time as he saw error in all their approaches (based on his study of the law).

Despite these assertions, though, al-Sharif had a relationship with Ayman al-Zawahiri that is the cause of much speculation. He met al-Zawahiri in 1968 when they were both students at the Faculty of Medicine in Cairo, but al-Zawahiri did not ask al-Sharif to join his organization until 1977. At this point, al-Sharif refused to join, arguing that al-Zawahiri's group did not have appropriate leadership, for there were no clerics or others proficient or trained in shariah law to direct them. Al-Sharif considered this type of traditional religious leadership as a critical component of a proper militant organization.[48] Although he did not join al-Zawahiri's group, the two still maintained enough of a relationship that the Egyptian government accused al-Sharif of participating in the plan to assassinate Anwar Sadat. The incident led to a clampdown on all Islamist elements in Egypt at the time, including al-Zawahiri's group. Both al-Zawahiri and al-Sharif fled to Pakistan—though several years apart—with the latter's being tried and eventually exonerated in absentia.[49]

While in Afghanistan, al-Zawahiri tried to convince al-Sharif that the Afghan jihad was an opportune time to build support for the jihad in Egypt (and the overthrow of the Egyptian regime). Al-Sharif, however, according to his recollection of the events, disagreed with al-Zawahiri, arguing that he could not form a group without those properly trained in Islamic law to help guide it in the appropriate ways. At that point, al-Zawahiri asked al-Sharif to take on that role for his group, and he agreed. By his account, though, he did not join formally. He attempted to dissuade the Egyptian jihadis in Afghanistan from fighting, as the organizations were not strong enough to reach their goals and the use of force would inevitably do more harm than good.

Al-Sharif claims that he continued to provide shariah guidance to the Egyptian and other groups that were in Afghanistan and became one of the most important religious leaders for the Arabs in the Afghan jihad. His counsel was related to matters of outreach and preaching—and not necessarily the use of force. In fact, he claims that al-Qaeda's leadership got to the point where "they would do nothing without consulting me," but he argued his role encompassed advising them only on shariah law.[50]

Al-Sharif's assessment of these events comes from a 2008 interview with *al-Hayat*; therefore, it is difficult to know with certainty if his claims are disingenuous. Al-Sharif's perspective on these events is hard (though not impossible) to believe. This is primarily because in 1988 while in Peshawar he had written "The Essential Guide for Preparation [for the jihad]," which was used in al-Qaeda training camps and, by all accounts, stressed a militant view for Muslim revitalization. He entrusted the publication and distribution of his second book, "The Compendium on Religious Study," to al-Zawahiri. In fact, this second book led to the final break between al-Sharif and al-Zawahiri, with al-Sharif accusing al-Zawahiri of bastardizing his ideas through a series of revisions and edits. According to al-Sharif, he was enraged particularly because al-Zawahiri and the other members of al-Qaeda's shariah council had no competence or training to edit a book on religious subjects. Al-Sharif then moved his family to Yemen and cut ties with militant groups. He was working quietly in a hospital in Sana'a, where Yemeni authorities questioned him after September 11. He turned himself in, spent three years in a Yemeni detention center, and in 2004 was transferred to an Egyptian prison, where he is currently serving a life sentence.[51]

Thus, this history colors al-Sharif's change of heart. In 2007 al-Sharif's new book, "Document of Right Guidance for Jihad Activity in Egypt and the World," vociferously critiqued al-Qaeda as well as the greater jihadi movement. It was published serially in both *Al-Jarida* (Kuwaiti daily publication) and *Al-Masri Al-Yawm* (Egyptian daily publication). It is important to note that al-Sharif, in this book, does not argue against the need for an Islamic state or against al-Qaeda's foundational interpretation of the pernicious policies of the West toward Islam. He indeed shares their mind-set and belief that the Muslim world is in a period of oppression and subjugation as a result of Western influence and power. For example, in part 1, al-Sharif writes that the Islamic nation,

> lived as one nation [united], and feared, for thirteen hundred years until the fall of the Ottoman Caliphate in the first world war (1914–18), when Muslims were weakened and scattered into fragments. And with the weakening of the Ottoman Caliphate at the end of the 19th century, the European nations captured most of the Muslim world, dividing it, weakening it, and plundering its wealth, depriving it of industrial progress, and keeping its people in a state of disunity, poverty, and underdevelopment, and imposed its culture and its law onto the land of Muslims by force of military occupation. Then these European nations proceeded to establish a state for the Jews (Israel) in the heart of the Muslim world in order to exhaust and to humiliate [the Muslim world].[52]

Thus, al-Sharif does not contest al-Qaeda's ends but its *means*. While al-Sharif asserts that Muslim weakness is attributed to the policies and interference of other others, he is quick to note that the nonviolent means to addressing these injustices are many. Important for our purposes, al-Sharif grounds his argument in Islamic reasoning. "There are many pathways," he writes, "for Muslims who are pursuing answers from shariah law in our present age, and in order to address the powerful nations that humiliate and weaken them." He insists too that the Shariah provides the guidance and the answers for responding to current Muslim ills. Moreover, he argues, violent means—particularly as undertaken by various militant Islamist groups, including al-Qaeda—are not only unacceptable but also contrary to the dictates of God. These groups, he contends, their ignorance of shariah law and what it requires and allows, have caused destruction and strife that clearly transgress Islamic law. He writes,

> Some of the Muslim groups have resorted to clashes with those in power in their own countries or with the great powers and their citizens—all in the pursuit of jihad in the name of God Almighty, so that they may elevate Islam. And they have spread this strife in various countries from the far east to the far west. These clashes have violated shariah rulings, such as the murder of innocent citizens, and the murder of people for reasons such as skin color or hair color, and murder over doctrinal differences and the murder of Muslims and non-Muslims whom it is prohibited to kill.[53]

Al-Sharif clearly warns that God will answer such destruction. "Nothing," he writes, "brings the wrath and indignation of the Lord than the unlawful spilling of blood and the destruction of treasury."[54] These jihadi groups, he argues, have succeeded only in killing innocents, bringing insecurity and havoc to Muslim countries, and engaging in unlawful acts while justifying these actions in terms of bringing about an Islamic state. For al-Sharif, it is not that the cause is wrong or unworthy, as he too asserts the need to institute shariah law in the political mechanisms of Muslim states. Rather, the militant Islamist groups are fighting a battle that is sure to fail and, in the process, are engaging in acts that are clearly unlawful or beyond the bounds of God's law. He therefore calls on these Muslims to observe the restrictions and limits on the use of force that he points out are unambiguously stated in the sources. Al-Sharif writes that he is publishing his book for this reason— to correct the multiple misperceptions of what these texts not only require but also what they allow for and from the believer.

> And the signatories of this document state their dissatisfaction of these transgressions against the shariah [caused by militant groups] . . . and

which has led to these evils, and they recall to themselves and to every Muslim the shariah restrictions . . . regarding the jihad, and declare their commitment to the restrictions contained in this document and call other Muslims, and especially the Muslim youth to commit to it . . . and the jihadist groups throughout the world to abide by them.[55]

For example, al-Sharif maintains that jihad requires permission from parents, from debtors, from spouses, and so on. He also disputes the al-Qaeda narrative, which commands that waging the jihad is one's duty above all else, and insists that the Muslim can engage in the process of bringing about an Islamic state in a number of other ways. Those who travel to other countries to wage the jihad—without these permissions and while neglecting their responsibilities to their spouses, children, parents, and so on—he says, are in transgression of God's law.[56] He is particularly critical of how the leaders of the militant organizations read the sources, arguing that these men are unqualified to derive rulings or guidance from the Quran or the hadiths and that, moreover, they are spreading this ignorance through the Internet.[57] Muslims, al-Sharif argues, have been led astray; they "are ruled by emotions and with their ears and now with their minds—that is, they admire what they hear without considering its true nature in their minds."[58] Those who claim to fight the United States—the force of oppression—have led them astray without considering the Shariah and its "knowledge concerning the conditions [required] for actions [to be permitted]."[59]

Al-Sharif is particularly critical of al-Qaeda, bin Laden, and al-Zawahiri, stressing the point that they had no qualified religious scholars among their inner circle. September 11, he argues, was characteristic of the type of chaos and damage created by militant Islamist groups. He chastises bin Laden for disobeying Mullah Omar and derides the September 11 operation as transgressing a legal agreement that the hijackers had with the United States. They had entered the United States on visas—a type of *aman,* or a "contract of safe passage and protection" (described in chapter 2)—and then violated that agreement by acting treacherously against the nation. Moreover, when the men compared their deed to Muhammad's actions against his enemies, they had mocked the religion and his example in ways that clearly indicated the illegal nature of the September 11 attack.

The followers of bin Laden entered America with his knowledge and by his order, and they acted perfidiously towards its people, and killed and destroyed. . . . Then they called their treachery and their perfidy a "raid" in order to compare their actions to the Prophet's raids. To tie their perfidy and treachery to the Prophet is to diminish him and to mock him, and the punishment for diminishing the worth of the Prophet is well-known to Muslims.[60]

Just as important, he maintains, their actions were catastrophic for Muslims. In fact, al-Sharif proposes convening a shariah court to try bin Laden and his associates for their crime. Al-Sharif wants a trial for two reasons: to hold the men accountable for their transgressions against God and the calamity they caused for Muslims and Islam, and to ensure that the general Muslim population understands the illegal nature of al-Qaeda and its operations so that those who are "ignorant in their religion do not repeat this futility."[61]

[Al-Qaeda] ignited strife that found its way into every home, and they were the cause of the imprisonment of thousands of Muslims in the prisons of various countries. They caused the death of tens of thousands of Muslims—Arabs, Afghans, Pakistanis, and others. The Taliban's Islamic Emirate was destroyed, and Al-Qaeda was destroyed. They were the direct cause of the American occupation of Afghanistan and other heavy losses which there is not enough time to mention here. They bear the responsibility for all of this.[62]

Conclusion

This chapter demonstrates the outlines of an ongoing and critical debate in the Muslim world. As noted, a wide cross section of influential Muslim thinkers contests al-Qaeda's narrative directly, particularly its insistence that Islam requires Muslims to take up arms and to participate in terrorist acts to regenerate their current societies. Although their positions are varied, all argue that al-Qaeda's insistence on the use of indiscriminate force is destructive, counterproductive, and, most important, based on a misunderstanding of what Islam requires.

If we conceptualize al-Qaeda as a theological narrative—one that gives meaning and direction to certain Muslims—then responding to al-Qaeda requires that we recognize and understand the alternative (and nonmilitant) ways that the vast majority of Muslim thinkers conceptualize the proper relationship between Islam, statecraft, and the use of force. To put it plainly, thinking of al-Qaeda as a theological narrative—that is, as a set of religious commitments that drive militant behavior—leads us to suggest that delegitimizing al-Qaeda necessitates alternative (nonmilitant) methods to counter it.

The fact that rampant opposition to al-Qaeda from influential Muslim voices exists then leads us to an important question: What part might the United States have (if any) in promoting the moderate position as a part of its strategic plan in the war against al-Qaeda?

Notes

1. While these figures use the terms "fundamentalist," "extremist," "puritan," and so on, to describe a train of intellectual thought and praxis in Islam, I retain the term "militant." I argue that it captures the characterizing feature of al-Qaeda's nature—that is, its insistence on using force to achieve its goals.

2. Kelsay, *Arguing the Just War*, 166.

3. For a brief summary of such statements, see Charles Kurzman, "Islamic Statements against Terrorism," http://kurzman.unc.edu/islamic-statements-against -terrorism/. See also Tahir-ul-Qadri, *Fatwa on Terrorism*, http://www.dailykos.com /story/2007/09/18/386670/-Saudi-Cleric-s-Ramadan-Letter-to-Osama-Bin-Laden -on-NBC.

4. See, for example, Haykel, "Salafi Thought and Action," in Meijer, *Global Salaf- ism*, 33–57.

5. An-Na'im, *Islam and the Secular State*, 16–20.

6. Abou El Fadl, *Great Theft*, 36.

7. Ibid. While Abou El Fadl is right to claim that the ulema's authority has eroded, it is important to note that the scholars still retain authority. For an excellent source on this point, see Zaman, *Ulama in Contemporary Islam*.

8. Abou El Fadl, *Great Theft*, 38–39.

9. Sachedina, *Islamic Roots*, 11.

10. Tibi, *Islam between Culture and Politics*, 24–68.

11. Ibid., 57. Abou El Fadl and An-Na'im also support the idea that the Islamic tradition is based on a set of shared beliefs.

12. Ibid., 65. Tibi is particularly insistent on what he terms the "post-Qur'anic" status of the hermeneutical methods (*qiyas, ijma, ijtihad*) of the early jurists, who, in their attempt to construct shariah law, "attached a law to the revealed word of God, the Qur'an."

13. Abou El Fadl, *Great Theft*, 150.

14. An-Na'im, *Islam and the Secular State*, 13.

15. Ibid., 31–32.

16. Sachedina, *Islamic Roots*, 84.

17. Quran 2:254.

18. Sachedina, *Islamic Roots*, 90.

19. Ibid., 22–63.

20. Quoted in ibid., 37.

21. Quoted in ibid., 39.

22. Abou El Fadl, *Great Theft*, 208.

23. Ibid., 213.

24. Ibid., 226.

25. Ibid., 231.

26. Stanley Kurtz, "Text and Context," in *The Place of Tolerance in Islam* (Boston: Beacon Press, 2002), 52.

27. An-Na'im, *Islam and the Secular State*, 53.

28. Al-Qaradawi, *Islamic Awakening*, 33.

29. Ibid., 33–46.

30. Ibid., 43–44. Explanation in brackets is mine.

31. Ibid., 83–95.

32. Ibid., 70–71.

33. Ibid., 50.

34. Al-Qaradawi's views on jihad are elaborated in a recently published book. He argues that while jihad in self-defense (i.e., the jihad of the Palestinians) is Islamically appropriate, the jihad of al-Qaeda—particularly in light of its indiscriminate targeting of civilians and its lack of established authority—is forbidden on Islamic grounds. This book has not, at the time of writing, been translated into English. For translated excerpts, see Gregory M. Reichberg, Henrik Syse, and Nicole M. Hartwell, ed. *Religion, War, and Ethics: A Sourcebook of Textual Traditions* (New York: Cambridge University Press, 2014), 379–80.

35. Al-Qaradawi, *Islamic Awakening*, 25.

36. Ibid., 25–26.

37. Ibid., 156.

38. Ibid., 82.

39. Ibid., 50–51.

40. Ibid., 163.

41. Ibid., 150–51.

42. Ibid., 151.

43. The "Muslim 500" is an annual report (Amman, Jordan: Royal Islamic Strategic Studies Center and the Prince al-Waleed bin Talal Center for Muslim-Christian Understanding at Georgetown University) that ranks influential Muslims throughout the world. See http://themuslim500.com/ (last accessed August 12, 2015).

44. Al-Ouda, "Ramadan Letter." My translation.

45. Ibid. My translation.

46. Al-Sharif, "Major Jihadi Cleric."

47. Ibid., 4.

48. Ibid., 5.

49. Ibid.

50. Ibid., 6.

51. Ibid.

52. Sayyed Imam al-Sharif, "Document of Right Guidance for Jihad Activity in Egypt and the World," (Arabic), part 1, 2007, http://www.qassimy.com/vb/show thread.php?t=161063. My translation.

53. Ibid.

54. Ibid.

55. Ibid.

56. Ibid., parts 4 and 5.

57. Ibid., part 2.

58. Al-Sharif, "Major Jihadi Cleric," 3.

59. Ibid.

60. Ibid.

61. Ibid.

62. Ibid.

Conclusion

Operationalizing Counter-narratives in the War against al-Qaeda

The War against al-Qaeda demonstrates the necessity of shifting focus to one that understands the al-Qaeda phenomenon through the religious narrative that gives it meaning and direction. It shows how a series of al-Qaeda ideologues have radicalized a narrative that references Islamic texts, symbols, and history, culminating in a tactical and strategic model of war that is diffuse, decentralized, and indiscriminate. This book also outlines various influential Muslim thinkers who contest the legitimacy of the al-Qaeda narrative, arguing that it departs severely from the normative moral restraints on war that are a part of the Islamic tradition.

Looking at al-Qaeda from this perspective—as a meaning-giving, action-guiding narrative that is *contested*—naturally requires that we consider the consequences of this conceptualization of al-Qaeda, and leads us to ask how it ought to be folded into the US response to the al-Qaeda phenomenon. In other words, if al-Qaeda is thought of as a religious narrative, and influential *counter-narratives* are available, then what are the implications for the US response to al-Qaeda?

Voices in the foreign policy community have argued for the need to respond to the narrative that drives the al-Qaeda phenomenon. Moreover, a trend in research on "radicalism" points toward the importance of narratives.[1] The idea has been presented through a variety of titles: "strategic communication," "responding to the ideology," "propaganda," "counter-messaging," and "counter-radicalization." The differences between these various labels are important to recognize, yet the general idea of these proposals is the same: There is a need to respond to the set of ideas that are undergirding the al-Qaeda phenomenon, often referred to as "militant Islam," "radical Islam," or another equivalent label indicating the militant and religious nature of the phenomenon described.

For clarity I continue to use the term "counter-narratives" as a general label for the work described in this chapter. I define *counter-narratives* as the attempt to delegitimize, deflate, disrupt, destroy, and dismantle the al-Qaeda narrative, which argues that indiscriminate violence and terrorism, at the hands of individuals, are not only justified and necessary but also part of a religiously mandated duty for all Muslims. I label the work that falls under this umbrella, generally, as the "counter-narrative initiative." These initiatives are not necessarily connected to each other in explicit ways (institutional or otherwise), but as I began to collect the information available, it became clear that a small but influential segment of policy influencers were arguing that responding to and fighting the "ideological battle" were critical and missing components of the US response to al-Qaeda.[2] The question, however, is if and how it can be done ethically, responsibly, and effectively.

Those arguing for the incorporation of counter-narratives in the US response have initiated a noteworthy discussion. And while the discussion remains relatively undertheorized—particularly in its use of certain terms (i.e., "radicalism," "radicalization," etc.) and its understanding of Islam—the voices that have joined the counter-narrative initiative raise significant points. Of critical importance, of course, is the question of whether the US government ought to incorporate the idea of counter-narratives in its policies formally and, if so, how it can be done in an ethical and appropriate manner given US commitments to a separation between religion and government. In this chapter, I begin by concentrating on the segment of the counter-narrative initiative that argues for direct US involvement in contested theological issues within contemporary debates about Islam. As one can imagine, a series of discomforts are involved when we consider the possibility of the US government's entering arenas that are theological by nature. In this way, our discussion in this concluding chapter, bolstered by the claims made in this book, help identify both the strengths and the vulnerabilities in the counter-narrative approach. I conclude by using this critical assessment to provide a set of recommendations for moving forward.

Counter-narratives: Recommendations and US Foreign Policy

The idea of counter-narratives in the war against al-Qaeda was initiated early after September 11. For example, a RAND Corporation study published in 2003 notes the importance of acquiring a "finely grained understanding of the ongoing ideological struggle within Islam, to identify appropriate partners and set realistic goals and means to encourage its evolution in a positive way."[3] Additionally, in 2004, the Center for Contemporary Conflict at the US Naval Postgraduate School published a paper on a "counter-narrative strategy." The United States, the authors argued, faces a "nascent insurgency" that has an "Islamic character." Its associated groups are built on "complicated political, economic, social and religious circumstance[s] that have been combined by Ayman Al Zawahiri into a sweeping narrative that forms a backdrop to the social networks that are now arguably driving Al Qaeda organizational structure."[4] Noting this, they continue, the US approach to al-Qaeda would profit from a "counter-narrative strategy." More specifically, such a strategy, they write, "would benefit from a comprehensive consideration of the stories terrorists tell; understanding the narratives which influence the genesis, growth, maturation and transformation of terrorist organizations will enable us to better fashion a strategy for undermining the efficacy of those narratives so as to deter, disrupt and defeat terrorist groups."[5]

The energy on this idea, however, did not pick up speed until 2007–08. In particular, Cheryl Benard's report in 2003 and Angel Rabasa and colleagues' study in 2007 provide an excellent outline for the counter-narrative policy discussion. Together they help demonstrate the strengths and challenges associated with counter-narrative work and, for this reason, are worth reviewing in detail. Both reports make the same point: The United States, as a part of its response to the al-Qaeda phenomenon, ought to recognize the ways in which religious ideas are a part of the conversation. The reports' recommendations encourage the United States to stake a claim in the ongoing "war of ideas" in the contemporary Muslim world. For example, Benard asserts,

> There is no question that contemporary Islam is in a volatile state, engaged in an internal and external struggle over its values, its identity, and its place in the world. Rival versions are contending for spiritual and political dominance. This conflict has serious costs and economic, social, political, and security implications for the rest of the world. Consequently, the West is making an increased effort to come to terms with, to understand, and to influence the outcome of this struggle.[6]

The 2007 report concurs. It affirms that "the struggle underway throughout much of the Muslim world is essentially a war of ideas. Its outcome will determine the future direction of the Muslim world and whether the threat of jihadist terrorism continues, with some Muslim societies falling back even further into patterns of intolerance and violence. It profoundly affects the security of the West." In fact, the authors assert, the war of ideas in Islam is one "of the central issues of our time."[7]

As Muslim-majority countries are important world actors, the 2003 report observes that the "international community as a whole would prefer an Islamic world that is compatible with the rest of the system: democratic, economically viable, politically stable, socially progressive, and follows the rules and norms of international conduct." Thus, it seems prudent, Benard argues, for the United States to focus actively on encouraging "the elements within the Islamic mix that are most compatible with global peace and the international community and that are friendly to democracy and modernity."[8] For Benard, "radical Islam" is clearly contributing to terrorism and militant groups that are affecting both the "Muslim world" and the national security of the United States. It seems only reasonable, then, to conclude that the United States ought to respond to this issue.

Both reports note that in the "ideological struggle in Islam," the radical and militant elements have the upper hand in terms of resources, attention, and financing, which allow them significant influence that is well beyond their marginal numbers. Consequently, they argue, the United States ought to do what it can to provide material resources and other forms of support to those Muslims who not only share its interests but also are amenable to liberal democratic beliefs and practices. These reports use the term "moderate Muslims" to refer to this group of potential partners in the war against the al-Qaeda phenomenon. It is important to note that the reports' interpretation of this term differs from how chapter 5 uses it to refer to a group of thinkers writing *against* the al-Qaeda phenomenon. The reports' authors use the term as a category to indicate agreement on a set of marker issues that help determine *which* Muslims are true "moderates" and therefore amenable to US interests. In fact, the primary aim in Benard's 2003 report was to provide a set of criteria that would help decision makers both correctly identify the Muslims who were most receptive to the US government's democratic goals and, once identified, determine the best ways of supporting them through funds and other means. The report identifies four categories of Muslims:

- "fundamentalists" (divided into "radical" and "scriptural"), who are hostile to the West, seek a state ruled by shariah law, and reject democratic values and contemporary Western culture;
- "traditionalists" (divided into "conservative" and "reformist"), who seek a conservative society and are ill at ease with modernity;
- "modernists," who want to reform the Islamic world so that it can "become part of global modernity"; and
- "secularists" (divided into "mainstream" and "radical"), who accept the division of religion and government.[9]

The report also provides a table of "'Marker Issues' and the Major Ideological Positions in Islam" that places Muslims into the appropriate category based on their positions on a set of key issues: democracy, human rights and individual liberties, polygamy, Islamic criminal penalties, hijab, beating of wives, status of minorities, Islamic state, public participation of women, jihad, and sources referenced for authority. For example, according to the report, on the issue of democracy, the radical fundamentalist position is that it is a "wrongful creed. Sovereignty and the right to legislate belong to God alone." The mainstream secularist position is "democracy is primary; Islam must (and can) bring itself into line with it and with the separation of church and state," while the modernist position is that "Islam contains democratic concepts that need to be brought to the forefront." On the issue of wife beating, the radical fundamentalist position is that the practice is "allowed and useful to control the behavior of women and to maintain hierarchy in the family." The mainstream secularist position does not permit it "because it is illegal, and against contemporary norms and human rights," while the modernist would argue that the practice is "not allowed, based on incorrect religious interpretation, and [is] clearly against the spirit of Islamic concept of marriage and gender relations."[10]

The table is meant for quick reference and as a tool for "mapping" positions on certain issues to determine where a particular Muslim falls on the spectrum outlined in the report. The report, moreover, goes on to elaborate in more detail each of these outlined marker issues and the various positions Muslims take. The idea is thus to help identify the appropriate partners in the US effort to assist moderate Muslims in amplifying their message above and beyond that of the radicals.

Noting that there is no easy fix, Benard's 2003 study suggests a "mixed approach that rests on firm and decisive commitments to our own fundamental values and understands that tactical and interest-driven cooperation is simply not possible with some of the actors and positions along the spectrum of political Islam."[11] Therefore, Benard continues, US policy regarding Islam ought to "support the modernists first, *enhancing their vision of Islam over that of the traditionalists* by providing them with a broad platform to articulate and disseminate their views. They, not the traditionalists, should be *cultivated and publicly presented as the face of contemporary Islam*" (emphasis mine).[12]

The report takes this position because the modernist vision is most amenable to the liberal, democratic values espoused by the United States. As Benard notes, it is "modernism, not traditionalism," that "worked for the West." By this, the author is referring to the fact that various forms of prescriptions and values contained in the Old Testament, for example, are abhorrent to modern sensibilities. As a result of modernism, a majority of Western people read those texts as historical documents written in a particular context and not as categorical prescriptions for conducting politics, family relations, or economic policy. A similar development, Benard argues, would suit Muslim people. Insofar as this is "exactly the approach that Islamic modernists propose," supporting them in their efforts makes sense.[13] After the modernists, secularists should be supported on a "case-by-case" basis, while traditionalists should be supported selectively and primarily to keep them viable against fundamentalists. The fundamentalists should be directly contested by "striking at vulnerabilities in their Islamic and ideological postures," thereby revealing "their corruption, their brutality, their ignorance, the bias and manifest errors in their application of Islam, and their inability to lead and govern."[14]

In their report, Rabasa and colleagues pick up and develop Benard's ideas. In much the same way, they argue that while "moderate Muslim networks and institutions would provide a platform to amplify the message of moderates," they lack the resources necessary to construct such networks and need an "external catalyst"—that is, funding, support, and other resources from the United States. The report notes, "The United States and Western countries can do little to affect the outcome of this 'war of ideas' directly, as only Muslims themselves have the credibility to challenge the misuse of Islam by extremists." Yet, Rabasa and colleagues continue, "Moderates will not be able to successfully challenge radicals until the playing field is leveled, which the West can help accomplish by promoting the creation of moderate Muslim networks."[15]

They develop this idea by pointing to the Americans' experience in the Cold War, when the US government exerted significant resources and energy in promoting individuals and organizations that were contesting communism in the Soviet Union. Their report provides a summary of US efforts in the Cold War to foster the intellectual movement against communism. When it was most successful, the US government acted similar to a foundation, providing money and resources to various anticommunist figures and organizations but in a "hands-off" approach. For example, it kept a low profile on its support to these organizations and, moreover, steered clear from their agendas and activities, ensuring that their decisions and leadership were relatively independent from US involvement.[16] In particular, the report describes the Congress for Cultural Freedom, a US-funded effort that had significant success until its financial link to the United States was exposed.[17] Using the US experience against communism during the Cold War as a model, the report recommends that the US federal government make the building of moderate Muslim networks an explicit goal.

Moreover, Rabasa and colleagues recommend concentrating US efforts to building moderate Muslim networks in places outside the Middle East, arguing that other parts of the Muslim world are more agreeable to this project and ought to be buttressed so that their influence can eventually be exerted on the more radical components of Islam found in Middle Eastern countries.[18] For example, the authors list intellectuals and programs in Europe, the United States, and Southeast Asia that are vital resources in the "ongoing war of ideas within the Muslims world, as well as in the effort to build moderate Muslim networks in this study."[19]

Additionally, the study notes a set of marker issues demonstrating characteristics of "moderate" Muslims: a commitment to democracy, implying a commitment to human rights and a rejection of the Islamic state; an acceptance of nonsectarian sources of law; a respect for women's and minority rights; and an opposition to terrorism and illegitimate violence.[20] Moderate Muslims are defined as those who share these "key dimensions of democratic culture" and those who support "internationally recognized human rights (including gender equality and freedom of worship) . . . [and] respect for diversity."[21] The report suggests that the United States ought to provide support to "liberal and secular" Muslim academics and intellectuals, "young moderate religious scholars," activists, women's groups that promote gender equality, and "moderate" journalists and writers, all in an effort to work toward the priorities of developing democratic education, gaining positive media coverage of moderate Muslims' ideas, achieving gender equality, and engaging moderate Muslims' voices more loudly in policy advocacy and the building of democratic civil society.[22]

Both reports recognize that supporting moderate and secular Muslims has its challenges. They point to the moderates' widely held belief that supporting these goals will discredit them and somehow taint their reputations and influence such that they will be seen as representatives of US, rather than Muslim, interests. Both reports, however, while acknowledging this challenge, also contend that the assumption may be overstated. Moreover, they both argue, in a world in which only imperfect policy tools and solutions exist, supporting moderate Muslims remains a strong policy option.[23]

One of the most interesting components of these reports is that their authors worry about the possibility that the United States will support false moderates, or Muslims who appear to be moderate in the ways the reports define this category (supporting democracy and human rights, taking a middle-of-the-road approach, and so on) but who, in response to certain events, have advocated using some form of violence. In particular, the authors are concerned that Muslims who fall into the traditionalist category are likely to present this danger. At first glance, they appear to be excellent partners to support because, according to Benard, they "enjoy widespread public legitimacy in the eyes of the Muslim population." Moreover, they "tend to be more middle-of-the-road, more moderate, [and] a calming influence," and they "are open to, and in fact often proactively seek, interfaith dialogue." Although the traditionalists "do not usually advocate violence," Benard cautions that some of them have sympathized with those who "have chosen that path, to the point of sheltering them, providing them with resources, and abetting their actions."[24] Moreover, certain groups attempt to pass themselves off as traditionalists when they are, in fact, "a front for more-radical affiliations." In addition, even "without a deliberate attempt to mislead," the "views and values" of traditionalists and fundamentalists are "often so close that only a very fine line divides them." Furthermore, they often share institutions and other types of infrastructure and space.[25]

Rabasa and colleagues continue this line of thought. Their reports list the dangers of supporting Muslims or Muslim organizations that posture as moderates but are, in fact, linked to extremist groups. For example, the study lists Nadeema Elyas, the former head of a German Muslim organization (Zentralrat der Muslime in Deutschland), as presenting

> an example of how difficult it can be to assess the true posture of self-identified moderates. In his public statements in the German press, Elyas—sarcastically referred to as the "darling of the dialogue crowd" by the newspaper *Die Welt*—skirts issues such as whether it would be desirable for *shari'a* law to be an option for Muslims in Europe (or even seems to answer them in the negative, saying that it is irrelevant to discuss *shari'a* law, since its application requires an Islamic state, which does not exist in Germany). On his Web site, however, *shari'a* law is described as eternal and binding on all Muslims. Asked about polygamy, he will say only that one does not need to push for its recognition in Europe since it is "not an Islamic duty"; about Islamic penalties such as stoning, that these "could be open to discussion." Elyas neither openly endorses nor directly renounces these practices.[26]

Critiques of Counter-narratives

The point about carefully choosing which Muslims to support demonstrates the challenges associated with segments of the counter-narrative initiative that argue for the direct involvement of American policymakers. The strength of these studies—and of the counter-narrative initiative more broadly—is that they recognize a foundational point: Religious ideas are part of the global al-Qaeda phenomenon. The problematic aspect of this, however, is that their proposed policy recommendations ask American decision makers to enter an arena that is explicitly theological in nature. Both reports seek to provide a set of criteria that will help determine the *right* type of Muslim to support. In the task of fomenting and creating "civil democratic Islam" or "moderate Muslim networks," the authors advocate that certain versions of Islam should be presented as appropriate or true and others as inappropriate or as grave deviations of the Islamic tradition. This effort involves taking a clear and unambiguous step into *theological* discussions regarding what is "true" Islam, an area that is explicitly confessional in nature and therefore beyond the bounds of responsible US domestic and international politics.

Interestingly, the 2003 report itself takes note of this point. Benard argues, "Distinctions that may appear relatively minor in the grand scheme of things take on enormous importance because they signify allegiance or nonallegiance, victory or stalemate." For example, a Muslim's stance on the hijab, or Islamic veiling—that is, his or her thinking on whether women ought to (or must) veil—is a prime example of one issue that places Muslims on certain parts of the spectrum developed by the reports. Such marker issues are, according to the study, evidence of the explicitly religious nature of these categories and the disputes between them. Therefore, as Benard notes, "When U.S. government agencies appear to endorse the head scarf, for example, considering this to be a minor matter of preference in dress code that cheaply enables them to signal tolerance, they are in fact unwittingly taking a major stand on a central, wildly contested symbolic issue." Moreover, "they are aligning themselves with the extreme end of the spectrum, with the fundamentalists and the conservative traditionalists, against the reformist traditionalists, the modernists, and the secularists."[27]

Benard takes issue with the fact that by appearing to endorse or tolerate the headscarf, American policymakers seem to be taking the side of Muslims who are not oriented toward the moderate end of the spectrum. Yet both Benard's report and that of Rabasa and colleagues fail to note that by aligning themselves with *any* interpretation of Islam, American decision makers are being asked to take an explicitly *theological* position (as defined that way by the reports themselves) on what is "true" Islam. Taking a stand either way on the issue of the headscarf, or any other theological position marker, on the part of the US government is equally objectionable. While certain positions might appear to align more closely with democratic, liberal commitments, declaring a position on theological issues—regardless of whether they offend certain sensibilities—is out of the question for American policymakers. Unlike the Cold War example, in these studies, policymakers are being asked to align themselves with *religious* camps that appear more likely to foster US interests and quell violent or extremist elements—a step that would clearly enter a space that is fraught with problems and difficulties. This critique is no way intended to detract from the spirit of what the authors suggest—that is, pointing out that religious arguments have a key role at the table. Rather, I argue that American decision makers cannot condone, support, or foster one vision of Islam over another regardless of how much more amenable "moderate Muslim networks" or "civil democratic Islam" may be to US policy interests and to the interests of the international community.

Additionally, it is important to recognize that supporting a broader array of Muslim voices does not necessarily ameliorate the issues involved. For example, a Brookings analysis paper written by Rashad Hussain (who serves as the US special envoy to the Organisation of Islamic Cooperation and as the coordinator for strategic counterterrorism communications in the US State Department) and al-Husein N. Madhany illustrates this point.

Hussain and Madhany argue that counter-narratives ought to be formulated not in terms that suggest the battle of ideas is between democracy and Islam, for this conception, they argue, somehow indicates that Islam needs to be watered down or sidelined to enable Muslims to accept democratic governments, human rights, and other liberal ideas. Rather, American foreign policy makers ought to frame the battle of ideas as a conflict "between terrorist elements in the Muslim world and Islam."[28] This interpretation, the authors feel, more clearly demonstrates the point that it is not Islam being marginalized; instead, terrorism—as a specific tactic—is the target of this foreign policy initiative. For example, they point out terms such as "Islamic extremism" or "Islamic terrorism" are counterproductive and obfuscating, as they contradict other statements (made by the administration) that indicate Islam is a peaceful tradition. In addition, such statements appear to give credence to the idea that Islam is tied to or inspires acts of terrorism. Moreover, terms such as "Islamic extremism" alienate segments of the population that the administration is attempting to reach and whose cooperation it needs and that are critical to counterterrorism efforts. For these reasons, the authors argue, policymakers ought to identify the battle as one against al-Qaeda or another group and not as one against Islam.[29]

This point is especially important, the authors maintain, insofar as suspicion regarding "Western intervention" already exists in the Muslim world. Therefore, "it is unlikely that Muslims will react positively to hegemonic orders to 'clean up' their societies by implementing Western-style democratic reforms." Moreover, those whom policymakers wish to reach, presumably those on the fence or those who are "attracted to terrorist ideologies," will find calls to Western-style democracy much less compelling when compared to arguments against terrorism that are rooted in Islamic texts, ideas, symbols, discourse, and so on.[30]

This last point regarding the critical role of Islamic symbols and ideas leads the authors to posit that Islam is the most important tool in the US counterterrorism tool box and that Muslims are the most important ally. For the effort to be effective, though, the Americans must frame the war of ideas in such a way that it does not appear interested in watering down the influence of Islam and replacing it with Western-style democracy. Rather, the authors contend that counterterrorism efforts must "emphasize that engaging in terrorism is antithetical to the *Shariah* or Islamic law."[31] Thus, the explicit promotion of Western-style freedom and democracy as alternatives to terrorism is not the linchpin answer—particularly as, according to Hussain and Madhany, Muslim societies are likely to interpret these categories as akin to secularism and reject them. Rather, the "first and foremost task" is the "promotion of mainstream Islam, which policymakers as notable as President [George W.] Bush have stated constitutes the promotion of peace."[32] Furthermore, they note, "it is the job of the global counterterrorism coalition to articulate the idea that Islam requires those dissatisfied with Western foreign policy and the perceived spread of immorality, as well as other political and non-political grievances, to reject terrorism as a means of addressing their concerns."[33]

Like Benard's report and the study by Rabasa and colleagues, Hussain and Madhany write that a key component of counterterrorism is the necessity of "discrediting terrorist ideology" and that focusing on and supporting Muslim voices and institutions that argue Islam unequivocally prohibits terrorism is the way to do so. However, their suggested means are different than those proposed by the RAND studies. Rather than supporting moderates and secularists, Hussain and Madhany recommend a "broad and diverse collation of partners" that is "not limited to those who advocate Western-style democracy."[34] The United States ought to build this coalition in a way that incorporates Muslims with different political views as long as they reject the use of violence. It also ought to distribute materials from Islamic authorities that clearly outline the prohibition of terrorism in Islam and ought to strengthen the "authoritative voice of mainstream Islam" by supporting and encouraging the development of organizations that advocate it.[35]

The strength of Hussain and Madhany's analysis is that it also recognizes the role of religious ideas in the al-Qaeda phenomenon; however, like the

RAND studies, they also call for American policymakers to make state-ments—tantamount to religious truth claims—about Islam. Although it certainly is true that "mainstream Islam," or the vast majority of Muslims, does not support terrorism, the authors' recommendations are asking poli-cymakers to side with a specific religious expression of Islam. This is not to say that religiously backed terrorism of the al-Qaeda variety is a legitimate form of Islamic expression and ought to be protected. Clearly, that is not the point I wish to make. Rather, I argue that American policymakers ought to refrain from taking *any* theological position on "proper" Islam.

Samuel J. Rascoff articulates this point well in a *Stanford Law Review* article. He writes,

> In the name of national security, the U.S. government as well as state and local governments are increasingly intervening in the religious lives of Muslims and into Islam itself. These interventions—which implicate initiatives from intelligence gathering and analysis to prison management to community outreach—form an essential part of what is not commonly called "counter-radicalization." While the concept remains open-ended and undertheorized, the core intuition behind counter-radicalization is that the prevention of future violence re-quires official involvement in shaping the ideational currents that are thought to underpin that violence.

According to Rascoff, this type of counter-radicalization carries serious potential for "significant legal tension and strategic confusion." More specif-ically, it conflicts with US commitments to religious freedom as contained in the First Amendment. Such policies carry the danger of the US federal government's promoting an "official Islam," which he defines as "a govern-ment sponsored account of 'mainstream Islam' offered by the state in place of radical doctrinal alternatives."[36] Such policies lead the "State to prefer one religious teaching over another" and creates "good" versus "bad" Muslims.[37] As he writes, "For the government to formulate (or to pick out from among rival options) and endorse a preferred conception of Islam—in effect to play the role of theologian and missionary—raises potentially serious concerns rooted in the Establishment Clause and the values it enshrines."[38]

It is well within the government's purview to engage in secular counter-terrorism methods, those aimed at effecting "changes in religious ideation by addressing what are seen as its marginal causes without direct reference to or interference in religion or ideology." For example, initiatives that address social, political, or economic concerns of marginalized or at-risk communities are secular; hence, they are appropriate counter-radicalization activities for the US government.[39] Other types of initiatives—for example, those that "pursue its ends through explicitly religious means"—are inappropriate methods that Rascoff labels under the heading of "proselytization."[40] He gives a series of examples to illustrate initiatives that fall under this label.

> Under the command of General Doug Stone, American officials charged with overseeing the detention of Iraqi prisoners of war produced a "directory" that juxtaposed "moderate" and "radical" Koranic passages "in order to refute detainees when they use certain passages to support a radical interpretation of Islam." They also created "the world's most moderate Hadith" in order to harmonize classical Islamic learning with American strategic objectives. The U.S. State Department has also sponsored trips to majority-Muslim countries by Muslim-American religious leaders as part of an official effort to "bring a moderate perspective to foreign audiences on what it's like to be a practicing Muslim in the United States." At a recent Senate committee hearing devoted in part to aspects of contemporary counter-radicalization, a veteran FBI and CIA official called for formal imam training (though not with respect to theology) as part of a larger strategy.[41]

Of particular note are instances in which the government makes statements that describe Islam and, in the process, "sets out its preferred tenets of Official Islam."[42] For example, Rascoff lists statements by National Security Adviser John Brennan and Ambassador Robert Godec that have indicated "jihad" does not mean holy war but refers instead to a spiritual nonviolent struggle to purify one's self and to cultivate moral excellence. As Rascoff notes, this interpretation is a standard way of understanding the term "jihad"—one elaborated by many Muslims—but that is not what is at issue. Rather, the issue is that representatives of the US government have made theological statements about Islam in the name of national security.[43]

Moreover, he adds, strategically speaking, the US government has neither the reputation nor the expertise to make such statements on Islam or other religious traditions. It simply lacks the credibility to do so.

> Effective counter-radicalization programs of this kind require immense amounts of insight into questions that merge theology with cutting-edge social science. It is questionable whether any institution—let alone a secretive government bureaucracy that lacks a track record of social scientific insight—is well positioned to develop that

sort of analytical account. Second, the government may fail at counter-radicalization because of the messenger, not the message itself. . . . As a British commentator recently noted, "It is one thing for Muslim countries like Indonesia or Saudi Arabia to promote scholar-led, Qur'an based deradicalisation programmes, but quite another for non-Muslim countries like the United Kingdom and the United States. It just isn't credible."[44]

Lessons from Europe

It is important to note that similar policy recommendations are being made in Europe. For example, a February 2008 report by the Change Institute for the European Commission sought to identify and provide recommendations for responding to the ideas that lead individuals to decide to participate in terrorist acts. This study reviewed online materials related to terrorism (documents, chat rooms, blogs, and so on). Conducting fieldwork in Denmark, France, Germany, and the United Kingdom, researchers interviewed a variety of significant stakeholders, including community organizers, academics, government representatives, and others who had some kind of relationship to terrorist narratives or who had worked on the issue. The researchers also attended "public and semi-public" events that were organized by local Muslim groups of all varieties.[45] They identified religious narratives and ideas as a primary component of terrorism. However, it cautioned that European Muslim communities experienced and internalized these narratives as their members felt the difficult effects of being marginalized minorities while under a great deal of suspicion by their fellow citizens. Importantly, the report recognized that some members held "radical" interpretations of Islam but, at the same time, repudiated violence.

Just as significant for our purposes, the Change Institute report highlights the relevance of religious narratives to this issue, arguing that "radical" interpretations of Islam have provided better explanatory power for the question of "why they/their co-religionists experience hostility, discrimination, and in some cases violence, from others and states across the globe."[46] According to this research, the "violent radicals" can provide compelling explanations and answers to this question and, moreover, to how they think Muslims ought to defend themselves.

Interestingly, the Change Institute report made similar but more extensive recommendations than those in the reports from Benard and Rabasa and others. The former has approximately twenty-one recommendations, but I review only a sample that pertains specifically to our discussion of the religious nature of certain types of counter-narrative work. For example, the reports suggest that the European Union's policy ought to do the following:

- Identify theologians/imams and significant religious voices who have effectively made the counter-radical case. . . . Our UK field-work indicates that it is possible to counter radicalisation of institutions through detailed theological argument by theologians who are seen as more learned than violent radicals. Representing a spectrum of Islamic orientations, these theological and ideological counterarguments, including those being developed by women, should be synthesised and made widely available. Additionally, it requires recognition that some Islamic orientations will provide a more effective counter weight than others.
- Support development programmes for the training of Muslim civic society leadership potential and associated networks to create an ideologically and theologically literate leadership and counter weight within community settings.
- Assist in the development and alignment of networks of European and Member State Muslim theologians, religious and community leaders—including women and young people—who are alive to respective Member State contexts, and who are deemed to be legitimate authenticators of a counter discourse to that promoted by violent radicals.
- Provide funding and infrastructure to "progressive" individuals, and organizations and for communities of practitioners.[47]

The report also suggests recommendations that seem to be much less involved in Muslim theological arguments. For example, it advocates providing exit strategies for those radicals who want to leave their respective organizations. It also encourages dialogue between governments and the various Muslim organizations that are working on issues of importance to their communities. Yet the report still finds itself making recommendations that, in light of the previous arguments, are out of line for governments that emphasize a separation of religion and state or, as in the case of Germany, for example, that understand themselves as neutral on the issue of religious belief.

Just as important, recent reports from the Global Center on Cooperative Security (formerly the Center on Global Counterterrorism Cooperation) and the Institute for Strategic Dialogue (based in London) note that counter-narrative work is most effective when governments take an indirect and facilitative role.[48] While writing that such work is still "in its infancy" (at least insofar as counter-narratives as public policy are concerned), both reports argue that government can play some role in terms of alternative narratives but is most effective in the arena of strategic communication. Other avenues are prohibitive in that the credibility gap makes such efforts "ineffective or even counter-productive." Of course, taking an indirect role does not necessarily preclude activities that would fall under Rascoff's label of promoting "official Islam," but it gestures toward this very important point.

Both reports make an important recommendation that speaks directly to these concerns: The United Nations and governments should think about counter-narratives in terms of "strategic communication." The Institute for Strategic Dialogue report provides a "counter-messaging" spectrum divided into three types: government strategic communication, alternative narratives, and counter-narratives. Government strategic communication involves "action to get the message out about what government is doing, including public awareness activities," in order to "raise awareness, forge relationships with key constituencies and audiences and correct misinformation." Alternative narratives are developed to "undercut violent extremist narratives by focusing on what we are 'for' rather than 'against,'" and counter-narratives "directly deconstruct, discredit and demystify violent extremist messaging" by challenging it "through ideology, logic, fact or humour."[49]

While government can work on alternative narratives, its primary sphere (and, I would argue, its most *appropriate* sphere) is in strategic communication—that is, using its resources to provide a clear, straightforward explanation and analysis of its foreign policy initiatives in ways that thoughtfully incorporate the perceptions and concerns of those whom the message is trying to reach. It requires thinking about how government messaging speaks to the preexisting narratives that its intended audience finds credible.

Conclusions and Recommendations for Moving Forward

To begin, it is important to recognize encouraging points to the small but growing research under the counter-narrative initiative. For one, the relevant and interested community of decision makers and foreign policy influencers are taking the religious elements of the al-Qaeda phenomenon seriously. This is a good development, as it will open up new ground for understanding the al-Qaeda phenomenon that complements the available research. Additionally, the initiative has commendable goals. It is hard to argue against the virtues of democratic governance, the recognition of rights, the building of civil society, and, of course, the support of national security and defense. Those working on the counter-narrative initiative have realized that the important work must be premised on a more nuanced understanding of the threat—one that I believe is more accurate—and must be invested in finding solutions that take this perspective into account.

Meanwhile, some of their recommendations must be critically analyzed and approached with care. As noted by one of the RAND reports, "It is not an easy matter to transform a major world religion." Indeed. If nation building is a daunting task, then "religion-building" is immeasurably more perilous and complex.[50] Moreover, as Rascoff argued, it is also an *inappropriate* task for the US government. I thus close by providing three points of criticism and suggestions for how this initiative may be reoriented to incorporate the critical importance of the al-Qaeda narrative while steering away from the legal and ethical challenges of certain aspects of the counter-narrative initiative.

First, the policy recommendations, as they stand, ask the US federal government to intervene in a set of *theological* issues. The questions they address are centered on a theological-ethical debate regarding Islamic discourse and positions on proper statecraft, the use of force, and justice. Recognizing this point also leads us to observe that by choosing certain types of Muslims to receive support, the US government is in fact choosing to support one vision of Islam over others. I certainly recognize that promoting those who are interested in civic institutions and democratization seems to be a good action to take. However, the case remains: Choosing a certain type of Muslim over another is asking the US federal government to intervene in a theological debate.

Identifying appropriate "working partners" requires determining the theological commitments of Muslims on these issues. In this way, selecting certain Muslims over others forces the US government to implicitly or explicitly make normative statements about the Islamic tradition. It is inappropriate—both legally and ethically—for the United States to do this; thus, it should refrain from any recommendations that require American policymakers, decision makers, or federal institutions to make confessional statements about what Islam *is* or what it *is not*. Such statements are appropriate for confessional Muslims. They are not the purview of the US government.

Second, in requiring US involvement in these ways, counter-narrative initiatives are recommending policies and actions that the federal government is not equipped to handle. Primarily it lacks personnel with the appropriate training or expertise to "categorize" Muslims. Furthermore, those with training would more than likely shy away from this activity given the ends to which this effort would be put. It is one thing for a researcher to place Muslim thought into some kind of typology to help further our understanding of Islamic history or discourse, but it is quite another to do it so that the federal government can provide funding and other aid to select Muslims in order to bolster their understanding and vision of Islam over that of others. Furthermore, the initiative does not take serious note of the historical facts of contestation and disagreement in religious traditions. Disagreement is part and parcel of the history of all religious tradition, and Islam is no exception. That different types of Muslims exist (or different types of Christians, Jews, Buddhists, Jains, Sikhs, and so on) is a material and historical fact that will never change. The debates happening in Islam, as described by these initiatives, demonstrate the type of debate that has occurred throughout history in all religious traditions. Is this debate influencing issues related to US security? Yes. But an affirmative response to this question does not necessarily mean that the US federal government ought to intervene in a way that interferes with, or plays into, the religious questions and issues at hand.

Third, the counter-narrative initiative, if it involves intervening in a set of religious questions by supporting certain Muslims over others, will prove unproductive at best and counterproductive at worst. The al-Qaeda phenomenon is based on a narrative that depends on a portrayal of the United States as an aggressor against Muslims and their religion. It depicts Western ideas (secularism and democracy) and US military and diplomatic policies as wanting to deplete the resources and power of Muslims and to destroy the Muslim people's moral fabric. The counter-narrative initiative, by arguing that the United States should support certain Muslims over others, will play directly into and add support to the arguments made by these militant groups.

The counter-narrative initiative thus demonstrates the challenge of the al-Qaeda phenomenon. Highlighting and acknowledging that it is driven by religious ideas presents a serious challenge regarding *how* the United States should construct its response. Unfortunately, the answer is not an easy one to accept: The US government ought not interfere in the ways that seem, at least at first blush, to hold significant potential—that is, to fund and support only certain types of Muslims to help steer the debate in ways that are amenable to US interests.

This counsel does not mean, however, that the United States should do nothing. Rather, it means the type of response constructed, one that takes the al-Qaeda phenomenon's religious undergirding into consideration, ought to be geared toward incorporating strategic messaging into US foreign policy, especially policy related to the war against the al-Qaeda phenomenon. This involves defining US foreign policy initiatives, including the use of force, in ways that thoughtfully heed and incorporate the perceptions of the intended audience. A thoughtful response requires forging relationships with key audiences and correcting misinformation. Most important, it calls for forging trust with important communities through policies that are transparent and honest regarding US interests and intentions.

The US federal government, for its part, initiated (and continues) its strategic communication work in the war against al-Qaeda by developing a temporary organization housed in the State Department that was dedicated solely to this task. The Center for Strategic Counterterrorism Communications (CSCC) was established by Executive Order 13584, "Developing an Integrated Strategic Counterterrorism Communications Initiative" (signed by President Obama on September 9, 2011). In explaining the need for the CSCC, the executive order notes,

> The United States is committed to actively countering the actions and ideologies of al-Qa'ida, its affiliates and adherents, other terrorist organizations, and violent extremists overseas that threaten the interests and national security of the United States. These efforts take many forms, but all contain a communications element and some use of communications strategies directed to audiences outside the United States to counter the ideology and activities of such organizations. These communication strategies focus not only on the violent actions and human costs of terrorism, but also on narratives that can positively influence those who may be susceptible to radicalization and recruitment by terror organizations.[51]

The task of the CSCC was to "coordinate, orient, and inform Government-wide public communications activities directed at audiences abroad and targeted against violent extremists and terrorist organizations, especially al-Qa'ida and its affiliates and adherents, with the goal of using communication tools to reduce radicalization by terrorists and extremist violence and terrorism that threaten the interests and national security of the United States."[52]

At the heart of the CSCC, now called the "Global Engagement Center," is the Digital Outreach Team, a group of individuals trained or who have native fluency in a variety of languages (Arabic, Farsi, Urdu, etc.). The team's task is to combat, respond, and critique terrorist narratives in the digital space. This work includes engaging with online terrorist supporters through social media and attempting to clarify misconceptions regarding US policy and to highlight the faults of terrorist groups. In addition, the team is responsible for producing a series of YouTube videos geared toward the same goals. Throughout the life of the CSCC, the videos have included a wide variety of content from "soft, positive stories (Ramadan greetings or US flood relief to Pakistan)" to what are referred to as "attack videos" in which a polemical point is made, often highlighting the hypocrisy of certain militant leaders (such as Ayman al-Zawahiri or Abu Bakr al-Baghdadi).[53] As noted by Ambassador Alberto Fernandez, the CSCC coordinator from March 2012 until February 2015, the center's work was somewhat encumbered by bureaucratic difficulties, and more work needs to be done.[54]

Additionally, beyond the center's specific work, the federal government can incorporate strategic communications into its work and messaging in other ways. This effort requires a direct focus on framing US policy so that it highlights what we are "for"—democracy, human rights, justice, development, security, and so on—rather than what we are "against." It entails presenting US liberties—particularly those related to religion—in ways that clearly demonstrate the United States is interested in dialogue with partners that are also interested in bolstering democratic societies and civic institutions and in promoting civil society but not in supporting certain types of religious visions of the good over others. *Soft capital not coerc[ive]*

Importantly, this work can, and ought to, happen outside the confines of the US federal government. Moreover, when this work happens outside the federal government, approaching the theological questions can be done with significantly more comfort. As noted in the acknowledgments, I organized a symposium on this very issue—that is, the ethical questions surrounding the counter-narrative initiative—at Western Kentucky University in October 2014. The papers were published in a special issue of *Soundings* (including the paper by Ambassador Fernandez), so I will not rehash the details here. Rather, to expand on the preceding points, I provide brief examples of the type of counter-narrative or strategic communications work discussed in the special issue that can directly and indirectly challenge the al-Qaeda narrative and that does not require the US government to engage in theological debate or make normative statements about Islam.[55]

To begin, research that contests the al-Qaeda phenomenon's narrative of jihad must be utilized and disseminated to interested parties. I do not necessarily mean research focused on counter-narrative initiatives only but the type of research that provides a sound basis for understanding the historical material from which the al-Qaeda phenomenon's narrative may be contested. For example, James Turner Johnson's and John Kelsay's works demonstrate how the al-Qaeda phenomenon's narrative may be engaged through the Islamic tradition's understanding of the just use of force. Johnson establishes that "jihad" is a widely contested term, one that has been discussed, debated, and deliberated throughout the life of the Islamic tradition. Moreover, as Kelsay notes, the connection that militants make between piety and violence is a place to begin challenging these arguments in a way that can clearly reference the history of the tradition and its argument on the just use of force. In short, this type of serious academic work on the Islamic historical discourse regarding the use of force provides the material that can help produce a nuanced and sophisticated understanding of Islamic thinking on the issue.

Second, it is important to highlight research that gives a more complete picture of the target audiences of the counter-narrative. The first audience is the militants themselves. Research that allows insight into these fighters is of critical concern so that those interested in strategic messaging and counter-narrative work may understand the various and multiple impulses that drive individuals and families to join militant groups. Adrian Shtuni provides demographic information on fighters from the Balkans who have chosen to join ISIS, noting the stories of these men and their reasons for leaving their homes to enter the fighting.

The second audience comprises those who may be sympathizers or fence-sitters. The extraordinary work of Mubin Shaikh—a self-described former militant who now uses his expertise to engage those who support ISIS or al-Qaeda online—demonstrates the highly personal nature of such work. He connects with individuals who sympathize or support militant narratives through relationships formed in social media platforms. Using various methods, he encourages these individuals to think critically about the al-Qaeda phenomenon and its narrative. In particular, he uses his prolific understanding of the Islamic textual tradition to contest positions that insist on the necessity of a militant jihad.

The third group covers audiences abroad who witness events unfold in their own countries while also watching the ramifications of US military campaigns in their own communities or those surrounding them. As demonstrated by David Pollock, the director of the Fikra Forum—a bilingual (Arabic and English) online platform dedicated to promoting discourse between Muslims, Arab democrats, and American decision makers—there is an appetite for dialogue on issues related to democracy, human rights, US foreign policy, and so on. Online forums such as this one—particularly in places where open dialogue is not available or where individuals want to connect with an American audience on such important issues—provide great potential for the types of conversations that, in and of themselves, help produce messaging and communication that are a vital part of counter-narrative work.

The last audience to address is the American public, which, of course, includes American Muslims. Their perspectives on these issues are vital to understanding how counter-narrative initiatives may be handled ethically and responsibly and with realistic goals and objectives. More broadly, though, the American public must also be educated on the issues that are involved in counter-narrative work. Reflecting on this leads to a critically important point: Counter-narrative work must involve the American public's general perceptions of Islam, and, here, much work remains to be done. Such work is not about convincing our neighbors that Islam is X and not Y. Rather, it entails encouraging our neighbors both to look beyond the short and reductive sound bites that provide misconstrued and truncated perceptions of this tradition and its adherents and to seek out information that is the product of careful and sustained research.

Counter-narratives, after all, are a two-way street. Dialogue requires hard conversation, and all of us must be willing to come to the table with the understanding that if we seek resolution, then we must be prepared to have our assumptions challenged—and often in ways that are uncomfortable.

The urgency of this work is becoming increasingly clear. As I finalize the work on this manuscript, President Obama has announced the introduction of American ground troops into Syria to serve, at least at this point, as military advisers to those groups fighting ISIS. Again, here I wish to stress the importance of recognizing the limits of using military means in responding to ISIS and other like-minded groups. It is imperative that we engage the set of ideas that are driving the proliferation of these groups if we are to have any hope of seeing the end of the al-Qaeda phenomenon.

I used to think that, in certain respects, reading Osama bin Laden's writing was akin to reading science fiction. Perhaps an Islamic "caliphate" run by the likes of him was possible in theory, but surely the actualization of such a thing was materially impossible. How could a marginal stream of thinking, such as that represented by the al-Qaeda narrative, muster the necessary support? Even bin Laden himself did not believe that it was an immediate possibility. Now, however, I cannot help but think that watching ISIS declare the caliphate is watching bin Laden's dream come to fruition. ISIS is proof that this narrative, one whose means include indiscriminate and wanton killing and destruction, will not, as many have hoped, die a quick death alone in the dark. Rather, this narrative has seen the light of day and continues to demonstrate its ability to grow and develop.

Ideas cannot be fought with weapons only. Iraq and Afghanistan have proven as much. Thus, those who wish to see the end of the al-Qaeda phenomenon must come together and, through smart and sensible policy making and grassroots engagement, contest the vision of the world that al-Qaeda seeks to produce.

Notes

1. For example, see Gunaratna and Hennessy, "Through the Militant Lens"; and Manning and La Bau, "In and Out of Extremism."

2. Carpenter et al., "Fighting the Ideological Battle."

3. Benard, *Civil Democratic Islam*, iii.

4. Casebeer and Russell, "Storytelling and Terrorism," 3.

5. Ibid.

6. Benard, *Civil Democratic Islam*, ix.

7. Rabasa et al., "Building Moderate Muslim Networks," iv.

8. Benard, *Civil Democratic Islam*, ix.

9. Ibid. These positions are summarized on p. x and elaborated in pp. 3–14.

10. Ibid., 8–12.

11. Ibid., 47.

12. Ibid.

13. Ibid., 37.

14. Ibid., 47–48. See also pp. x–xii.

15. Rabasa et al., "Building Moderate Muslim Networks," 3.

16. Ibid., chaps. 2 and 3.

17. Ibid., 18–22.

18. Ibid., 85.

19. Ibid., 109. See also pp. 79–113.

20. Ibid., 66–68.

21. Ibid., 66.

22. Ibid., see esp. 81–84.

23. Ibid., 78; and Benard, *Civil Democratic Islam*.

24. Benard, *Civil Democratic Islam*, 29.

25. Ibid., 30.

26. Rabasa et al., "Building Moderate Muslim Networks," 94.

27. Benard, *Civil Democratic Islam*, 14.

28. Hussain and Madhany, "Reformulating the Battle of Ideas," ix, 5.

29. Ibid., 5–7.

30. Ibid., 8.

31. Ibid.

32. Ibid., 9.

33. Ibid.

34. Ibid., ix.

35. Ibid., ix, 8.

36. Rascoff, "Establishing Official Islam?," 126–27.

37. Ibid., 171, 173.

38. Ibid., 129–30.

39. Ibid., 138.

40. Ibid., 139.

41. Ibid., 139–40.

42. Ibid., 159.

43. For his argument in detail, see ibid., 162–66.

44. Ibid., 167.

45. Change Institute, "Studies into Violent Radicalisation," 11–19.

46. Ibid., 6, 138.

47. Ibid., 138–47.

48. Fink and Barclay, "Mastering the Narrative"; and Briggs and Feve, "Review of Programs."

49. Briggs and Feve, "Review of Programs," 6.

50. Benard, *Civil Democratic Islam*, 3.

51. Office of the Press Secretary, the White House, "Executive Order 13584—Developing an Integrated Strategic Counterterrorism Communications Initiative," September 9, 2015, https://www.whitehouse.gov/the-press-office/2011/09/09/executive-order-13584-developing-integrated-strategic-counterterrorism-c.

52. Ibid.

53. Fernandez, "'Contesting the Space,'" 490–91.

54. Ibid.

55. All the research described in the following paragraphs is found in a special issue on counter-narratives in *Soundings* 98, no. 4 (2015).

Selected Bibliography

'Abd-al-Hakim, 'Umar (Abu Mus'ab al-Suri). *Afghanistan, the Taliban, and the Battle for Islam Today*. The Issues of the Revealers of the Truth series. Foreigners' Center for Islamic Studies, 1998. [Arabic and English] Combating Terrorism Center, US Military Academy, West Point, NY. https://www.ctc.usma.edu/posts/afghanistan-the-taliban-and-the-battle-for-islam-today-english-translation-2.

Abd Al Hakim, Omar (Shaykh Abu Mus'ab As Suri). "Muslims in Central Asia and the Coming Battle of Islam." Jihadology.net, August 2, 2010. https://azelin.files.wordpress.com/2010/08/abu-musab-al-suri-muslims-in-central-asia-and-the-coming-battle-of-islam.pdf.

Abou El Fadl, Khaled. *The Great Theft: Wrestling Islam from the Extremists*. New York: HarperCollins, 2005.

Abu'l-Hasan al-Mawardi. *Al-Ahkam as-Sultaniyyah: The Laws of Islamic Governance*. Translated by Asadullah Yate. London: Ta-Ha Publishers Ltd., 1996.

Afsaruddin, Asma. *Striving in the Path of God: Jihad and Martyrdom in Islamic Thought*. New York: Oxford University Press, 2013.

Alston, Philip. "Report of the Special Rapporteur on Extrajudicial, Summary or Arbitrary Executions; Addendum: Study on Targeted Killings." United Nations General Assembly, Human Rights Council, Fourteenth Session, Agenda Item 3, May 28, 2010. http://www2.ohchr.org/english/bodies/hrcouncil/docs/14session/A.HRC.14.24.Add6.pdf.

An-Na'im, Abdullahi Ahmed. *Islam and the Secular State: Negotiating the Future of Shariah*. Cambridge: Harvard University Press, 2008.

Azzam, Abdullah. *Defence of the Muslim Lands: The First Obligation after Imam*. [English.] Religioscope, 2002. http://www.religioscope.com/info/doc/jihad/azzam_defence_3_chap1.htm.

———. *Join the Caravan*. London: Azzam Publications, 2001.

Ballen, Ken. *Terrorists in Love: True Life Stories of Islamic Radicals*. New York: Free Press, 2011.

Beckett, Ian F. W. *Encyclopedia of Guerrilla Warfare*. Santa Barbara: ABC-CLIO, 1999.

Bellamy, Alex J. *Fighting Terror: Ethical Dilemmas*. London: Zed Books, 2008.

Benard, Cheryl. *Civil Democratic Islam: Partners, Resources, and Strategies*. Santa Monica: RAND National Security Research Division, 2003.

Benjamin, Daniel, and Steven Simon. *The Age of Sacred Terror: Racial Islam's War against America.* New York: Random House, 2002.

Bergen, Peter. *Holy War, Inc.: The Secret World of Osama bin Laden.* New York: Free Press, 2001.

Bin Laden, Osama. "Declaration of War against the Americans Occupying the Land of the Two Holy Places." *NewsHour*, PBS, 1996. http://www.pbs.org/news hour/updates/military-july-dec96-fatwa_1996/.

———. "Open Letter to Shaykh Bin Baz on the Invalidity of His Fatwa on Peace with the Jews." [English.] December 29, 2014. Translated by the Counterterrorism Center, US Military Academy, West Point, NY. https://en.wikisource .org/wiki/Open_Letter_to_Shaykh_Bin_Baz_on_the_Invalidity_of_his_Fatwa _on_Peace_with_the_Jews.

———. "Second Letter to Shaykh Bin Baz." [English.] January 29, 1995. https://en .wikisource.org/wiki/Second_Letter_to_Shaykh_Bin_Baz.

Bin Laden, Osama, Ayman al-Zawahiri, Abu-Yasir Rafa'i Ahmad Taha, Shaykh Mir Hamzah, and Fazlur Rahman (World Islamic Front). "Jihad against the Jews and Crusaders." [Arabic] *Al-Quds Al-Arabi*, February 23, 1998. https://www.library .cornell.edu/colldev/mideast/fatw2.htm. [English] February 23, 1998. Federation of American Scientists, Washington, DC. http://fas.org/irp/world/para/docs /980223-fatwa.htm.

Brennan, Rick. "Withdrawal Symptoms: The Bungling of the Iraq Exit." *Foreign Affairs* 88, no. 4 (July–August 2009).

Briggs, Rachel, and Sebastian Feve. "Review of Programs to Counter Narrative of Violent Extremism: What Works and What Are the Implications for Government?" London: Institute for Strategic Dialogue, 2013. https://www.counter extremism.org/resources/details/id/444/review-of-programs-to-counter -narratives-of-violent-extremism-what-works-and-what-are-the-implications -for-government.

Burke, Jason. *Al-Qaeda: The True Story of Radical Islam.* London: I. B. Tauris, 2004.

Callwell, C. E. *Small Wars: Their Principles and Practice.* Tales End Press, 2012 (first published in 1896). http://www.talesendpress.com/2012/08/small-wars-by -charles-edward-callwell.html.

Carpenter, Scott J., Matthew Levitt, Steven Simon, and Juan Zarate. "Fighting the Ideological Battle: The Missing Link in U.S. Strategy to Counter Violent Extremism." Washington, DC: Washington Institute for Near East Policy, July 2010. http://www.washingtoninstitute.org/policy-analysis/view/fighting-the -ideological-battle-the-missing-link-in-u.s.-strategy-to-counte.

Casebeer, William D., and James A. Russell. "Storytelling and Terrorism: Towards a Comprehensive 'Counter-narrative Strategy.'" *Strategic Insights* 4, no. 3 (March 2005).

Change Institute. "Studies into Violent Radicalisation: The Beliefs, Ideologies, and Narratives." London: The Change Institute for the European Commission–Di-

rectorate General Justice, Freedom and Security. February 2008. http://www
.changeinstitute.co.uk/images/publications/changeinstitute_beliefsideologies
narratives.pdf.

Clarke, Richard A. *Against All Enemies: Inside American's War on Terror.* New
York: Free Press, 2004.

Cruickshank, Paul, and Mohammad Hage Ali. "Abu Musab Al-Suri: Architect of the
New Al Qaeda." *Studies in Conflict and Terrorism* 30 (2007): 1–14.

Donner, Fred McGraw. *The Early Islamic Conquests.* Princeton: Princeton University Press, 1981.

———. *Narratives of Islamic Origins: The Beginnings of Islamic Historical Writing.*
Princeton: Darwin Press, 1998.

———. "The Sources of Islamic Conceptions of War." In *Just War and Jihad: His-
torical and Theoretical Perspectives on War and Peace in Western and Islamic
Traditions.* Edited by John Kelsay and James Turner Johnson, 31–69. Westport,
CT: Greenwood Press, 1991.

Emmerson, Ben. "Report of the Special Rapporteur on the Promotion and Protec-
tion of Human Rights and Fundamental Freedoms while Countering Terrorism."
United Nations Human Rights Council, Twenty-Fifth Session, Agenda Item 3,
February 28, 2014. https://www.justsecurity.org/wp-content/uploads/2014/02
/Special-Rapporteur-Rapporteur-Emmerson-Drones-2014.pdf.

———. "Statement of the Special Rapporteur Following Meetings in Pakistan."
Islamabad: United Nations Human Rights Office of the High Commissioner,
March 14, 2013. http://www.ohchr.org/EN/NewsEvents/Pages/DisplayNews
.aspx?NewsID=13146&LangID=E.

Fernandez, Alberto. "'Contesting the Space': Adversarial Online Engagement as a
Tool for Combating Violent Extremism." *Soundings* 98, no. 4 (2015): 488–500.

Fink, Naureen Chowdhury, and Jack Barclay. "Mastering the Narrative: Counterterrorism Strategic Communication and the United Nations." Center on Global
Counterterrorism Cooperation, 2013. http://www.globalcenter.org/publications
/mastering-the-narrative-counterterrorism-strategic-communication-and-the
-united-nations/.

Gessen, Masha. *The Brothers: The Road to an American Tragedy.* New York: River-
head Books, 2015.

Gunaratna, Rohan, and Orla Hennessy. "Through the Militant Lens: The Power
of Ideology and Narratives." The Hague: International Centre for Counter-
Terrorism, June 2012. https://www.clingendael.nl/publication/Through-militant
-lens-power-ideology-and-narratives.

Haykel, Bernard C. F. "On the Nature of Salafi Thought and Action." In *Global
Salafism: Islam's New Religious Movement.* Edited by Roel Meijer, 33–57. New
York: Columbia University Press, 2009.

Hodgson, Marshall G. S. *The Venture of Islam: Conscience and History in World
Civilization.* Vol. 1, *The Classical Age of Islam.* Chicago: University of Chicago
Press, 1977.

Holder, Eric. Speech at Northwestern University School of Law. Chicago, March 5, 2012. http://www.cfr.org/terrorism-and-the-law/attorney-general-holders -speech-targeted-killing-march-2012/p27562.

Hourani, Albert. *Arabic Thought in the Liberal Age, 1798–1939*. Cambridge: Cambridge University Press, 2006.

Hussain, Rashad, and al-Husein N. Madhany. "Reformulating the Battle of Ideas: Understanding the Role of Islam in Counterterrorism Policy." No. 13. Washington, DC: Saban Center at Brookings, August 31, 2008.

Ibrahim, Yasir S. *Al-Tabari's Book of Jihad: A Translation from the Original Arabic*. Lewiston, NY: Edwin Mellin Press, 2007.

Jacobs, Sally, David Fillipov, and Patricia Wen. "The Fall of the House of Tsarnaev." *Boston Globe*, December 15, 2013. http://www.bostonglobe.com/Page/Boston /2011-2020/WebGraphics/Metro/BostonGlobe.com/2013/12/15tsarnaev /tsarnaev.html.

Jansen, Johannes J. G. *The Neglected Duty: The Creed of Sadat's Assassins and Islamic Resurgence in the Middle East*. New York: Macmillan, 1986.

Johnson, James Turner. "Aquinas and Luther on War and Peace." *Journal of Religious Ethics* 31, no. 3 (Spring 2003): 3–20.

———. *Just War Tradition and the Restraint of War: A Moral and Historical Inquiry*. Princeton: Princeton University Press, 1981.

———. *Morality and Contemporary Warfare*. New Haven: Yale University Press, 1999.

———. "On Keeping Faith: The Use of History for Religious Ethics." *Journal of Religious Ethics* 7, no. 1 (1979): 97–115.

Kelsay, John. *Arguing the Just War in Islam*. Cambridge: Harvard University Press, 2007.

———. "Islam and the Distinction between Combatants and Noncombatants." *Cross, Crescent, and Sword: The Justification and Limitation of War in Western and Islamic Tradition*. Edited by John Kelsay and James Turner Johnson, 197–220. Westport, CT: Greenwood Press, 1990.

———. *Islam and War: A Study in Comparative Ethics*. Louisville, KY: Westminster John Knox Press. 1993.

Khadduri, Majid. *The Islamic Law of Nations: Shaybani's Siyar*. Baltimore: Johns Hopkins University Press, 1966.

———. *War and Peace in the Law of Islam*. Baltimore: Johns Hopkins University Press, 1955.

Kilcullen, David. *The Accidental Guerrilla: Fighting Small Wars in the Midst of a Big One*. Oxford: Oxford University Press, 2009.

———. "Countering Global Insurgency." *The Journal of Strategic Studies* 28, no. 4 (2005): 597–617.

———. "Twenty-Eight Articles: Fundamentals of Company-Level Insurgency." *Small Wars Journal*, March 2006.

Koh, Harold Hongju. Speech at the Annual Meeting of the American Society of

International Law. Washington, DC, March 25, 2010. http://www.state.gov/s/l /releases/remarks/139119.htm.

Lacey, Jim, ed. *A Terrorist's Call to Global Jihad: Deciphering Abu Musab Al-Suri's Islamic Jihad Manifesto.* Annapolis: Naval Institute Press, 2008.

Lav, Daniel. *Radical Islam and the Revival of Medieval Theology.* New York: Cambridge University Press, 1983.

Lawrence, T. E. *Seven Pillars of Wisdom: A Triumph.* New York: Anchor Books, 1991.

Lia, Brynjar. *Architect of Global Jihad: The Life of Al-Qaida Strategist Abu Mus'ab al-Suri.* New York: Columbia University Press, 2008.

Lieberman, Joseph I., and Susan M. Collins. "A Ticking Time Bomb: Counterterrorism Lessons from the U.S. Government's Failure to Prevent the Fort Hood Attack." Washington, DC: US Senate, Committee on Homeland Security and Governmental Affairs, February 3, 2011. http://www.hsgac.senate.gov//imo /media/doc/Fort_Hood/FortHoodReport.pdf?attempt=2.

———. "Violent Islamist Extremism, the Internet, and the Homegrown Terrorist Threat." Washington, DC: US Senate, Committee on Homeland Security and Governmental Affairs, May 8, 2008. http://www.hsgac.senate.gov//imo/media /doc/IslamistReport.pdf?attempt=2.

Maass, Peter. "Professor Nagl's War." *New York Times Magazine,* January 11, 2004.

Manning, Ruth, and Courtney La Bau. "In and Out of Extremism: How Quilliam Helped 10 Former Far-Right and Islamists Change." London: Quilliam, August 2015. http://www.quilliamfoundation.org/wp/wp-content/uploads/publications /free/in-and-out-of-extremism.pdf.

Mao Tse-tung. *On Guerrilla Warfare.* Translated by Samuel B. Griffith. Westport, CT: Praeger, 2007.

———. *Selected Military Writings of Mao Tse-Tung.* Peking: Foreign Language Press, 1966.

Martin, Richard C. "The Religious Foundations of War, Peace, and Statecraft in Islam." In *Just War and Jihad: Historical and Theoretical Perspectives on War and Peace in Western and Islamic Traditions.* Edited by John Kelsay and James Turner Johnson, 91–117. Westport, CT: Greenwood Press, 1991.

McCants, Will. *The ISIS Apocalypse: The History, Strategy, and Doomsday Vision of the Islamic State.* New York: St. Martin's Press, 2015.

McChrystal, Stanley A. "COMISAF's Initial Assessment." Headquarters, International Security Assistance Force Afghanistan, June 26, 2009.

Miller, Flagg. *The Audacious Ascetic: What the Bin Laden Tapes Reveal about Al-Qa'ida.* New York: Oxford University Press, 2015.

Mitchell, Richard P. *The Society of the Muslim Brothers.* Oxford: Oxford University Press, 1969.

Moosa, Ebrahim. "My Madrasa Classmate Hated Politics, Then He Joined the Islamic State." *Washington Post,* August 21, 2015.

Morris, Michael F. "Al-Qaeda as Insurgency." US Army War College Strategy

Research Project. Carlisle Barracks, PA: US Army War College, March 18, 2005.

Nagl, John A. "Let's Win the Wars We're In." *Joint Force Quarterly,* 52 (2009).

———. "Winning the Wars We're In." Philadelphia: Foreign Policy Research Institute, Temple University, Center for the Study of Force and Diplomacy, November 2009.

Nagl, John A., and Paul L. Yingling. "New Rules for New Enemies." *Armed Forces Journal,* October 2006.

Obama, Barack Hussein. "The Future of Our Fight against Terrorism." Speech at National Defense University, Washington, DC, May 23, 2013. http://www .theguardian.com/world/2013/may/23/obama-drones-guantanamo-speech-text.

Osanka, Franklin Mark, ed. *Modern Guerrilla Warfare: Fighting Communist Guerrilla Movements, 1941–1961.* New York: Free Press, 1962.

Al-Ouda, Salman b. Fahd. "A Ramadan Letter to Osama bin Laden (September 14, 2007)." *Islam Today,* September 18, 2007. [Arabic] http://www.islamtoday.net /salman/services/printart-78-10136.htm. [English] http://en.islamtoday.net /artshow-417-3012.htm.

Pape, Robert. *Dying to Win: The Strategic Logic of Suicide Terrorism.* New York: Random House, 2005.

Al-Qaradawi, Yusuf. *Islamic Awakening between Rejection and Extremism.* Herndon, VA: International Institute of Islamic Thought, American Trust Publications, 1991.

Rabasa, Angel, Cheryl Benard, Lowell H. Schwartz, and Peter Sickle. "Building Moderate Muslim Networks." Santa Monica: RAND Center for Middle East Policy, 2007. http://www.rand.org/content/dam/rand/pubs/monographs/2007 /RAND_MG574.pdf.

Rascoff, Samuel J. "Establishing Official Islam? The Law and Strategy of Counter-Radicalization." *Stanford Law Review* 64 (2012): 125–90.

Reichberg, Gregory M., Henrik Syse, and Endre Begby, eds. *The Ethics of War: Classic and Contemporary Readings.* Malden, MA: Blackwell, 2006.

Sachedina, Abdulaziz A. "The Development of Jihad in Islamic Revelations and History." In *Cross, Crescent, and Sword: The Justification and Limitation of War in the Western and Islamic Tradition.* Edited by James Turner Johnson and John Kelsay, 35–50. Westport, CT: Greenwood Press, 1990.

———. *The Islamic Roots of Democratic Pluralism.* Oxford: Oxford University Press, 2005.

Sageman, Marc. *Leaderless Jihad: Terror Networks in the Twenty-First Century.* Philadelphia: University of Pennsylvania Press, 2004.

Schanzer, Jonathan. *Al-Qaeda's Armies: Middle East Affiliate Groups and the Next Generation of Terror.* New York: Specialist Press International, 2005.

Al-Sharif, Sayyed Imam. "Major Jihadi Cleric and Author of Al-Qaeda's Shari'a Guide to Jihad: 9/11 Was a Sin." Special Dispatch Series No. 1785. Washington,

DC: Middle East Media Research Institute, September 14, 2007. Made available to author by special request.

Simon, Steven. "Can the Right War Be Won?" *Foreign Affairs* 88, no. 4 (July–August 2009).

Simon, Steven, and Jonathan Stevenson. "Afghanistan: How Much Is Enough?" *Survival* 15, no. 5 (October–November 2009).

Stern, Jessica, and J. M. Berger. *ISIS: The State of Terror.* New York: HarperCollins, 2015.

Al-Suri, Abu Musab. *The Global Islamic Resistance Call.* [Arabic.] Online. Brynjar Lia dates the publication to January 2005, while Paul Cruickshank, Mohammad Hage Ali, and Jim Lacey date its publication on jihadi websites to late 2004.

Al-Tabari, Ibn Jarir. *Al-Tabari's Book of Jihad.* Translated by Yasir S. Ibrahim. Lewiston, NY: Edwin Mellen Press, 2007.

———. *The History of al-Tabari.* Vol. 6, *Muhammad at Mecca.* Translated by W. Montgomery Watt and M. V. McDonald. Albany: State University of New York (SUNY) Press, 1988.

———. *The History of al-Tabari.* Vol. 7, *The Foundation of the Community.* Translated by W. Montgomery Watt and M. V. McDonald. Albany: SUNY Press, 1987.

———. *The History of al-Tabari.* Vol. 8, *The Victory of Islam.* Translated by Michael Fishbein. Albany: SUNY Press, 1997.

———. *The History of al-Tabari.* Vol. 9, *The Last Years of the Prophet.* Translated by Ismail K. Poonawala. Albany: SUNY Press, 1990.

———. *The History of al-Tabari.* Vol. 10, *The Conquest of Arabia.* Translated by Fred M. Donner. Albany: SUNY Press, 1993.

———. *The History of al-Tabari.* Vol. 11, *The Challenge to the Empires.* Translated by Khalid Yahya Blankinship. Albany: SUNY Press, 1993.

———. *The History of al-Tabari.* Vol. 12, *The Battle of al-Qadisiyyah and the Conquest of Syria and Palestine.* Translated by Yohanan Friedmann. Albany: SUNY Press, 1992.

———. *The History of al-Tabari.* Vol. 13, *The Conquests of Iraq, Southwestern Persia, and Egypt.* Translated by Gautier H. A. Juynboll. Albany: SUNY Press, 1989.

———. *The History of al-Tabari.* Vol. 14, *The Conquest of Iran.* Translated by G. Rex Smith. Albany: SUNY Press, 1994.

Tahir-ul-Qadri, Muhammad. *Fatwa on Terrorism and Suicide Bombing.* London: Minhaj-ul-Quran International, 2010.

Thompson, Robert. *Defeating Communist Insurgency: The Lessons of Malaya and Vietnam.* New York: Frederick A. Praeger, 1966.

Tibi, Bassam. *Islam between Culture and Politics.* New York: Palgrave Macmillan, 2005.

Totten, Mark. *First Strike: America, Terrorism, and Moral Tradition.* New Haven: Yale University Press, 2010.

Tovo, Ken. "From the Ashes of the Phoenix: Lessons for Contemporary Counter-insurgency Operations." In *Strategic Challenges for Counterinsurgency and the Global War on Terrorism*. Edited by Williamson Murray, 17–42. Carlisle, PA: Strategic Studies Institute, September 2006.

US Army and US Marine Corps. *The U.S. Army/Marine Corps Counterinsurgency Field Manual*. Chicago: University of Chicago Press, 2007.

Walzer, Michael. *Just and Unjust War: A Moral Argument with Historical Illustrations*. New York: Basic Books, 1997.

Watt, W. Montgomery. *Muhammad at Mecca*. Oxford: Oxford University Press, 1953.

———. *Muhammad at Medina*. London: Oxford University Press, 1956.

———. *Muhammad: Prophet and Statesman*. London: Oxford University Press, 1974.

Weiss, Michael, and Hassan Hassan. *ISIS: Inside the Army of Terror*. New York: Regan Arts, 2015.

West, Bing. *The Wrong War: Grit, Strategy, and the Way Out of Afghanistan*. New York: Random House, 2011.

Wickham, Carrie Rosefsky. *Mobilizing Islam: Religion, Activism, and Political Change in Egypt*. New York: Columbia University Press, 2002.

Wright, Lawrence. *The Looming Tower: Al-Qaeda and the Road to 9/11*. New York: Vintage Books, 2006.

Zaman, Muhammad Qasim. *The Ulama in Contemporary Islam: Custodians of Change*. Princeton: Princeton University Press, 2002.

Index

Arabic names beginning with the prefix 'al-' are alphabetized by the name itself.

Abbasid Caliphate, 68, 138n22
Abd al-Qadir Setmariam, Mustafa. *See* al-Suri, Abu Musab
Abduh, Muhammad, 70–71
Abdullah ibn Abi Quhaafah (Abu Bakr), 61–62, 63, 65, 76n26
Abdulmutallab, Umar Farouk, 32
Abou El Fadl, Khaled: on core beliefs, 169n11; on the crisis of authority, 144, 147–48, 169n7; on diversity, 154; Kelsay on, 145; Kurtz on, 155; on militant Islamists, 154–55; on reasoning, 156; on *Shari'ah*, 150–51
abrogation (*naskh*), 153
Abu Bakr (Abdullah ibn Abi Quhaafah), 61–62, 63, 65, 76n26
Abu Hanifa, 65, 102n9
Abul Husayn Muslim, 102–3n26
Abu Talib, 58
Abu Yusuf, 102n9
Accidental Guerrilla (Kilcullen), 22, 47n11, 47n18
al-Adnani, Abu Muhammad, 2, 133
al-Afghani, Jamal al-Din, 70–71
Afghanistan: Azzam and, 86–88, 90, 91–94; bin Laden in, 87–88, 95; counterinsurgency campaign in, 7, 18, 20–21, 24–25, 44, 47n15, 48n32; drone strikes in, 39; killing of noncombatants in, 121–22; McChrystal on, 23; open fronts in, 118; political instability in, 30; post-9/11 invasion of, 110; reasonable hope of success in, 29–31; safe havens in, 22–23, 27–28, 31–32; al-Sharif and, 164; Soviet-Afghan War and, 86–89, 90, 91–94, 109–10, 118; al-Suri and, 108, 109–10, 138n19
Afghan Services Bureau (*Makhtab al-Khidamat*), 87–88, 108

Afsaruddin, Asma, 14–15n18, 57
Algerian jihad, 108
Ali, Mohammad Hage, 137n1, 137n2
Alston, Philip, 37–38
aman, 67
American Muslims, 127, 185, 194. *See also* Hasan, Nidal Malik; Tsarnaev, Tamerlan
An-Na'im, Abdullah: on colonialism, 151; on core beliefs, 169n11; on the crisis of authority, 148; on the Islamic state, 155–56; Kelsay on, 144–45; on secularism, 152; vs. the traditionalist moderates, 146
apostate rulers, 81, 82–84, 113, 136
apostate tribes, 63–64
AQI (Al-Qaeda in Iraq), 132–33, 135
armed conflict, 24, 34, 36, 37–39, 91. *See also* jihad; just war; use of force
Audacious Ascetic (Miller), 13n8
Augustine, Saing, 26
authority: crisis of, 144, 147–48, 169n7; of the ulema, 146, 147–48, 157–59, 169n7. *See also* legitimate authority criterion; political authority
al-Awlaki, Anwar: Hasan and, 127–28, 141n77; "How to Make a Bomb in the Kitchen of Your Mom," 130, 140n68; *Inspire* magazine and, 122, 123; killing of, 33; Shahzad and, 126
Azzam, Abdullah Yusuf: Afghan Services Bureau and, 55–56; bin Laden and, 87, 88, 95–96, 100; biography of, 87; "Defence of Muslim Lands," 87, 89; on defensive jihad, 87, 89, 91, 93; on the global jihad, 80, 86, 91–92, 93–94, 101; on individual jihad, 89–91, 93–94, 114–15; on innocents, 89, 103n35; ISIS and, 135; on jihad, 88, 89–91, 93–94, 100, 101, 103n35, 103–4n51, 114–15; "Join

Azzam, Abdullah Yusuf (*continued*)
the Caravan," 87, 89, 93; on Muhammad, 89–90; on noncombatants, 101; al-Qaeda narrative and, 9, 80, 86–94, 103n35; Soviet-Afghan War and, 86–88, 89, 90, 91–94; al-Suri and, 88, 108, 117; on the use of force, 88–89, 93

al-Baghdadi, Abu Bakr, 1–2, 133, 134
al-Baghdadi, Abu Omar, 132, 133
banditry, 115–16
"Basic Principles of Counter insurgency" (Thompson), 20, 45n6
Battle of al-Qadisiyyah, 64
bayah, 132
Bellamy, Alex, 8, 45n1
Benard, Cheryl, 175–78, 179–80, 183, 186
benevolent societies, 84
Benjamin, Daniel, 6
Bergen, Peter, 138n14
Berger, J. M., 12–13n3
bin Laden, Osama: Afghan Services Bureau and, 87–88; Azzam and, 87, 88, 95–96, 100; biography of, 94–95; "Declaration of Jihad against Jews and Crusaders," 98–100; "A Declaration of Jihad against the Americans Occupying the Land of the Two Holy Sanctuaries," 5; Faraj and, 96, 100; on indiscriminate killing, 101, 104n62; on individual jihad, 99–101; ISIS and, 135; on jihad, 55–56, 98–101; "Jihad against the Jews and Crusaders," 5–6, 13n9; al-Ouda and, 146, 160, 161–62; al-Qaeda narrative and, 9, 80, 94–101; al-Qaeda organization under, 12–13n3, 95; radicalization by, 70; on the "route of the journey," 95, 104n52; on Saudi Arabia, 95, 96, 98–100, 116; al-Sharif and, 163, 167–68; al-Suri and, 108, 109–10, 117, 137–38n11; on the United States, 5–6, 97, 98–100; writings of, 194; al-Zarqawi and, 132
bombings. *See* terrorist attacks
Boston Globe, 131
Boston Marathon Bombing (2013), 123, 128–31
Brennan, John, 185
Buchanan, Allen, 50–51n69
al-Bukhari, Muhammad, 60
Burke, Jason, 13n11
Bush, George W., 32, 112, 183
Byman, Daniel, 43

caliphate: Azzam on, 90; establishment of, 1–2, 3, 133–36, 137, 194; Faraj on, 84–85; juristic tradition and, 68. *See also* Islamic state
The Call. See The Global Islamic Resistance Call (al-Suri)
Callwell, C. E., 45n5
Camp Bucca (Iraq), 133
Center for Contemporary Conflict, 175
Center for Strategic Counterterrorism Communications (CSCC), 191–92
Central Intelligence Agency (CIA), 41, 43
Change Institute, 186–87
CIA (Central Intelligence Agency), 41, 43
civilian casualties: from drone strikes, 39, 40, 41, 42, 50n62, 50n64; Muhammad on, 60. *See also* innocents; noncombatant immunity
Clarke, Richard A., 6
classical period (570–1258 CE), 56
Clausewitz, Carl von, 19
clerical class, 117
Cold War, 178–79, 182
Collins, Susan, 122
colonialism, 151, 155
combatants: choices given, 64; as drone strike targets, 35; military uniforms and, 127, 140n71; vs. noncombatants, 60, 64, 65, 69, 80, 101; war rights of soldiers and, 26
Combatant Vanguard, 107
"Commander's Summary" (McChrystal), 23
communism, 178–79
community obligation (*fard kifaya*), 67
"The Compendium on Religious Study" (al-Sharif), 165
Confederate forces, 48n28
Congress for Cultural Freedom, 178
conscience, freedom of, 152–54
"Constitution of Medina," 74n11
"Countering Global Insurgency" (Kilcullen), 47n11
counterinsurgency: in Afghanistan, 18, 20–21, 24–25, 44, 47n15, 48n32; concepts and theories of, 6, 17, 18–20, 45n5; global scale for, 31, 45–46n9, 47n11; in Iraq, 18, 20–21, 24–25, 44, 47n15; just war tradition and, 7, 17–18, 25–31, 44; Kilcullen on, 21–22, 23, 29, 45–46n9, 47n11, 47n18; legitimate authority criterion and, 17, 25–28; local populations and, 23, 24–25,

28, 44; McChrystal on, 23; Nagl on, 22, 23–24, 47n15, 47n19; partner governments and, 29, 48–49n33; proportionality of ends criterion and, 28–31; Thompson's principles for, 20, 45n6; Tovo on, 46–47n10; war against al-Qaeda and, 20–25
Counterinsurgency Field Manual (US Army and Marine Corps), 24, 28
counter-narratives, 173–96; Benard on, 175–78, 179–80, 183, 186; Change Institute on, 186–87; critiques of, 180–86; debate within Islam and, 143–47, 176; definition of, 174; ethical questions for, 192; Europe and, 186–88; Global Center on Cooperative Security on, 187–88; Hussain and Madhany on, 182–84; Institute for Strategic Dialogue on, 187–88; as proselytization, 185; Rabasa on, 175, 176, 178–80, 183, 186; RAND Corporation on, 174–75, 183, 189; Rascoff on, 184, 189; role of, 11–12, 188–95; strategic communication for, 188, 191–94; target audience for, 193. *See also* moderate Muslims
counter-radicalization, 184–86, 187
counterterrorism: analysis of, 17; concepts and theories of, 31–37; extraordinary tools of, 6; Hussain and Madhany on, 183; just war tradition and, 7, 17–18, 37–44; legitimate authority criterion and, 17, 37–41, 44–45; proportionality of ends criterion and, 41–44; right of self-defense and, 39; war against al-Qaeda and, 31–33. *See also* drone strikes
Cronin, Audrey Kurth, 43
Cruickshank, Paul, 137n1, 137n2
Crusader alliance. *See* Jewish-Crusader Alliance
CSCC (Center for Strategic Counterterrorism Communications), 191–92

Dabiq (magazine), 134–35
dar al-harb (territory of war), 66–67, 69–70, 155
dar al-Islam (territory of Islam), 66–67, 69–70, 102n9, 155
"Declaration of Jihad against Jews and Crusaders" (bin Laden), 98–100
"A Declaration of Jihad against the Americans Occupying the Land of the Two Holy Sanctuaries" (bin Laden), 5

"Defence of Muslim Lands: The First Obligation after Iman" (Azzam), 87, 89
defensive jihad: Azzam on, 87, 89, 91, 93; bin Laden on, 100; Ibn Taymiyyah on, 103n35; juristic tradition on, 85; al-Qaradawi on, 170n34; al-Suri on, 114
democracy, 177, 179, 183
denial of sanctuary, 22–23, 27–28
Digital Outreach Team, 191–92
discrimination: apostate tribes and, 63; drone strikes and, 42, 43, 45; jihad and, 55, 68; just war tradition and, 8, 9, 17; against Muslims, 127, 186
diversity, 146, 154, 179
"Document of Right Guidance for Jihad Activity in Egypt and the World" (al-Sharif), 165–68
Donner, Fred, 62, 75n23, 76n34
drone strikes, 32–44; al-Awlaki's death and, 123; civilian casualties from, 39, 40, 41, 42, 50n62, 50n64; controversies about, 33, 41; criteria for use of, 35, 42–43; future use of, 43–44; legal justification for, 33–37; legitimate authority criterion and, 37–41, 44–45; necessity for, 35, 36–37; in Pakistan, 32, 39, 40–41, 42, 50n62, 50n64; proportionality of ends criterion and, 41–44; statistics on, 32, 49n40, 50n62; targets for, 37–38, 40, 41–43; transparency and, 43, 50–51n69
due process, for terrorists, 32–33, 34
duty (*fard 'ayn*): assassination of Sadat as, 81; Azzam on, 89–91, 93–94; bin Laden on, 97, 99–101; of defensive war, 100; Faraj on, 84–86; Hasan on, 128; of individual jihad, 55, 80, 89–91, 113, 115, 116, 136; individual vs. collective, 89; Islamic state and, 53, 88–89; al-Suri on, 115–16, 117; use of force and, 54

Egypt, 71–72, 79, 80–81, 82, 165
El Khalifi, Amine, 32
Elyas, Nadeema, 180
Emmerson, Ben, 38–40, 41, 50n62
"The Essential Guide for Preparation" (al-Sharif), 164–65
ethics, religious, 8, 13n6
Europe, 70–71, 111, 186–88
European Commission, Change Institute report, 186–87
Executive Order 13584, 191
extremists. *See* militant Islamists

Fadl, Dr. *See* al-Sharif, Sayyed Imam
failed states, terrorists in, 22–23
Faraj, Muhammad abd-al-Salam: on apostate
  rulers, 81, 82–84; vs. Azzam, 87, 91; bin
  Laden and, 96, 100; on individual jihad,
  84–86; ISIS and, 135; on an Islamic state,
  81–82, 83–85, 102n9; on jihad, 83–84,
  100, 101, 103–4n51; on the Muslim-wide
  struggle, 86; "The Neglected Duty," 80–81,
  84–85, 86, 102–3n26; on noncombatants,
  101; al-Qaeda narrative and, 9, 55–56,
  80–86, 93; on *Shari'ah*, 82, 85–86, 102n9;
  al-Suri and, 117
fard 'ayn. See duty
fard kifaya (community obligation), 67
"al-Faridah al-Ghaibah ("The Neglected
  Duty") (Faraj), 80–81, 84–85, 86,
  102–3n26
fatwa, 134
Federal Reserve Building plot (2012), 32
Feinstein, Dianne, 42
Fernandez, Alberto, 192
Fikra Forum, 193
al-Filistini, Abu Qatada, 134
fiqh, 87, 150–51
First Gulf War, 5, 96, 111
fitra (the good), 152–53
force. *See* use of force
foreign policy: bin Laden on, 97, 98; Cold
  War and, 178–79, 182; counter-narratives
  for, 12, 174–80; counter-radicalization
  and, 184–86; CSCC and, 191–92; just war
  tradition and, 8; occupation of holy sites
  and, 97; al-Qaeda narrative and, 11–12,
  173; recommendations for, 188–95; Saudi
  Arabia and, 97, 111; Shahzad on, 125;
  strategic communication for, 188, 191–94;
  al-Suri on, 111; on terrorists, 182–83;
  theological position and, 181–82, 185–86,
  189; Tsarnaev brothers on, 130, 131
Fort Hood shooting (2009), 123, 126–28,
  140n71
freedom of religion, 152–54, 184
Free Officers revolution, 71–72
fundamentalists, 169n1, 176, 177, 178, 180.
  See also militant Islamists

Gadahn, Adam Yahiye, 105
Genghis Khan, 82–83
Gessen, Masha, 131
Ghailani, Ahmed, 32

Ghani, Ashraf, 30
Global Center on Cooperative Security,
  187–88
The Global Islamic Resistance Call (al-Suri),
  110–13; on global jihad, 105–6, 112–13,
  116–17, 121, 136; on individual jihad,
  10–11, 113, 123–24; Islamic state and,
  135; on jihadi websites, 137n2; rise of ISIS
  and, 123; translation of, 106; writing of,
  110
global jihad/revolution: Azzam on, 80, 86,
  91–92, 93–94, 101; bin Laden and, 95–98;
  counterinsurgency and, 24, 30–31, 44;
  drone strikes and, 39; al-Qaeda phenomenon as, 24, 30–31, 39, 44; al-Suri on,
  105–6, 112–13, 116–17, 121, 136; terrorist school of, 119–21
Global Justice Clinic, 42
Godec, Robert, 185
the good (*fitra*), 152–53
governments, partner, 29, 48–49n33. *See
  also* political authority
gradation, 159, 160
Grotius, Hugo, 26
guerrilla tactics, 19–20, 22, 26, 45n5
Guevara, Che, 19

hadiths: Azzam on, 93; Faraj on, 85, 86,
  102–3n26; on Islamic revitalization, 71;
  moderate Muslim thinkers on, 145, 149;
  al-Qaradawi on, 159; *sahih*, 90; on war, 56
Hague Convention IV, "Laws and Customs
  of War on Land," 48n28
Hanafi school, 89, 115, 147
Hanbali school, 82, 89, 115
Hasan, Nidal Malik, 6, 126–28, 136; radicalization of, 123, 126–27, 141n77; targets of,
  127, 140n71
Hashmi, Sohail, 74–75n12
al-Hayat, 164
headscarf, 181
hijrah (immigration), 58, 135, 142n85
Holder, Eric, 34–35
holy sites, occupation of, 5, 96, 97–98, 99,
  111
Holy War, Inc. (Bergen), 138n14
"How to Make a Bomb in the Kitchen of
  Your Mom" (al-Awlaki), 130, 140n68
Huband, Mark, 138n14
human agency, 144, 151
human rights, 38, 39, 177, 179

Human Rights Council (UN), 39
Hussain, Rashad, 182–84

Ibn Kathir, 83
Ibn Taymiyyah, 83, 102n9, 103n35
IHL (international humanitarian law), 38.
  See also international law
immigration (*hijrah*), 58, 135, 142n85
indigenous populations. *See* local populations
indiscriminate use of force: bin Laden on,
  101, 104n52; duty for, 136; by Hasan,
  140n71; religious narrative on, 3; al-Suri
  on, 124, 131; by the Tsarnaev brothers,
  131
individual jihad: Azzam on, 89–91, 93–94,
  114–15; bin Laden on, 99–101; duty of,
  55, 80, 89–91, 113, 115, 116, 136; Faraj
  on, 84–86; *Inspire* magazine on, 140n68;
  juristic tradition and, 67–68, 85; al-Qaeda
  narrative and, 80, 100–101; religious
  foundation for, 114–16; *Shari'ah* on, 113,
  115–16; al-Suri on, 10–11, 106, 113–17,
  119–21, 136; terrorist school of, 119–21;
  training for, 119, 125, 126, 140n68. *See
  also* lone-wolf jihadists; terrorists
infidels. *See* non-Muslims
infrastructure, 23, 46–47n10, 187
innocents: Azzam on, 89, 103n35; bin
  Laden on, 101, 104n62; vs. combatants,
  60, 64, 69, 80, 101; juristic tradition on,
  69; Muhammad on, 60, 65; al-Ouda on,
  161–62; al-Qaeda narrative on, 80, 162;
  al-Sharif on, 166–68; al-Suri on, 121–22.
  See also civilian casualties; noncombatant
  immunity
Inspire (magazine), 122, 123, 140n68
Institute for Strategic Dialogue, 187–88
insurgencies: concepts and theories of,
  18–20, 45n5; definition of, 24; focus of, 24;
  global scale of, 31; in Iraq and Afghanistan, 21; legitimate authority criterion
  and, 25–28, 48n28; political and military
  challenges of, 24, 46n10; al-Qaeda organization as, 27–28. *See also* counterinsurgency
intelligence personnel, 40, 43
international humanitarian law (IHL), 38
International Human Rights and Conflict
  Resolution Clinic, 42
international law, 7, 33–41

international order, 54, 145, 148, 151–52, 155
In the Shade of the Quran (Qutb), 72
Iraq: counterinsurgency in, 18, 20–21,
  24–25, 44, 47n15; Islamic state in,
  132–33; lack of progress in, 7; political
  instability in, 30; reasonable hope of
  success in, 29–31; safe havens in, 22–23,
  27–28; sectarian violence in, 21, 132–33;
  al-Zarqawi and, 132
irregular actors, 17, 19, 26–27, 48n28
ISIL. *See* Islamic State
Islam: Azzam on, 88; the call (invitation)
  to, 61, 63, 68–69, 86, 102–3n26; camp
  of, 72–73; core beliefs of, 150, 169n11;
  crisis of authority in, 144, 147–48, 169n7;
  ideological struggle in, 175, 176, 181–82;
  mainstream, 183, 184; preferred concept
  of, 181–82, 184, 185, 189; proper practice
  of, 110–12
Islamic history: classical period (570–1258
  CE), 56; early stages of, 9, 61–65, 74n4; on
  the jihad tradition, 56–69; leadership in,
  62, 76n26; marginal interpretation of, 3,
  13n6; militant Islamists on, 149; normative
  claims of, 155–56; al-Qaeda ideologues
  and, 79; revivalist movements in, 70–71,
  73; scope of authority for, 144. *See also*
  Islamic textual tradition; juristic tradition
Islamic law. *See Shari'ah*
Islamic Organization (Tanzim al-Jihad),
  80–81
Islamic revivalist movements, 56, 70–71,
  73, 85
Islamic state: Azzam on, 88–89, 91–92; bin
  Laden on, 100, 101; conflation model of,
  156; establishment of, 1–2, 3, 133–36;
  Faraj on, 81–82, 83–85, 102n9; in Iraq,
  132–33; juristic tradition and, 66, 76n37;
  moderate Muslim thinkers on, 145, 179;
  Muslim revitalization and, 3, 54, 96–97;
  An-Na'im on, 155–56; necessity for, 53–
  54, 113–14, 133, 136, 151–52; al-Qaeda
  narrative on, 80; al-Qaradawi on, 159–60;
  under *Shari'ah*, 53, 82, 85, 102n9, 113, 136,
  151–52; the Taliban as, 109–10
Islamic State (ISIS), 132–36; allegiance to,
  134–35; appeal of, 2, 3, 193; authority
  and legitimacy of, 3, 136; background of,
  132–33; *Dabiq* (magazine), 134–35; declaration of a caliphate by, 1–2, 3, 133–36,
  137, 194; differences from al-Qaeda, 2–3,

Islamic State (ISIS) (*continued*)
12–13n3; *hijrah* to, 135, 142n85; in Iraq
and Syria, 30; military force and, 2, 3, 194;
organizational structure of, 12–13n3; rise
and spread of, 1, 7; al-Suri and, 15n19, 106,
123, 135, 140n67
Islamic State in Iraq and the Levant. *See*
Islamic State
Islamic textual tradition: crisis of authority
in, 144, 147–48, 169n7; just war and, 9,
14–15n18, 69, 193; moderate vs. militant
thinkers on, 148–50; Muslim democrats
and, 145, 150–55; normative claims of history and, 155–56; al-Ouda and, 160–62;
post-Quranic methods of, 169n12;
al-Qaradawi and, 156–60, 170n34;
reexamination of, 144–45; al-Sharif and,
163–68; strategic communication and,
193; traditionalist moderates and, 145–47,
156–68; on the use of force, 4–5, 10–11,
64, 69, 193. *See also* juristic tradition
Islam Today (newspaper), 160

Jabhat al-Nusrah, 133
jahiliyya, 72–73, 81, 86
Jamaat al-Tawhid wal-Jihad (Organization of
Monotheism and Jihad), 132
al-Jarida, 165
Jewish-Crusader Alliance, 95, 96, 99, 116
jihad: apostate rulers and, 83–84, 113, 136;
Azzam on, 88, 89–91, 93–94, 100, 101,
103n35, 103–4n51, 114–15; bin Laden
on, 97–98, 99–101; *dar al-Islam* and,
67; decentralization of, 45, 120, 123, 136;
duty of, 54, 55, 66, 67, 80, 89–91; early
caliphate and, 61–65; Faraj on, 83–84,
100, 101, 103–4n51; historical tradition of,
53–73; ideologues of, 55–56; individual
vs. collective, 89; invitation to Islam and,
86, 102–3n26; juristic tradition and, 56,
65–69, 76n34, 85, 98; legitimate authority
criterion and, 55, 64–65, 69; moral
constraints on, 56–69, 101; Muhammad's
conduct and, 57–61; open fronts type of,
118, 120–21; "open source," 140n68; al-
Qaeda narrative on, 9–10, 55, 80, 101–2;
al-Qaradawi on, 146, 170n34; secret
military organization school of, 118, 120;
Shari'ah on, 56, 113, 115–16; al-Sharif on,
166–67; small cell school of, 119–21; al-
Suri on, 10–11, 106, 110, 113–22, 136–37;

territorial expansion and, 58–59, 62–64,
74–75n12; types of, 67–68. *See also*
defensive jihad; global jihad/revolution;
individual jihad; lone-wolf jihadists
"Jihad against the Jews and Crusaders" (bin
Laden), 5–6, 13n9
jihadi, vs. *takfiri* or *mujahideen*, 22
jizyah (poll tax), 61, 75n21
Johnson, James Turner, 14n16, 14–15n18,
192–93
"Join the Caravan" (Azzam), 87, 89, 93
Jomini, Antoine-Henri, 19
juristic tradition: of abrogation (*naskh*), 153;
development of, 56, 65–69; Islamic state
and, 66, 76n37; jihad and, 76n34, 85, 98;
of political authority and legitimacy, 68;
post-Quranic methods of, 169n12; traditionalist moderates on, 146
jus ad bellum, 8
jus in bello, 8, 17
just war: academic studies on, 14–15n18;
counterinsurgency and, 7, 17–18, 25–31,
44; counterterrorism and, 7, 17–18, 37–
44; discrimination and, 8, 9, 17; historical
and moral tradition of, 14n16; irregular
actors and, 17; Islamic traditions and, 9,
14–15n18, 69, 193; legitimate authority
criterion and, 17, 25–28; moral anchorages of, 8, 17, 45n1; reasonable hope of
success and, 29; territorial expansion
and, 62–63; Western tradition of, 7–9,
14–15n18, 25–28

Karzai, Hamid, 30, 48n32
Kelsay, John, 14–15n18, 145, 192–93
Keohane, Robert O., 50–51n69
Khadduri, Majid, 65, 67
Khalid ibn al-Walid, 60–61
Khan, Samir ibn Zafar, 123
Kilcullen, David: *Accidental Guerrilla*,
22, 47n11, 47n18; "Countering Global
Insurgency," 47n11; on counterinsurgency,
21–22, 23, 29, 45–46n9, 47n11, 47n18;
on denial of sanctuary, 27–28; on a global
insurgency, 31; Thompson's principles
and, 45n6
Koh, Harold Hongju, 33–34, 35
Kurtz, Stanley, 155

Lacey, Jim, 106
Lawrence, T. E., 19

leadership, 62, 76n26, 90, 116–17. *See also* legitimate authority criterion; political authority

legal reasoning, 39, 65, 147. *See also* juristic tradition

legitimate authority criterion: Afghanistan and, 30, 90; counterinsurgency and, 17, 25–28; counterterrorism and, 17, 37–41, 44–45; drone strikes and, 37–41, 44–45; insurgencies and, 25–28, 48n28; jihad tradition and, 55, 64–65, 69; juristic tradition and, 67; just war and, 17, 25–28; Muhammad and, 59–60, 75n20; territorial expansion and, 63

Lia, Brynjar, 106, 137n2

Lieberman, Joseph, 122

literacy rates, 148

local populations: counterinsurgency and, 23, 24–25, 28, 44, 48n32; insurgencies and, 19–20

lone-wolf jihadists: Nidal Malik Hasan, 6, 123, 126–28, 140n71, 141n77; increase in, 6, 122; indiscriminate use of force by, 140n71; ISIS and, 135; model for, 123–31; Faisal Shahzad, 6, 32, 123, 124–26; al-Suri's influence on, 106, 123–24, 126, 131, 136; Tsarnaev brothers, 6, 32, 123, 128–31

Long War (war against al-Qaeda), 4–9, 12, 24, 44, 45. *See also* counterinsurgency; counter-narratives; counterterrorism

Looming Tower (Wright), 13n8

Madhany, al-Husein N., 182–84

Madrid (2004) terrorist attacks, 6, 105, 137n1

Makhtab al-Khidamat (Afghan Services Bureau), 87–88, 108

al-Maliki, Nouri, 30, 133

Maliki school, 67–68, 82, 89, 115

Mao Tse-tung, 19

al-Maqdisi, Abu Muhammad, 132, 134

Martin, Richard C., 76n37

Al-Masri Al-Yawm, 165

al-Mawardi, 68

McCants, William, 12–13n3, 15n19

McChrystal, Stanley, 21, 23, 45n6

Medina, 58–59, 74n9, 74n10, 74n11

Milestones (Qutb), 72, 79

militant Islamists: Abou El Fadl on, 154–55; colonialism and, 155; counter-narratives

for, 193; crisis of authority and, 148; on the international order, 145; on the Islamic state, 151–52; moderate Muslim thinkers on, 143–44, 148–50; normative claims of history and, 156; al-Qaradawi on, 156–60; *Shari'ah* on, 149; al-Sharif on, 166–68; terminology of, 169n1; traditionalist moderates on, 145–47. *See also* al-Qaeda phenomenon

military counter-models, 8–9, 18. *See also* counterinsurgency; counterterrorism

military strategy, 11, 59, 62, 75n23, 106

military uniforms, 127, 140n71

Miller, Flagg, 13n8

moderate Muslim networks, 178, 179, 181

moderate Muslims, 143–71; authority of, 155; characterization of, 144, 179; critical issue for, 155–56; debate within Islam and, 143–47, 176; definition of, 179; false, 179–80; on freedom of religion, 152–54; vs. militant Islamists, 148–50; Muslim democrats, 145, 146, 150–55; al-Ouda, 160–62; al-Sharif, 163–68; traditionalist moderates, 145–47, 156–68, 170n34

modernism, 177–78

modernists, 176, 177–78

Mongol rulers, 82–83

Monis, Man Haron, 135

moral anchorages, of just war, 8, 14n16, 17, 45n1

Morris, Michael F., 46n10

Mueller, Robert, 122

al-Muhajir, Abu Hamzah, 132

Muhammad: Azzam on, 89–90; death of, 61, 62; early followers of, 58, 74n8; Faraj on, 81, 83, 84, 85, 86; first successors to, 61–65; Islamic state and, 155–56; jihad tradition and, 56, 57–61; militant Islamists on, 149; move to Medina by, 58–59, 74n9, 74n10, 74n11; on noncombatant immunity, 60–61; on non-Muslims, 60–61, 75n21; al-Ouda on, 162; political authority of, 58–59, 74n11, 75n20; al-Qaradawi on, 159; Quraysh tribe and, 58, 59–60; revelations to, 58, 74n5, 74n7; the "route of the journey" and, 95, 104n52; territorial expansion by, 58–59, 74–75n12; white banner of, 59, 75n13, 85

mujahideen: Afghan, 86–87, 93–94, 95; Azzam on, 90–91, 93–94; bin Laden on, 95, 100; Bosnian on, 118; Hasan on, 128;

mujahideen (continued)
recruitment of, 88; terminology for, 47n13;
al-Zarqawi and, 132
Mujahideen Shurah Council, 132–33
Muslim 500, 160, 170n43
Muslim-Americans, 127, 185, 194. *See also*
Hasan, Nidal Malik; Tsarnaev, Tamerlan
Muslim Brotherhood, 72, 107, 163
Muslim democrats, 145, 146, 150–55
Muslims: categories of, 176, 189–90; current
situation of, 88, 116, 136; decline of, 85,
88, 100, 110–12, 138n22, 165–67; obliga-
tion to ISIS, 134–35
Muslim-wide revolution. *See* global jihad/
revolution

Nafis, Quazi Mohammad Rezwanel Ahsan, 32
Nagl, John, 21, 23–24, 27–28, 45n6, 47n15,
47n19
naskh (abrogation), 153
Nasser, Gamal Abdel, 71–72, 79
nationality, al-Suri on, 117
nation-building, 24, 28–29, 44
al-Nawawi, 102–3n26
"The Neglected Duty" ("al-Faridah al-
Ghaibah") (Faraj), 80–81, 84–85, 86,
102–3n26
New America, International Security Program, 49n40
New World Order, 10–11, 110, 112–13, 114,
122, 136
Nixon, Richard, 20
noncombatant immunity: bin Laden on,
101, 104n62; vs. combatants, 60, 64, 65,
69, 80, 101; drone strikes and, 42; juristic
tradition and, 69; Muhammad on, 60–61;
al-Qaeda narrative on, 55, 80; al-Suri on,
121–22. *See also* innocents
non-Muslims: assumed state of hostilities
with, 65–68; Faraj on, 82; in the holy sites,
96; invitation to Islam and, 61, 63, 68–69,
86, 102–3n26; Muhammad on, 60–61,
75n21
nonviolent methods, 67, 84, 165–66, 185
al-Numan, 64

Obama, Barack: on Afghanistan, 30; drone
strikes and, 32, 33–37, 41, 42–43; Executive Order 13584, 191; on Iraq, 30; Nobel
Peace Prize speech by, 8; on Syria, 194
obligatory duty. *See* duty (*fard 'ayn*)

occupied lands, 5, 96, 97–98, 99, 111, 113
Old Testament, 178
Omar, Mohammed, 110
online forums, 186, 191–92, 193
open fronts, 118, 120–21, 135
"open source" jihad, 140n68
Organization of Monotheism and Jihad
(Jamaat al-Tawhid wal-Jihad), 132
Ottoman Empire, 70, 147
al-Ouda, Salman bin Fahd bin Abdullah,
145–47, 160–62

pacifism, just war tradition and, 8
Pakistan: drone strikes in, 32, 39, 40–41,
42, 50n62, 50n64; safe havens in, 31, 32;
Shahzad in, 125
Palestine, 5, 86, 87, 92
Pape, Robert, 13n11, 13–14n12
peace treaties, 63, 67
People of the Book, 154
Petraeus, David, 24, 45n6
Phoenix Program, 46–47n10
pluralism, 144, 153, 156
political authority: apostate rulers and, 81,
82–84, 113, 136; conflation model of, 156;
insurgencies and, 19–20, 24, 46n10; irregular actors and, 26; Islamic state and, 66,
76n37; juristic tradition on, 68; legitimate
authority criterion and, 25; of Muhammad, 58–59, 74n11, 75n20; al-Qaeda
narrative and, 55; *Shari'ah* and, 149. *See
also* legitimate authority criterion
political instability, 30
Pollock, David, 193
poll tax (*jizyah*), 61, 75n21
population, local. *See* local populations
post-9/11 world, 10–11, 110, 112, 119
poverty, 111, 165
proportionality of ends criterion, 28–31,
41–44
proselytization, 185
protected class, 61
puritans. *See* militant Islamists

al-Qaeda (organization): attacks by, 6; bin
Laden and, 12–13n3, 95; decentralized
nature of, 53, 101–2, 104n63; definition
of, xiii; history of, 5–6, 13n8, 70, 95;
as an insurgency, 27–28; vs. ISIS, 2–3,
12–13n3; legitimate authority criterion
and, 27–28; as a network of networks,

12, 17, 21–22, 46–47n10; organizational
structure of, 12–13n3, 13n11; al-Ouda
on, 160; radicalization by, 70; al-Sharif on,
163, 165–68; al-Suri and, 108. *See also* al-
Qaeda narrative; al-Qaeda phenomenon;
war against al-Qaeda
Al-Qaeda in Iraq (AQI), 132–33, 135
Al-Qaeda in the Land of Two Rivers. *See*
Al-Qaeda in Iraq
al-Qaeda narrative: definition of, xiii; dual
nature of, 9, 55, 101–2; early Islamic history and, 10, 79; five theological commitments of, 80; foreign policy and, 11–12,
173; growth and development of, 173,
194; ideologues of, 3–4, 9–10, 53, 79–80;
ISIS and, 1, 135–36; on jihad, 9–10, 55,
80, 101–2; moderate Muslim thinkers on,
145, 168–69; noncombatant immunity
and, 55, 80; political authority and, 55;
Qutb and, 79, 80; research on, 192–93;
al-Sharif on, 165–68; strategic and tactical
model of, 10–11; on the United States,
190; on the use of force, 10, 54, 80, 101.
See also Azzam, Abdullah Yusuf; bin
Laden, Osama; counter-narratives; Faraj,
Muhammad abd-al-Salam; religious
narrative
al-Qaeda phenomenon: American citizens
in, 35; conceptual model for, 4, 6–7,
13n11, 13–14n12; counter-narratives to,
11–12, 181, 183–84, 188–95; decentralized nature of, 53, 80; declaration
of a caliphate and, 133; definition and
description of, xiii, 3–4; driving force
behind, 9, 12; dual nature of, 4; global
scale of, 24, 30–31, 39, 44; infrastructure and, 46–47n10; as an insurgency,
46n10; ISIS and, 123; legitimate authority
criterion and, 27–28; radicalization of,
70; religious narrative for, 3, 5, 7, 9, 12,
13n11, 13–14n12, 181; response to, 4, 5;
Soviet-Afghan War and, 95; al-Suri's influence on, 106, 117; traditionalist moderates
on, 146; as a transnational organization,
21–22, 46–47n10; understanding of, 173.
See also global jihad/revolution
al-Qaradawi, Yusuf, 11, 145–47, 156–60,
170n34
Quran: Azzam on, 93; compilation of, 58,
74n6; Faraj and, 84; on freedom of religion, 152–54; on gradation, 159, 160; on

jihad, 56, 115; moderate Muslim thinkers
on, 145, 149; Muslim revitalization and,
71; Surah 5, 83
Quraysh tribe, 58, 59–60
Qutb, Sayyid, 71–73; execution of, 79, 163;
Faraj and, 80, 85; on the global jihad, 86;
ISIS and, 135; *Milestones*, 72, 79; *In the
Shade of the Quran*, 72; al-Suri and, 117

Rabasa, Angel, 175, 176, 178–80, 183, 186
radicalism, research on, 173
radicalization: counter-narratives to,
184–86; of Hasan, 126–27, 141n77; locations for, 122–23; of lone-wolf jihadists,
123; of the al-Qaeda narrative, 173, 194; of
Shahzad, 124–26; of Tamerlan Tsarnaev,
130
RAND Corporation, 174–75, 183, 189
Rascoff, Samuel J., 184, 189
realism, just war tradition and, 8, 14n16
reasoning, 144, 149–50, 151, 156
recruitment: bin Laden and, 87–88; drone
strikes and, 43; for individual jihad, 119,
120; by ISIS, 3; by al-Qaeda, 13n11; safe
havens for, 23; strategic communication
and, 191; by the Taliban, 20. *See also*
radicalization
religion, freedom of, 152–54, 184
religious ethics, 13n6
religious narrative, 3–4, 5, 9–10, 79–104;
declaration of a caliphate and, 133; on
the duty to use force, 54; early caliphate
and, 61–65; foreign policy and, 181–82,
185–86, 189; on individual jihad, 114–16;
ISIS and, 135–36; juristic tradition and,
65–69; military theories connection
with, 11; moderate Muslim thinkers
on, 168–69; moral constraints on war,
53–73; Muhammad and, 57–61; al-Qaeda
phenomenon and, 3, 5, 7, 9, 13n11,
13–14n12, 181; responding to, 11; al-Suri
on, 106. *See also* Azzam, Abdullah Yusuf;
bin Laden, Osama; Faraj, Muhammad
abd-al-Salam
revitalization, Muslim, 3, 73, 96–97, 156,
161–62, 165
revivalist movements, Islamic, 70–71, 73, 85
ribat, 67–68
Riddah Wars (Wars of Apostasy), 62–63
rulers, apostate, 81, 82–84, 113, 136
Russell, Katherine, 129–30

Sachedina, Abdulaziz, 76n34, 144, 146, 152–54
Sadat, Anwar, 79, 80–81, 82, 86, 164
al-Sadr, Muqtada, 21
safe havens, 22–23, 27–28, 31, 32
Sageman, Marc, 13n11, 13–14n12
Sahih (al-Bukhari), 60
Saudi Arabia: bin Laden on, 95, 96, 98–100, 116; counterinsurgency, 97–98; foreign policy and, 97, 111; holy sites in, 5, 96, 97–98, 99; al-Ouda on, 160–61; al-Suri on, 111, 116
SAWS, 90, 103n39
Schanzer, Jonathan, 13n11
secret military organizations, 118, 120
secularists, 176, 177, 178, 179, 185
secularization, 111, 152
self-defense, right of, 34, 39. *See also* defensive jihad
September 11, 2001 attacks, 6, 162, 167–68
Serbian genocide, 118
Shafi school, 62, 88, 89, 115
Shahzad, Faisal, 6, 32, 123, 124–26, 136
Shaikh, Mubin, 193
Shari'ah: authority to interpret, 144, 147–48, 157–59, 169n7; Azzam on, 92; bin Laden on, 101; Elyas on, 180; Faraj on, 82, 85–86, 102n9; *fiqh* and, 150–51; Hanafi school of, 89, 115, 147; Hanbali school of, 82, 89, 115; Islamic state ruled by, 53, 82, 85, 102n9, 113, 136, 151–52; on jihad, 56, 65–69, 113, 115–16; Maliki school of, 67–68, 82, 89, 115; militant Islamists on, 149; multiple schools of, 147; necessity to live under, 53–54, 85–86, 113–14, 136; Shafi school of, 62, 88, 89, 115; al-Sharif on, 164, 166; territory of war in, 66–67; terrorism and, 183; traditionalist moderates on, 146–47. *See also* Islamic textual tradition; juristic tradition
al-Sharif, Sayyed Imam (Dr. Fadl), 145–47, 163–68
al-Shaybani, Muhammad ibn al-Hasan, 65, 67
Shiites, 21
Shtuni, Adrian, 193
Simon, Steven, 6, 31–32
siyar, 65–66
small cells, 119–21
Small Wars (Callwell), 45n5
social media, 186, 191–92, 193

soldiers, war rights of, 26. *See also* combatants
Soviet-Afghan War, 86–89, 90, 91–94, 95, 109–10, 118
Stanford Law Review, 184
state, definition of, 3
statecraft, 4, 8, 54, 65–68, 160, 189
states, failed, 22–23
Stern, Jessica, 12–13n3
Stevenson, Jonathan, 31
Stone, Doug, 185
strategic communication, 188, 191–94
Striving in the Path of God (Afsaruddin), 14–15n18
success, reasonable hope of, 18, 28, 29–31
suicide terrorism, 13n11, 13–14n12
Sunnah (tradition), 150, 153
Sunnis, 30, 66, 82, 132
al-Suri, Abu Musab, 102, 105–23; Afghanistan and, 108, 109–10, 138n19; Azzam and, 88, 108, 117; bin Laden and, 108, 109–10, 117, 137–38n11; biography of, 107–8, 138n14; capture of, 105; on the decline of Muslims, 110–12, 138n22; on duty (*fard 'ayn*), 115–16, 117; on global jihad, 105–6, 112–13, 116–17, 121, 136; on individual jihad, 10–11, 106, 113–17, 119–21, 136; influence of, 105–6, 117, 122–23; ISIS and, 15n19, 123, 135, 140n67; jihad model of, 10–11, 106, 110, 113–22, 136–37; on killing innocents, 121–22; lone-wolf jihadists and, 106, 123–24, 126, 131, 136; Madrid terrorist attacks and, 105, 137n1; on military strategy, 106; personal website of, 105, 137n2; religious narrative of, 106; on Saudi Arabia, 111, 116; studies on, 106; on training, 105, 108, 113, 118, 120–21, 122; writings of, xiii. *See also The Global Islamic Resistance Call*
symbols, Islamic, 150, 183
Syria, al-Suri's life in, 107
Syrian civil war, 133, 194

al-Tabari, Ibn Jarir, 63, 64, 68, 69
tafsir, 56
al-Tahtawi, Rifaa, 70–71
Taif, 83
takfiri, 22, 47n13
Taliban, 20–21, 31, 109–10
Tanzim al-Jihad (Islamic Organization), 80–81

Tanzim Qadat al-Jihad fi Bilad al-Rafi dayn. *See* Al-Qaeda in Iraq
targets: for drone strikes, 37–38, 40, 41–43; military uniforms and, 127, 140n71; al-Suri on, 121. *See also* noncombatant immunity
Tehrik-i-Taliban, 125
territorial expansion: choices given during, 63–64; duty and obligation for, 66; by ISIS, 133; jihad and, 58–59, 62–64, 74–75n12; just war tradition and, 62–63; Muhammad and, 58–59, 74–75n12
territory of Islam (*dar al-Islam*), 66–67, 69–70, 102n9, 155
territory of war (*dar al-harb*), 66–67, 69–70, 155
terrorist attacks: Boston Marathon Bombing (2013), 123, 128–31; Fort Hood shooting (2009), 123, 126–28, 140n71; by Jamaat al-Tawhid wal-Jihad, 132; by lone-wolf jihadists, 122, 123–31, 140n71; Madrid (2004), 6, 105, 137n1; September 11, 2001, 6, 162, 167–68; *Shari'ah* and, 183; statistics on, 104n63; Times Square Bombing attempt, 32, 123, 124–26; training for, 125; US Capitol bomb plot (2012), 32
terrorists: American citizens as, 35; counter-narratives to, 182–83; due process for, 32–33, 34; in failed states, 22–23; individual jihad school of, 119–21; online forums for, 186. *See also* counterterrorism; drone strikes
theological narrative. *See* religious narrative
Thompson, Robert, 20, 45n6
Tibi, Bassam: on core beliefs, 150, 169n11; Muslim democrats and, 144; on post-Quranic methods, 169n12; as a secularist, 11; on the system of symbols, 150; vs. the traditionalist moderates, 146
Times Square Bombing attempt, 32, 123, 124–26
Totten, Mark, 7
Tovo, Ken, 46–47n10
traditionalist moderates, 145–47, 156–68; al-Ouda, 145–47, 160–62; al-Qaradawi, 11, 145–47, 156–60, 170n34; al-Sharif, 145–47, 163–68
traditionalists, 176, 178, 180
training: Abou El Fadl on, 147, 148; Azzam on, 93; Hasan and, 140n71; for individual jihad, 119, 125, 126, 140n68; for

Islamic jurisprudence, 10, 144; al-Suri on, 105, 108, 113, 118, 120–21, 122; by Tehrik-i-Taliban, 125; traditionalist moderates on, 157; for the ulema, 147
training camps: al-Qaeda, 10–11, 164–65; radicalization and, 122, 128; safe havens for, 23; al-Suri and, 107, 110; al-Zarqawi and, 132
transnational organizations, 21–22, 46–47n10
Treaty of Hudabiyya, 60
Tsarnaev, Anzor, 128–29, 130
Tsarnaev, Dzhokhar "Jahar," 6, 32, 123, 128–31, 136
Tsarnaev, Tamerlan, 6, 123, 128–31, 136
Tsarnaev, Zubeidat, 128–29, 130

ulema, authority of, 146, 147–48, 157–59, 169n7
Umar bin al-Khattab (Umar), 61–62, 63, 64, 65
ummah, 93, 133
United Nations (UN), 37–41, 188
United States: American Muslims in, 127, 185, 194; bin Laden on, 5–6, 97, 98–100; counter-narrative initiative for, 11–12, 194; just war tradition and, 7–9; post-9/11 invasion of Afghanistan, 110; al-Qaeda attacks against, 6; al-Qaeda narrative on, 190; Qutb on, 71; radicalization in, 122–23; al-Sharif on, 167–68; al-Suri on, 111, 112, 121. *See also* drone strikes; foreign policy; war against al-Qaeda
United States Naval Postgraduate School, 175
US Army's General Order no. 100, 48n28
US Capitol bomb plot (2012), 32
use of force: Azzam on, 88–89, 93; bin Laden on, 97; duty and obligation for, 54; indiscriminate, 3, 101, 104n52, 124, 131, 136, 140n71; Islamic traditions on, 4–5, 10–11, 69, 193; by Muhammad, 59, 61; proportionality of ends criterion and, 28–31, 41–44; al-Qaeda narrative on, 10, 54, 80, 101; right of self-defense and, 34; al-Suri on, 115–16; war planning efficacy and, 18; Western tradition of, 4–5. *See also* jihad; just war
US foreign policy. *See* foreign policy
US Senate Committee on Homeland Security and Governmental Affairs, 122
Usul al-fiqh, 151

veiling, 181
Vietnam War, 20, 46–47n10, 47n15

al-Wahhab, Muhammad ibn Abd, 70
Wahhabist movement, 70
Walzer, Michael, 26
war. *See* armed conflict; jihad; just war; use
    of force
war against al-Qaeda (Long War), 4–9, 12,
    24, 44, 45. *See also* counterinsurgency;
    counter-narratives; counterterrorism
war planning, feasibility and efficacy of, 18
*Warriors of the Prophet: The Struggle for
    Islam* (Huband), 138n14
Wars of Apostasy (Riddah Wars), 62–63, 156
West, Bing, 48n32
Western culture & traditions: on just war,
    7–9, 14–15n18, 25–28; of law, 147; of
    modernism, 177–78; al-Qaeda narrative
    on, 190; Qutb on, 71; al-Suri on, 111, 121;
    on the use of force, 4–5

white banner, 59, 75n13, 85
wife beating, 177
World Islamic Front for Jihad against Jews
    and Crusaders, 109
Wright, Lawrence, 13n8, 79
Wrong War (Bing), 48n32

Yazadagird, 64
Yemen, 32, 39, 50n62, 165
Yingling, Paul, 23
YouTube, 192

al-Zarqawi, Abu Musab, 132
al-Zawarhiri, Ayman: Azzam and, 88; Center
    for Contemporary Conflict on, 175; ISIS
    and, 133–34, 135–36; al-Qaeda organiza-
    tion and, 12–13n3; al-Sharif and, 163, 164,
    165, 167–68; on al-Suri, 105
Zentralrat der Muslime in Deutschland, 180
Zionist-Crusader alliance. *See*
    Jewish-Crusader Alliance

About the Author

Nahed Artoul Zehr is executive director of the Faith & Culture Center in Nashville, Tennessee. Previously she was assistant professor of Islam and Religious Studies at Western Kentucky University, where she taught courses on Islam, the Qur-an, Comparative Religious Ethics, and Religion and Violence. In 2011–2012 she was Minerva Research Chair at the United States Naval War College.